W9-DAT-512

PUBLICATIONS OF
THE INSTITUTE OF HIGHER EDUCATION

A New Trimester Three-Year Program
Thad L. Hungate and *Earl J. McGrath*

Are School Teachers Illiberally Educated?
Earl J. McGrath and *Charles H. Russell*

Are Liberal Arts Colleges Becoming Professional Schools?
Earl J. McGrath and *Charles H. Russell*

The Liberal Arts as Viewed by Faculty Members
in Professional Schools
Paul L. Dressel, Lewis B. Mayhew, and *Earl J. McGrath*

Attitudes of Liberal Arts Faculty Members Toward
Liberal and Professional Education
Paul L. Dressel and *Margaret F. Lorimer*

The Evolving Liberal Arts Curriculum:
A Historical Review of Basic Themes
Willis Rudy

The Graduate School and the Decline of Liberal Education
Earl J. McGrath

The Quantity and Quality of College Teachers
Earl J. McGrath

Memo to a College Faculty Member
Earl J. McGrath

Liberal Education in the Professions
Earl J. McGrath

Liberal Education and Nursing
Charles H. Russell

Liberal Education and Journalism
Paul L. Dressel

Liberal Education and Engineering
Edwin J. Holstein and *Earl J. McGrath*

LIBERAL EDUCATION AND PHARMACY
James Newcomer, Kevin P. Bunnell, and Earl J. McGrath

LIBERAL EDUCATION AND MUSIC
Willis J. Wager and Earl J. McGrath

LIBERAL EDUCATION AND BUSINESS
William M. Kephart, James E. McNulty, and Earl J. McGrath

LIBERAL EDUCATION AND HOME ECONOMICS
Jeanette A. Lee and Paul L. Dressel

THE ACADEMIC DEANSHIP
John Wesley Gould

COOPERATIVE LONG-RANGE PLANNING IN
LIBERAL ARTS COLLEGES
Earl J. McGrath

THE PREDOMINANTLY NEGRO COLLEGES AND UNIVERSITIES IN TRANSITION
Earl J. McGrath

LIBERAL EDUCATION IN THE SERVICE ACADEMIES
William E. Simons

LIBERAL EDUCATION AND SOCIAL WORK
Gordon J. Aldridge and Earl J. McGrath

SELECTED ISSUES IN HIGHER EDUCATION: AN ANNOTATED BIBLIOGRAPHY
L. Richard Meeth

Copies of these reports may be purchased from the
Bureau of Publications, Teachers College, Columbia University

THE PREDOMINANTLY NEGRO

COLLEGES AND UNIVERSITIES

IN TRANSITION

EARL J. McGRATH

Executive Officer, Institute of Higher Education
Teachers College, Columbia University

PUBLISHED FOR THE
INSTITUTE OF HIGHER EDUCATION

BY THE
BUREAU OF PUBLICATIONS
TEACHERS COLLEGE, COLUMBIA UNIVERSITY

FOREWORD

IN OCTOBER 1963 THE OFFICERS OF THE CARNEGIE CORPORATION OF NEW York made a grant to the Institute of Higher Education to finance a study of the predominantly Negro institutions of higher education and expressed the hope that a report could be finished late in 1964. The potential usefulness of such a study to the many individuals and organizations interested in these institutions and in the welfare of their students has become abundantly clear in the intervening months. In fact, without such a body of relevant facts it is patent that the present widespread attempt to help them could in part at least be abortive or even damaging.

At the time of the grant the character of the inquiry, its scope, the range of its various subdivisions, and the nature of the prospective report were thoroughly discussed. These exploratory discussions led to the conclusion that it would not be feasible in a little over a year to make complete institutional analyses of some one hundred colleges and universities. Although individual profiles accompanied by qualitative ratings might prove helpful in some ways, they would necessarily be difficult to make in the time available and they would have to include many subjective evaluations. Moreover, the amount of data needed from the institutions themselves to support such detailed analyses would have imposed prohibitive expenditures of time and money on their part and would actually have deterred some from taking part in the inquiry. Indeed, only a deep sense of commitment prevented some presidents from declining to participate even in the present study because of the burdens it necessarily imposed on their staffs. Consequently it was decided not to attempt qualitative, comparative institutional ratings, but rather to try to provide an overview of the characteristics, the needs, and the prospects of the predominantly Negro institutions.

To be sure, this type of general aproach which often results in the portrayal of general features rather than catalogues of individual institutional characteristics has some disadvantages. Since in many features of institutional life the averages fall below those for the colleges and universities of the nation at large, some may feel that the figures do an injustice to the better institutions or even to all of them. This position rests on an assumption of questionable validity; namely, that if the weaknesses of some are exposed all will be commensurately depreciated and some or all of the Negro colleges will unfairly lose prospective additional financial and moral support. This report rests on the opposite view that the revelation of the weaknesses of some and the needs of all will generally swell the flow of new support. In fact, many foundations, as the following pages will reveal, have already made substantial grants to these institutions and indeed have been adding to these subventions during the preparation of this publication. If some of the newest developments in these colleges do not appear in this report, it is because they have occurred while the manuscript was being prepared.

There is abundant evidence that the public mind and conscience have been aroused to the absolute social and moral necessity of improving educational opportunities for Negro youth. The knowledge that all these colleges, like their sister institutions, are deficient in some respects, and some shockingly below the average for the nation at large, will in this day deter few citizens from coming to their aid. In fact, one of the reasons for several months' delay in the publication of this report has been the persistent demands on those who have been doing the work for information on how help could be provided to needy colleges and universities, their faculties, and their students.

The facts presented here do not cover every aspect of the programs, personnel, and facilities in these colleges. But any person or organization wanting to discover how help can be provided to these institutions and to the young people attending them will here find a set of facts and recommendations on which they can confidently proceed. Additional research, however, indeed nothing less than continuing study, will be indispensable for a period of years, because more detailed analysis ought to be made of some of the items investigated, and because the swiftly changing social, economic, and political forces impinging on these institutions and their clientele will require constant review. Accordingly, it was decided at this time to paint the picture of the condition of these institutions in broad strokes rather than in minute detail. At best the latter technique would have involved invidious distinctions more harmful to individual institutions than anything that has or has not been said in this type of report.

The reader will observe that the generalizations arrived at are often derived from varying numbers of institutions. Sometimes an average or median will relate to seventy-five and at other times to eighty-nine institutions or their subdivisions. These variations occur because not all institutions answered all questions or supplied complete data on them. These differences do not, however, invalidate the conclusions drawn with respect to particular characteristics.

Nothing would be gained by describing these institutions as a group in more glowing terms than the facts permit, nor in suppressing weaknesses that all informed persons know or presume to exist. As the report repeatedly states, on any measure of faculty competence, library facilities, salaries, physical equipment, and a host of other characteristics, the predominantly Negro institutions run the entire gamut from the highest to the lowest. When compared with the predominantly white colleges they can be matched institution by institution. If some of the facts and comments in this report seem unduly negative and discouraging it should be recognized that they represent the condition of American higher education in its entirety with the qualification that a larger proportion of these institutions need strengthening than of the whole family of colleges and universities.

At the very outset, therefore, it should be said that anyone who thinks that a significant percentage of them can be substantially helped by an expenditure of a few million dollars sadly deludes himself. The presently predominantly Negro colleges will need several hundred million dollars in the next five or ten years merely to keep step with the growing needs of their potential student bodies and the unprecedented advancements in higher education. The full efforts of individuals, corporations, philanthropic groups, foundations, and the state and Federal governments will be required to reach the goal of providing a better higher education for Negro youth, and for their white contemporaries who will increasingly attend these institutions. Anything less than such efforts will result in continuing restrictions nearly as demeaning and privational as segregation itself. And the time to begin to eradicate the present inadequacies in service is now, not five or ten years hence when several additional generations of young Americans will have been denied a suitable higher education and the social, economic, and cultural benefits flowing from it.

This study could not include an analysis of the Negro youth attending the predominantly white institutions. They are scattered among more than a thousand institutions throughout the United States. It was possible, however, to obtain fairly reliable figures on the number of such students by direct inquiry among the administrative officers concerned with enrollments and by making estimates for those institutions which did not reply or said they did not keep enrollment statistics on the basis of race. Even though the figures gathered present a reasonably reliable picture of the present situation a more searching survey of Negro youth in all colleges and universities ought to be made. In this report on the predominantly Negro colleges and universities the word "predominantly" will often be omitted in the interest of economy of wording, but this usage should not suggest an endorsement of any policy designed to preserve racial separatism.

Gratitude is due many individuals who in one way or another contributed to this study. Needless to say, they have no responsibility for the conclusions or recommendations which represent the sincere, even if at times the controversial, views of the author, the Executive Officer of the Institute of Higher Education. Not all those who helped can be mentioned. The institutions which supplied some or all of the data requested are listed in Appendix A. Without their unswerving cooperation the study could not have been made. At times special advice was obtained from the Southern Regional Council, the Southern Association of Colleges and Schools, the United States Office of Education, the General Education Board of the Methodist Church, the College Entrance Examination Board, the Woodrow Wilson Foundation, the Southern Regional Education Board, and the Phelps-Stokes Fund.

Special thanks should go to Dr. Frederick D. Patterson, founder of the United Negro College Fund, for wise counsel and help in finding basic material related to the investigation. The Fund, representing among its membership the top institutions in the predominantly Negro colleges and universities, has for a number of years given strong leadership in interpreting these institutions and their needs to the general public and to potential donors, in conducting conferences on the most significant developments in higher education, in advising member institutions about the merits of various educational policies and practices, and in conducting studies of the condition and the development of its constituent members. Under Dr. Patterson's distinguished leadership the Fund has taken vigorous and sound steps to strengthen the whole enterprise of Negro education. It was only natural, therefore, that he should have been consulted as this project has progressed.

A number of persons helped with special aspects of this study, including L. Richard Meeth, William R. O'Connell, Jr., and John W. Rembert who visited many of the cooperating institutions; and Henry G. Badger, W. Robert Bokelman, Warren J. Haas, Thad L. Hungate, Joseph F. Kauffman, and William G. Land took responsibility for preparing basic data for several chapters of the report. JB Lon Hefferlin was of immense assistance in reorganizing the material, recasting several chapters, and writing several others anew. To Dr. William K. Selden, Executive Director of the National Commission on Accrediting, who made arrangements to release Dr. Hefferlin from his regular duties for more than a month, special thanks are due.

The manuscript was read by W. Robert Bokelman, James A. Colston, Frank G. Dickey, Frederick D. Patterson, John W. Rembert, Arthur L. Singer, Jr., and Stephen J. Wright, all of whom made valuable suggestions which improved the accuracy and cogency of the report.

The author also wishes to express his personal thanks to the officers of the Rockefeller Foundation for arranging a month's residence at the Villa Serbelloni on Lake Como in Italy where, in the quiet and beauty of this unique establishment, he was able to devote his undivided efforts to the preparation of a first draft of this report, and to Mr. and Mrs. John Marshall whose gracious hospitality made this period highly productive as well as pleasant.

This report deals with more controversial ideas and issues than most other studies of higher education. For example, some educators think that closing from a third to a half of the predominantly Negro colleges would, more than any other one thing, improve the higher education of Negroes; others, including the author, believe such an action would be a profound disservice to both the Negro and white youth who constitute their potential student bodies. Some believe that larger numbers of the faculty members in the predominantly Negro colleges and universities, especially the most accomplished scholars, should be immediately engaged by the white northern colleges and universities; others, including the author, who unqualifiedly endorse integration believe that such a one-way migration would greatly damage the total program of higher education for Negroes. Some believe that admissions standards in these institutions, especially the private colleges, ought to be rapidly raised to narrowly restrictive levels, and scholarships provided for able but poor students; others, including the author, believe that such a step would exclude not only many of the poor but also of the potentially able youth who could not meet the higher standards. The list of these issues on which judicious and honorable men can and do hold opposing views could be extended. No reasonable person can expect the author of a treatise on this difficult subject, if he is to say anything worth reading, to do more than look at the evidence and express such objective judgments as seem to him calculated to advance the educational opportunities of Negro youth and their white contemporaries who will increasingly attend these institutions. This spirit has animated the preparation of this report on an immensely complicated subject.

The author believes the substance of this report to be intimately related not only to the welfare of this and future generations of Negroes, but also to the welfare of our country and its position among the nations. He hopes, therefore, that it will be widely read and critically analyzed, and, most importantly, that individuals and groups will be energized at once into action to achieve the recommended objectives.

EARL J. McGRATH
Executive Officer

CONTENTS

TABLES

THE PREDOMINANTLY NEGRO
COLLEGES AND UNIVERSITIES
IN TRANSITION

Chapter 1

THE BACKGROUND OF THE STUDY

BARRING SOME PRESENTLY UNFORESEEABLE SOCIAL CATACLYSM, THE DECADE
of the sixties, although studded with a host of significant and dramatic
events at home and abroad, will be most vividly signalized in the United
States by swift and lasting advances toward racial equality. Already the
Federal Government has enacted legislation guaranteeing certain basic
civil rights and has taken other steps to establish political equality for
all citizens regardless of race. Equally important, the conscience of the
people generally has been aroused to the evils of discrimination and
its attendant violations of the moral principles basic to a truly democratic society. Now aware of the racial injustice which has so long existed
throughout our commonwealth, more and more individuals and organizations are throwing their efforts into a great variety of activities to
close the gap between our professed egalitarian principles and our dis-
criminatory practices. These activities assail abuses along the whole
spectrum of rights—from voting privileges and equal access to education,
to employment practices, housing conditions, and consumer services.

The struggle for equal educational opportunities demonstrates how
advances in any of these areas of social life affect the others. In the
past, major progress toward the goal of free and open access to education
has had to await legal action in the courts, but now educational opportunities are expanding as the result of wider and more telling use of
political power and social pressure. These educational opportunities are
themselves necessary before comparable advances can be made in employment opportunities, for in modern society, education and technological
training are the keys which unlock the doors to the preferred occupa-

1

tions. Fair-employment practices will not, by themselves, guarantee admittance to higher occupations. Without open access to education at all levels, to the untutored and unskilled the right to employment without regard to race will largely remain an empty hope.

The salutary effects of increased educational opportunity extend beyond employment and housing and voting: Education also gives renewed strength to the entire movement for equal opportunities. Negro college students dramatized this role of education in the early 1960's when they began to demonstrate for equal consumer services. First in North Carolina, then in Alabama and Georgia, students joined in protests at lunch counters and movie theaters, bringing arrests, jailings, publicity, and further protests. The sit-in demonstrations, together with the enrollment of the first Negro students in previously segregated state universities in Mississippi and Georgia, focused the eyes of the nation on the colleges that these students attended and inspired an interest among many in the character of the education they provided. Questions arose. What were these colleges like? What role did they play in the whole enterprise of American higher education? What were their standards and what were their needs?

At least four times in the past half-century analysts of American higher education undertook to answer these questions. In 1917, the Phelps-Stokes Fund sponsored a study of these institutions by Thomas Jesse Jones of the United States Bureau of Education.[1] Eleven years later, in 1928, under the direction of Arthur J. Klein of the United States Office of Education, a somewhat similar review resulted in further recommendations to strengthen and improve them.[2] In 1942, staff members of the United States Office of Education completed a comprehensive four-year survey of the higher education of Negroes, and reported extensively on related socioeconomic matters as well as on the condition of education in the Negro institutions.[3] Most recently, in 1960 and 1962,

[1] Thomas Jesse Jones, *Negro Education: A Study of the Private and Higher Schools for Colored People in the United States* (Washington: Bureau of Education, 1917), 2 volumes.

[2] Arthur J. Klein, "Survey of Negro Colleges and Universities," prepared in the Division of Higher Education, U.S. Office of Education *Bulletin*, 1928, no. 7 (Washington: U.S. Government Printing Office, 1929).

[3] *National Survey of the Higher Education of Negroes:* Ina Corinne Brown, *Socio-Economic Approach to Educational Problems* (Misc. no. 6, vol. 1); *General Studies of Colleges for Negroes* (Misc. no. 6, vol. 2); Lloyd E. Blauch and Martin D. Jenkins, *Intensive Study of Selected Colleges for Negroes* (Misc. no. 6, vol. 3); Ambrose Caliver, *A Summary* (Misc. no. 6, vol. 4) (Washington: U.S. Government Printing Office, U.S. Office of Education, 1942 and 1943).

college administrators and scholars contributed to two symposia in *The Journal of Negro Education* on the past, present, and future of Negro public and private and church-related colleges.[4]

All these reports in one form or another contain many facts about higher education for Negroes, state by state and institution by institution. Like its predecessors, the present report concerns itself primarily with colleges and universities attended predominantly by Negro students. It does not report on the education of Negroes who attend predominantly white institutions, except to provide estimates of their numbers, nor does it survey the progress of desegregation in the white and Negro institutions. Both of these subjects deserve investigation, but they could not be included within the scope of the present inquiry. Unlike its predecessors, this report is not highly detailed. It aims to provide a general overview of the kinds of higher education now available in predominantly Negro institutions and the numbers and types of students who take advantage of their offerings. It also attempts to suggest policies and procedures to extend existing opportunities and to improve their quality. Whenever possible it compares the range of variation among these institutions with the larger company of American colleges and universities.

Similar studies and reports can be and have been made for other specific groups of institutions—for example, those established for women or those attended largely by members of particular religious denominations. But there is one overriding reason why the nation's predominantly Negro institutions today deserve special analysis and description. Because of poverty and discrimination, Negro youth make up a large proportion of the seriously disadvantaged youth in the nation, and our people generally have now determined to eradicate these unjust privations and the handicaps they impose. *Although the Negro colleges and universities include less than six per cent of American institutions of higher education, and their enrollments comprise less than 3 per cent of all college students, these Negro colleges enroll over half of all Negroes attending the nation's institutions of higher education.* Under the impact of P.L. 441 the percentage of white enrollments, especially in the publicly supported institutions, will doubtless rise with increasing acceleration as they should. *But regardless of the speed or extent of racial integration many of these institutions will, for the foreseeable*

---

[4] "The Negro Private and Church-Related College," *The Journal of Negro Education*, vol 29, no. 3, Summer 1960; "The Negro Public College," *The Journal of Negro Education*, vol. 31, no. 3, Summer 1962.

future, continue to be a major avenue to higher education for Negro youth.

It should be made unmistakably clear at the outset that no one officially associated with this inquiry has assumed that any American institution of higher education will be perpetuated on a segregated basis. On the contrary, this report and its recommendations rest on the conviction that *all* American colleges and universities will increasingly be open on an equal basis to *all* citizens regardless of race, creed, color, class, social origin, or financial status. Unquestionably, the present predominantly Negro institutions will admit more and more white students, and predominantly white institutions will admit larger numbers of Negroes. Thus in time institutional differences will reflect not racial differences, but student variations in ability, intellectual interest, and vocational goals. Eventually both Negroes and whites of the requisite ability from all sections of the country will be able to get their higher education at the institutions of their choice.

Despite this prospect, it is likely that for an unpredictable number of years many of the colleges and universities in this study will be attended largely by Negroes. Quite apart from legal and financial obstructionism, neither of which can be immediately uprooted, strong psychological and social factors as well as those of finance and geography will cause many Negro students to gravitate toward these institutions. A number of persons who have made thoughtful and unbiased analyses of the situation have reached this conclusion. For example, in summing up a series of papers presented at a conference on *Educational Imperative: The Negro in the Changing South*, Freda H. Goldman states:

However paradoxical it may seem to look to colleges established expressly to serve a segregated Negro community as the central institution to lead the educational movement for integration, it is a fact of life, as Marion Wright points out in the opening statement, that the Negro community "for as long as any of us will be alive" will have to rely on these colleges for most of its educational needs. It may also be true, however, that being closer to the problems of Negroes and more experienced in dealing with them, they may already have established patterns that give them a kind of advantage, psychologically and organizationally, for the huge job that needs to be done. Thus, while it is expected that the process of desegregation of both the white and Negro colleges will continue, our writers assume that the major burden of responsibility for the educational implementation of the transition to integration and a good society for Negro southerners will remain on the schools predominantly serving Negroes.[5]

If, therefore, many Negro young people, particularly those in the southern region, are to receive *any* higher education, the institutions now primarily serving Negroes must for a considerable span of years furnish it. The facts and recommendations in this report are designed to initiate the actions which need to be taken to assure the adequacy of the education they provide.

If this report does nothing else, it should establish the fact that, except at the topmost level of excellence represented by a few celebrated institutions, the Negro institutions run the entire gamut of quality within American higher education. Some educators as well as laymen unfamiliar with the Negro colleges seem not to realize this fact. Occasionally they appear to believe that the nation's predominantly Negro colleges make up a small isolated band of institutions at the end of the American academic procession—the procession of colleges and universities that David Riesman has depicted so graphically as a snake-like line, led by the experimental avant-garde institutions, followed by a multitude of colleges attempting to keep up with the first, and tapering to a long, trailing line of weaker institutions that form the tail.[6] But instead of forming a separate unitary group near the end of this procession, the Negro institutions lie all along the line. Some are exceptionally far forward and others far behind, but beside each of them stands some institution attended predominantly by white students.

An objective review of the facts discloses, however, that a not inconsiderable number of Negro institutions now struggle along toward the rear of the academic procession. The scope and recency of the training of their faculties, the character and the level of their students' preparatory education, and under present conditions the prospects of improvement in some of these institutions are not reassuring, even to the most sympathetic observer. Reviewing the relevant facts some educators and laymen as well have already concluded that both their students and society at large would be better served if a number of

[5] Freda H. Goldman, "Integration and the Negro College," *Educational Imperative: The Negro in the Changing South* (Chicago: The Center of Liberal Education for Adults, 1963), pp. 2–3.

[6] David Riesman, "The Academic Procession," *Constraint and Variety in American Education* (Lincoln: University of Nebraska Press, 1956).

Negro colleges closed their doors. To be sure, some of the bare, unin-
terpreted facts in this report would seem to support the argument that
a considerable number of these institutions ought to be disestablished.
Such a drastic proposal is, however, of such portentous significance that
it ought to be acted upon only after the most thoughtful, informed, and
restrained judgment.

*Contrary to the proposal for disestablishment, a deliberate weigh-
ing of the evidence in this study leads to the conclusion that most of
the predominantly Negro institutions ought to be preserved and
strengthened. In any event none should be allowed to die unless and
until their present and prospective students can be assured of better
educational opportunities elsewhere.* In one southern state where the
board controlling the institutions of higher education proposed phasing
out a Negro college the Negro citizenry as well as one of the state's
most prominent newspapers rejected this proposal and countered with
the suggestion that the institution be assimilated on an integrated basis
into the entire state system of colleges and universities. Mergers among
some neighboring colleges would doubtless create stronger educational
programs, and such possibilities should be objectively explored. In
some communities, the joining either of two or more predominantly
Negro or of Negro and white institutions, particularly at the junior
college level, would be advantageous. But in towns and countryside
where no other college is readily available to Negroes, these institutions
should be maintained despite their limited programs while energetic
efforts are made to enable them to provide a better higher education
for local youth.

The arguments of those who advocate institutional euthanasia for
the weaker institutions deserve careful appraisal. Some contend that
these weak institutions provide education of indefensibly low quality
and by so doing delude their students into believing that they are gaining a higher education when, in fact, their intellectual experiences are
hardly more stimulating and rewarding than those of a moderately
good high school. Hence, when these students graduate they may find
themselves inadequately prepared either for further education in a
graduate or professional school, for immediate gainful employment in
any but unskilled occupations, or for the demanding responsibilities of
public and private life in the modern world. If these colleges did not
exist, it is reasoned, their students would either attend institutions of
better quality or, if unable to gain admission elsewhere, they would

in any event not spend valuable years and scarce funds pursuing a delusive educational goal.

Second, the proponents of disestablishment maintain that the predominantly Negro college of low quality tends to create a false and handicapping image of the whole company of these institutions. This image, it is contended, prevents prospective donors from contributing directly to the colleges or to such assisting organizations as the United Negro College Fund, which gathers support for thirty-three private institutions. The elimination of the less fit, so the argument goes, would brighten the image of the Negro colleges as a whole, strengthen the survivors through increased support, and thus on the average improve the higher education of Negro youth.

Third, some observers hold that weak Negro colleges have the effect of perpetuating segregation. These institutions will become integrated, it is reasoned, only to the extent that they are able to offer white students instruction equal or superior to that available in the better predominantly white institutions. In this view, preserving Negro colleges of low quality is in fact tantamount to excluding white students and hence in effect nearly as objectionable as compulsory segregation. By closing the weaker institutions, the inadequate resources available to them would, in many instances, flow to the stronger, whose student bodies *ipso facto* would more quickly become genuinely multiracial.

Before attempting a rebuttal of these arguments for closing institutions, it cannot be denied that the present image of the Negro college probably drives away some able students, both Negro and white, and restrains some potential donors. It must be admitted that, with a few notable exceptions, the Negro institutions have not thus far attracted large numbers of white students. It does not ineluctably follow, however, that closing the weaker institutions would materially change these patterns of attendance and improve the educational opportunities for Negro students in general. Would the closing of, say, a fourth or a fifth of existing institutions, and the shifting of support to those which remain, provide greater opportunity for better higher education for the *entire population* of Negro youth? Surely not. An indeterminable but small percentage of students who now attend the lower-quality institutions would go to other predominantly Negro colleges or to some other institutions. But the facts in this study relating to the previous education and the financial ability of Negro students indicate that at present and, to a lesser degree, for some years to come, the majority of students in the weaker colleges could not gain admission to the stronger nor afford to attend them even if admitted. *Hence the closing of the weaker institutions would deprive thousands of Negro youth of any opportunity for higher education.*

Consider first the facts of finance. A number of community studies have convincingly demonstrated a close relationship between the nearness of higher education and the percentage of local young pople who continue their education beyond high school. This relationship is particularly high among low-income families. Poorer families can afford neither the expenses of living away from home nor the generally larger tuition and other fees in the "prestige" institutions. For these reasons many students in the predominantly Negro colleges are attracted by their proximity to home and their relatively low costs. With the exception of the extremely able youth who can obtain large scholarships it is delusive and visionary to expect poor Negro boys and girls from rural Alabama or South Carolina to attend Fisk or Howard universities, or for that matter, Harvard or Yale.

The idea that either private gifts or public funds can provide enough scholarships of sufficient value to enable the thousands of potentially eligible Negro youth to attend major institutions is equally deceptive. Moreover, it cannot be forgotten that even the institutions which for the most part attract students with low high school records and poor qualifying test scores invariably have in their classes a modest but socially significant percentage of young people of the very highest academic potential. And American history testifies abundantly to the fact that these students have often achieved positions of high status in their occupations and in public life generally. The hard fact remains that unless relatively inexpensive higher education is near at hand, the majority of these young people will not be able to continue their formal schooling beyond high school. Hence, as many as possible of the existing colleges should be preserved while strenuous efforts are made to improve them.

Consider next the factor of earlier education. The evidence gathered in this inquiry indicates that, like thousands of young people in poor areas throughout the country, many Negro youth, regardless of their latent ability, simply have had neither the type of elementary and secondary education nor the cultural stimulation in the home to prepare them for exacting higher education. As a result, until education in the lower schools is greatly improved, they will be unable to gain admission either to predominantly white institutions or to selective Negro colleges. In the meantime they can receive a satisfactory if not a distinguished education at the presently weaker institutions, if the latter are dedicated to the ideal and equipped for the task of offering superior instruction to students whose earlier education is inadequate. Special programs in New York City and elsewhere have fully proved that with individual attention, dedicated teachers, and superior teaching procedures, disadvantaged children can make impressive intellectual progress even in one school year. Four years of such college teaching could lift youth of limited academic preparation to high levels of achievement and send a normal proportion on to further formal education, to major positions of responsibility, and to distinguished service in American society.

Finally, consider the dramatically mounting enrollments and the consequent need for higher education. The elaborate statistics on future college enrollments need not be displayed again to demonstrate that the demands on all the constituent units of the enterprise of American higher education will increase intensively and irresistibly in the years ahead. The nation will need every existing establishment, and many more, to accommodate the young people who seek and deserve the advantages of higher education. All the existing Negro colleges and many more institutions will be required to accommodate these oncoming legions. It would be neither economical nor in the national interest, in fact it would be patent foolishness, to close existing colleges while establishing new institutions.

In short, student finances, educational preparation, and growing enrollments argue compellingly for preserving, strengthening, and integrating existing Negro institutions and against closing them or allowing them to wither on the academic vine. To keep these institutions in being and to enhance the quality of their programs will, as the information presented in the following pages demonstrates, require large additional funds. But both social necessity and humane considerations persuasively demonstrate that obtaining these urgently needed resources is a work to which foundations, government at the local, state, and Federal levels, and individual philanthropists can with deep satisfaction dedicate their efforts.

As far as disadvantaged Negro and other youth are concerned, the concept of excellence can be realized, not by the application of the negative philosophy of casting out all those who do not come up to elitist standards—and this view appears to be gaining popularity among many American educators—but by taking students where they are socially, economically, and educationally, and developing their abilities to the fullest. This is the affirmative philosophy from which our educational system and our social and political institutions have sprung. This is the only foundation stone on which our national well-being can securely rest. This is the doctrine which should illuminate any decision to preserve or close the weaker Negro institutions or, indeed, their counterparts in the higher education establishment.

Chapter 2

THE INSTITUTIONS

THE PRESIDENT OF ONE PREDOMINANTLY NEGRO INSTITUTION HAS SAID THAT the major task of the Negro colleges is one of "taking students who have experienced cultural deprivation and preparing them in the short span of the college experience to compete on a basis of equality with other American college graduates."[1] His statement highlights three major facts about these institutions: (1) They arose to serve a disadvantaged group in American society, as a result of which (2) they have had to devote much of their effort to remedial work, and (3) in the past they have had to place the emphasis in their curricula on a limited number of utilitarian and vocational ends.

These generalizations which still hold for many Negro institutions must be qualified in two respects. First, the same statements could be made about a number of other American colleges which provide similar educational opportunities to equally disadvantaged students. Second, such generalizations cover up the diversity among the predominantly Negro colleges, the wide variations in the backgrounds of their students, and the range of their programs. In this respect, too, they are representative of other institutions of higher education. This report will reveal the diversity of the Negro colleges and at the same time show their commonality with all American colleges and universities. Hence, when central tendencies with respect to any of their features are cited the fact should not be overlooked that they differ greatly among themselves and yet in many respects resemble other institutions.

[1] Martin D. Jenkins, *The Morgan State College Program—An Adventure in Higher Education* (Baltimore, Md.: Morgan State College Press, 1964), p. 3.

11

Succeeding chapters present facts about their students and their courses of study in some detail. This chapter describes more general features such as their public or private control, location, enrollments, and financial conditions.

THE NUMBER OF INSTITUTIONS

Although it may seem strange, one major problem in studying the predominantly Negro colleges and universities was simply the difficulty of identifying those institutions in which Negro students comprise from 50 to 100 per cent of the full-time enrollments. For some with long-standing national reputations, such as Tuskegee, Fisk, Howard, or Atlanta, no such difficulty arises. But others are only regionally or locally recognized. To identify all of them, the Institute of Higher Education initially obtained the help of a number of agencies and individuals: the Southern Regional Council, the United Negro College Fund, and the United States Office of Education, to name but three. From all available sources an original list of 107 institutions was assembled. Lists of colleges in *The Journal of Negro Education* and conversations in visits to eighty-nine of these institutions revealed eighteen others which raised to a total of 123 the number of colleges and universities in the United States enrolling a predominance of Negro students in 1963–64.[2]

The closing of one and the merging of two institutions have already changed this figure. Further closings and mergers may reduce the number in the future as they have in the past, and some now predominantly Negro institutions will enroll increasing proportions of white students to the point that their student bodies will no longer be predominantly Negro. In two traditionally Negro institutions in West Virginia, Bluefield State and West Virginia State colleges, the racial balance has already shifted from Negro to white. On the other hand, some new or currently largely white institutions, particularly those serving the inner core of great metropolitan centers, may become pre-

---

[2] All 123 are listed in Appendix A on pages 172–177. One hundred and twelve of them are included in Part 3 of the U.S. Office of Education's *Education Directory 1963–64* which limits its listings to accredited colleges and universities and any unaccredited institutions whose credits are accepted on transfer by at least three accredited institutions. The eighty-nine institutions which supplied detailed information to the Institute of Higher Education for this report comprise 72 per cent of all 123 institutions, and serve over 85 per cent of the aggregate enrollment. The junior colleges were more largely represented among the group which did not take part in the study, and in two states, Alabama and South Carolina, less than half of the eligible institutions participated.

dominantly Negro, as have three of the eight new campuses of Chicago City Junior College.[3] Even if the number of predominantly Negro colleges increases in the future, their proportion of all institutions in the United States is not likely to grow; in fact, since over 180 new institutions have come into being during the past five years, the predominantly Negro colleges will inevitably constitute an ever-shrinking percentage of the whole enterprise of American higher education.

The future expansion of predominantly Negro junior colleges is in doubt. These institutions have generally not flourished and yet, like their sister institutions, they could perform important functions, especially for young people who cannot afford to go away from home for their college education or who ought to have special types of technical instruction not available in four-year colleges. But as this study progressed it became obvious that the Negro junior or community colleges were virtually untouched by the mainstream of higher educational expansion and development. They serve a mere 7,000 students in comparison with the 100,000 enrolled in the Negro senior institutions and the nearly one million attending predominantly white junior and community colleges. The general enthusiasm and excitement found in many white junior colleges and in the communities which have been caught in the spirit of this relatively new educational venture are almost totally absent in the Negro junior colleges and their communities.

One of the strongest restraining influences in this situation is the attitude of most Negro senior colleges toward the two-year institutions. This has often been one of depreciation, expressed practically in their refusal to grant fair credit to students who attempt to transfer from the junior to the senior institutions. There are notable exceptions, but generally the senior institutions seem to consider the two-year colleges beneath college grade. Perhaps this attitude stems from the fact that most of the junior colleges are unaccredited, and therefore their work cannot generally be accepted in transfer. In any event the student's inability to get credit for his junior college work has caused many of the administrators, teachers, and students interviewed in the predominantly Negro junior colleges to be unenthusiastic about their programs, services, and prospects for development.

It is regrettable that such a stifling influence on the junior colleges exists because the latter ought to be performing several crucial functions

[3] Chicago's junior college is not included in the list of 123 institutions, since its enrollment at large is predominantly white, while Bluefield and West Virginia State are listed because of their continuing large full-time Negro enrollment.

other than preparing their students for work beyond the first two college years. Regardless of the pace of desegregation, it is essential to maintain some of the existing Negro junior colleges as educational centers with the unique responsibilities of (1) meeting certain peculiar needs of Negro students in the interim and (2) carrying out a deliberately designed program of desegregation of the educational system in their own communities. In fulfilling this latter responsibility the Negro junior college can enhance its educational contribution by becoming a deseg- regated center whose interracial and intercultural innovations can serve as examples worthy of emulation in other institutions. For these reasons some of the present Negro junior colleges should be considerably ex- panded and improved.

PROPORTION OF NON-NEGRO STUDENTS

Although this study made no attempt to investigate the rate and extent of desegregation, it was recognized that an understanding of the present functions and the future prospects of the predominantly Negro colleges would to a degree depend on knowledge of the per- centage of their present students who are not Negroes. Hence statistical information was gathered on this matter. The aggregate figures revealed that between 2.5 and 3.5 per cent of the students enrolled in pre- dominantly Negro institutions in 1963–64 were non-Negro. Although a small minority of these students were Oriental, most were Caucasians. Seventy-five of the 123 institutions reported that they had no non- Negro students. As the figures in Table 1 show, in the remaining forty-eight colleges integration has advanced to various levels; in two

Table 1   PERCENTAGE OF NON–NEGRO ENROLLMENTS AT PREDOMINANTLY NEGRO INSTITUTIONS, 1963–1964[a]

PERCENTAGE OF TOTAL ENROLLMENTS	NUMBER OF INSTITUTIONS
50–55%	2
40–50	1
30–40	0
20–30	3
10–20	4
5–10	4
any to 5	34

[a] The total full-time and part-time enrollments have been combined but not equated.

institutions, in fact, the proportion of non-Negroes exceeds one-half, and in terms of enrollments they are actually no longer predominantly Negro institutions. Moreover, another twelve institutions report that more than 5 per cent of their students are non-Negroes. Thirty-four have less than 5 per cent of non-Negro students.

As might be expected, most of the Negro institutions with large proportions of non-Negro students are located in the northeastern or border states, at Bluefield and West Virginia State colleges, and at Lincoln University in Pennsylvania.

LOCATION

The geographical distribution of all 123 institutions is shown on page 16 and in Appendix A. Of the 123 Negro institutions, 119 are located in the seventeen southern states and the District of Columbia, where the Negro population has been heavily concentrated and where until recently segregation has been severely enforced. Only four of the 123 are located in northern states: Wilberforce University and Central State College on adjoining campuses in Wilberforce, Ohio, and Lincoln University and Cheyney State College in southeastern Pennsylvania. It is significant that Wilberforce and Lincoln are the oldest of all the Negro institutions, both having been established before the Civil War, one in 1854 and the other in 1856.

LEVEL OF OFFERING

Some inferences can be drawn concerning the kind and level of education these predominantly Negro institutions offer by an analysis of their structure and the degrees they grant. In this connection it is important to recall that most of the older Negro colleges began their work after the Civil War at the elementary and secondary school level and only later moved into the collegiate sphere while at least in principle discontinuing preparatory education. The figures in Table 2 reveal several significant facts about the level of the present educational programs in these 123 institutions. First, the percentage of those with programs of no more than two years beyond the high school is almost identical with similar figures for the institutions of higher education at large in the United States and in the southern states. Nearly a third of the predominantly Negro colleges, 30.9 per cent, are junior or community colleges. But these figures could be misleading without a

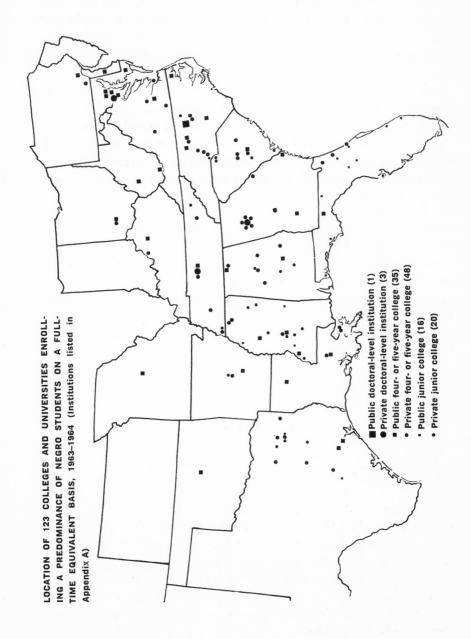

LOCATION OF 123 COLLEGES AND UNIVERSITIES ENROLL-
ING A PREDOMINANCE OF NEGRO STUDENTS ON A FULL-
TIME EQUIVALENT BASIS, 1963-1964 (Institutions listed in
Appendix A)

■ Public doctoral-level institution (1)
● Private doctoral-level institution (3)
▪ Public four- or five-year college (35)
• Private four- or five-year college (48)
▪ Public junior college (16)
• Private junior college (20)

scrutiny of the enrollments in these junior colleges. Actually their position among the Negro colleges is less prominent than the 30.9 per cent might suggest, for they serve only an aggregate of about 7,000 students. The other junior and community colleges of the country, however, accommodate nearly a million students, over a fifth of the total enrollments in all types of institutions. These figures show that the predominantly Negro junior colleges are, on the average, small institutions, in many instances too small to provide the rounded educational program so common in other junior colleges. Because of this lack of enterprising development a considerable number of Negro youth must inevitably be deprived of the various types of academic and technical programs so richly provided for thousands of others.

Table 2   LEVEL OF CURRICULAR OFFERING IN PREDOMINANTLY NEGRO AND IN OTHER INSTITUTIONS

	PREDOMINANTLY NEGRO INSTITUTIONS	ALL INSTITUTIONS IN THE 17 SOUTHERN STATES	UNITED STATES INSTITUTIONS[a]
I. Two but less than four years	30.9%	30.8%	30.5%
II. Only the B.A. or first professional degree	51.2	33.3	37.5
III. M.A. and/or second professional degree	15.4	27.2	21.5
IV. Ph.D. and equivalent degree	2.4	8.2	10.5

[a] Table 1, page 9, *Education Directory 1963–1964, Part 3.* Not included are twenty-five institutions offering degrees other than these four types.

An examination of categories III and IV in Table 2 documents the view that these 123 colleges serving Negro youth preponderantly offer only undergraduate four-year programs. In the United States at large, 32 per cent of the institutions of higher education grant master's or doctor's degrees, but in these 123 institutions the comparable figure is only 17.8. More importantly, of the latter, 15.4 per cent are at the master's level and highly concentrated in fields directly related to professional teacher education. In only 2.4 per cent, actually three of the predominantly Negro institutions, can a student earn the doctoral degree. That this is not a peculiar geographical condition is clear from the figures relating to the institutions serving predominantly white students in the South. The undergraduate character of these 123 colleges and universities is borne out by their enrollment figures. Only 4.9 per cent of their students are enrolled at the graduate level, while the comparable figure for the United States at large is 9.7.

The figures in Table 2 also show that the higher education enterprise serving Negro youth is a lopsided effort, or rather it has too large a bulge in the middle. Just as the history of these institutions to a large extent explains their past programs and clientele, the changing circumstances of American life and the position of the Negro in it, foretell a shift in emphasis within their courses of study, institutional structures, and the use of their resources. *The four-year undergraduate liberal arts and professional curricula need to be expanded and strengthened. More diversified programs should be provided in more serviceably located junior colleges. More graduate and postbaccalaureate curricula in the professional fields should be established and the related existing courses of study strengthened.*

In the years immediately ahead, however, the multiplication of graduate programs leading to the Ph.D. degree should proceed only with the most judicious appraisal of need and potential support. Perhaps a dozen or fifteen of the stronger liberal arts colleges could, within the next ten years, extend their offerings into the graduate fields covered by the large universities. But to do so they will require large additional resources if they are to match the quality of the graduate specializations elsewhere. Nothing will be gained by creating a false image of superiority through the initiation of graduate programs of secondary or lower quality. Only institutions which already have strong undergraduate departments and the prospects of obtaining the large additional financial resources to sustain high-quality graduate work should undertake it. If they can obtain large foundation, government, or corporate support, a limited number of these institutions appears to have that potential. The others should enhance the quality of their undergraduate offerings and send their qualified students on to other institutions for graduate degrees.

SPONSORSHIP

The auspices under which institutions of higher education are established and sustained influence the type of students they serve, their programs, and, in latter years, the probability that they can gain the resources essential for good service or even survival. Most of the Negro colleges are the outgrowth of three major historical forces in higher education: the missionary work of the American churches, the land-grant legislation and the development of the normal schools, and more recently the junior college movement. Today, of the 121 institutions which supplied relevant information, the largest proportion, fifty-six, or 46.3 per cent, are controlled by religious denominations.

Table 3 shows the denominational affiliation of these fifty-six institutions classified by the level of their instruction. Long the backbone of Negro higher education, these fifty-six colleges are the survivors of over two hundred which sprang from nineteenth-century missionary efforts. Begun in 1846 with the formation of the American Missionary Association, these endeavors helped to establish six educational institutions for Negroes prior to 1860 and organized scores more in cooperation with the Freedmen's Bureau following the Civil War. Currently, the strength of their denominational ties varies considerably; some, like Dillard, Fisk, and Morehouse, receive relatively little denominational

Table 3   NEGRO COLLEGES SUPPORTED BY RELIGIOUS DENOMINATIONS, 1963–1964

DENOMINATION	JUNIOR COLLEGES	SENIOR COLLEGES	DOCTORAL INSTITU- TIONS	TOTAL
Baptist	6	7		13
Methodist	3	6½		9½
African Methodist Episcopal	4	5½		9½
Christian Methodist Episcopal		4		4
Protestant Episcopal	2	2		4
American Missionary Association		3		3
African Methodist Episcopal Zion		1		1
Church of Christ	1			1
Church of God	1			1
Disciples of Christ		1		1
Interdenominational		1		1
Lutheran	1			1
Presbyterian US		1		1
United Presbyterian	1	3		4
Roman Catholic		1		1
Seventh-Day Adventists		1		1
Total	19	37	0	56

support and their governing boards are not religiously dominated; others, like Bennett or Lane, are largely church supported and governed.

Of the fifty-one institutions operated under public auspices, shown in Table 4, thirty-six are supported and operated by states, twelve by counties, and two by cities. About half of the thiry-four senior colleges under the auspices of public bodies evolved out of normal schools established to train school teachers; the other half were brought into being by the Land-Grant Acts of 1862 and 1890 which encouraged instruction in agriculture and the mechanic arts. Sixteen of these fifty-one are two-year community colleges, most of them in Florida and almost all established since the Second World War.

Table 4   **TYPE OF CONTROL IN FOURTEEN INDEPENDENT AND FIFTY-ONE PUBLIC NEGRO COLLEGES**

	JUNIOR COLLEGES	SENIOR COLLEGES	DOCTORAL INSTITUTIONS	TOTAL
INDEPENDENT	2	9	3	14
PUBLIC				
State	2	33	1	36
County	12			12
City	2	1		3

Like other such institutions in this country, many of the *private* Negro colleges and universities are among the very best in terms of their educational programs, their faculty preparation, their student selection, and the quality of their leadership. They will continue to serve an indispensable role in the education of American youth, and they deserve a greatly enlarged financial and moral support. But, as is true in the other branches of our system of higher education, the *publicly* supported institutions will be called on to serve an ever-increasing proportion of college-age youth. If they are to meet these additional obligations, public bodies, and our people generally, must be prepared to increase the tax funds required to supply the needed financial support. Integration will require substantial financial underpinning of both white and Negro state colleges; indeed, larger support of both will give desirable impetus to the integration movement.

ENROLLMENTS

As is true in the nation generally, enrollments at the public Negro institutions are increasing more rapidly than at private colleges. Despite the fact that the seventy-two private outnumber the fifty-one public colleges by twenty-one, they enroll only three-fifths as many students—in 1963–64, about 41,000 compared to over 69,000. In 1958, Negro students in public colleges comprised 61 per cent of the total enrollments, but in 1964 they made up 63 per cent, and by 1970 this figure will probably rise to 65 or possibly 67. While the four-year Negro institutions were increasing their enrollments significantly the Negro junior colleges lagged considerably behind the former and behind the two-year institutions at large. While the two-year Negro colleges have been increasing only slightly, junior college enrollments throughout the country have been rising dramatically. In the fifteen years since 1949–50, while the number of junior college students in the nation at large was increasing by over 175 per cent, Negro junior college enrollments rose less than 7 per cent. These figures bear out the view expressed earlier that the Negro junior colleges have not risen to the position they ought to occupy in the whole enterprise of American higher education.

Significantly, Negro institutions as a whole have expanded at a higher rate from 1948 to 1963 than colleges and universities generally; enrollments in the former grew by over 60 per cent, in the latter by only about 50 per cent. Even at this rate of expansion, however, numerically they are playing a smaller and smaller role in the total services of American higher education. Their enrollments rose to nearly 3.2 per cent of the national total in 1952, but by 1960 this figure had fallen to 2.6 per cent, and in the fall of 1964 dropped still further to 2.4 per cent. Unless these institutions receive substantial help in expanding their educational offerings, in attracting highly qualified faculty members, and in enlarging their plant facilities, they will quite likely play a less and less prominent role in the education of Negro, or, for that matter, white students. Last year they enrolled about 58 per cent of the estimated 185,200 Negro college and university students in the United States.[4] This proportion of the total is likely to decline because (1) Negro migration will probably continue from the South into other regions with predominantly white institutions, (2) northern colleges and universities will intensify their recruiting of Negroes in southern high schools, and (3) desegregation within the South will bring

[4] Estimates of Negro college attendance have varied as much as 75,000. This estimate was made by the Institute of Higher Education from replies from 1,400 of the nation's 2,100 colleges and universities and from extrapolations by type of institution and state for the others.

greater numbers of Negro graduate students to desegregated state universities, while most of the predominantly Negro institutions concentrate their efforts at the undergraduate level.

This apparent anomaly of playing a smaller role in higher education generally and also in the education of Negroes while expanding at a higher than average rate is accounted for largely by the disproportionately small size of many of the Negro colleges. In 1963–64, eleven of the 123 institutions enrolled fewer than one hundred students, the smallest only twelve, and two others only seventeen. Fifty-seven others had fewer than five hundred students. In only thirty of the colleges were there over a thousand students, and even Howard University—the largest, with a student body of 6,288—fell far below the size of other private and public universities such as New York University and the University of Illinois. In contrast, only 36 per cent of the nation's colleges and universities were as small as the 51 per cent of the Negro institutions, with fewer than five hundred students, and 40 per cent of the former enrolled over a thousand students in contrast to 24 per cent of the latter.

The small size of Negro colleges becomes even more evident by comparing the percentage of students in institutions of various sizes. Thirty-five per cent of the students in Negro colleges attend institutions with fewer than a thousand students, in contrast to less than 12 per cent of students in other institutions. The most dramatic figures relate to the students who attend very large universities. Only 10 per cent of the students in Negro institutions attend the two Negro universities which enroll over five thousand students (Howard and Southern), while over 58 per cent, almost three out of five, of the nation's students are now enrolled in institutions of at least this size.

There has been much discussion in recent years of the economic and educational advantages and disadvantages of small and large institutions of higher education. Because of the paucity of reliable facts the issues cannot be definitively resolved. It can be said, however, with considerable assurance, that an institution with fewer than a thousand or twelve hundred students must operate on a costly scale. Moreover, no one has proved that raising enrollments from four or five hundred to something over a thousand lowers educational standards. In fact, such evidence as does exist suggests that a small enrollment, in the absence of inordinately large endowments or other sources of income, impoverishes the educational program by restricting the range of curricular offerings and suppressing the level of faculty compensation. Small institutions usually limit the breadth of their programs, expect teachers to be competent in several fields, and impose heavy teaching schedules. Small enrollments necessitate uneconomically small classes, and disproportionately increase costs for supporting services such as plant upkeep and administration. *Hence, the Negro colleges should make an effort to enroll at least a thousand students in order to improve their fiscal and educational efficiency.*

Increasing the size of student bodies should not be difficult in the years ahead. The need for higher education is greatest in the South where most of these colleges are located. In 1960, only 29 per cent of all college-age youth of both races in the South were attending college, compared to 39 per cent for the nation as a whole. The Southern Regional Education Board has estimated that if present trends continue, by 1970, 34 per cent of the region's youth may be in college, while the national proportion is rising to 45 per cent. The Board believes that the South should attempt to halve the gap of 11 per cent between the region and the nation by raising its college attendance rate to 39 per cent.[5] This enlarged attendance, coupled with over a 50 per cent increase in the number of college-age youth, should double the rate of growth in enrollments in higher education in the South over the decade. To meet this demand for additional schooling, all educational facilities in the South will have to be extensively expanded. The integration of the institutions which are now either predominantly Negro or white will not diminish the need for more places in the colleges and universities. Hence the opportunity to make fuller and more efficient use of the small Negro colleges is at hand.

INTERINSTITUTIONAL COOPERATION

A variety of devices will have to be used to accommodate the services of the predominantly Negro institutions to these enlarged student bodies. One of these is interinstitutional cooperation. At least twenty predominantly Negro institutions already share their resources. Although it is not possible to completely catalogue these joint efforts, examples will illustrate the range and kinds of cooperation that might profitably be adopted elsewhere. The most prominent example of cooperation and

[5] The Commission on Goals for Higher Education in the South, *Within Our Reach* (Atlanta: Southern Regional Education Board, 1963), p. 38.

partial merger is to be found at the Atlanta University Center, where six institutions—Clark, Morehouse, Spelman, Morris Brown, Interdenominational Theological Center, and the graduate school, Atlanta University, all located within several blocks of each other—share courses and library holdings. Five other predominantly Negro institutions participate in the sixteen-member Piedmont University Center of North Carolina which has established an interchange of professors, a visiting scholar program, an artists and lecture series, joint use of library resources, and sponsored faculty research. In Richmond, Union Theological Seminary and Virginia Union University share library facilities and student fellowships. In Florida, the five Associated Mid-Florida Colleges which have united in mutual assistance include two predominantly Negro institutions. Bishop College belongs to the Dallas Inter-University Council, and Howard University is one of five Washington universities organized in a Joint Graduate Consortium to coordinate their graduate programs.

Opportunities have long existed for similar combinations of effort among other predominantly Negro institutions, and possibilities increasingly present themselves for cooperation with other colleges and universities. *These arrangements for cooperation with white and other Negro institutions should be expanded. Since duplication of functions and resources incur costs beyond the limits of even the most generous philanthropy, foundations and individuals could well condition potential grants on the ability and willingness of institutions, wherever possible, to make joint use of faculties and facilities.*

In some instances outright fusion would be even more beneficial than joint operation. A duplication of educational facilities and services in the same locality is not only wastefully expensive, usually it is poorer in quality than unified programs could be. Doctrinal differences now stand in the way of mergers of neighboring denominationally affiliated colleges, but these institutions could combine their offerings, faculties, and facilities, while maintaining separate departments or courses in religion. Mergers should not be limited to institutions serving a predominantly Negro clientele. *Religious denominations which now maintain separate colleges for Negro and white students predominantly should explore the economic and educational advantages of merger, especially when two or more institutions are located within commuting distance of one another.*

In the past, such combinations of public white and Negro colleges and schools has meant the loss of jobs to some of the Negro teachers and administrators. Mergers would still cause some displacements of top administrators, but with the increased demand for higher education and the opportunity for assistance in self-improvement through graduate study, the number of teachers depressed in position in the academic community or displaced should be minimal.

PLANNING

The 1942 *National Survey of the Higher Education of Negroes* concluded that

with a few notable exceptions, the colleges and universities studied are operating in a traditional way without giving much thought to their aims and objectives. They go on from year to year sometimes changing somewhat the work they do but without clearly formulating the basis for their programs of service. This of necessity has a profound influence on the quality of educational service they render.[6]

Contemporary critics are expressing similar views about colleges throughout the United States. They apply to many of the Negro institutions. Among the eighty-nine predominantly Negro institutions visited by the staff of the Institute of Higher Education, it was evident that at least a fourth of them were undertaking no programmed institutional research to provide basic information essential in a revision of their educational offerings and practices to meet emerging needs. A dozen more engage only periodically in self-study, usually to assemble data required for accreditation. A few have initiated research and critical analysis of their operations to develop a ten-year plan as proposed in Sidney Tickton's *Needed: A Ten Year College Budget*. A small group of colleges engages in systematic institutional research, conducted in most cases by members of the faculty or the administration on a casual or part-time basis, occasionally by the president himself. *Only four institutions in this group employ a specially designated director of institutional research to make systematic and continuous analyses of their operations.*

Administrators now generally agree that long-range planning based on sound research is essential if institutions of higher education are to

[6] Ambrose Caliver, *National Survey of the Higher Education of Negroes: A Summary* (Washington: U.S. Office of Education, 1942), p. 26.

keep abreast of the changing needs of the society which supports them and if they are going to operate within their prospective resources. Such studies are even more needed in the institutions included in this inquiry because they are going to be subjected to more exigent social pressures than their sister institutions and because their financial needs will be so large as to make efficient management imperative. Hence these institutions should inaugurate internal research activities to provide continuing analyses of their operations. *Since for a time some institutions will be unable to establish such research offices, large institutions like the Atlanta University Center should organize a broad program of cooperative institutional research. Additional resource centers should be established in Nashville and other strategic locations where persons capable of directing research related to finance, the curriculum, the faculty, student personnel services, and physical facilities could assist smaller institutions as consultants.*

FINANCE

Many of the predominantly Negro colleges could eliminate or at least mitigate their present shortcomings and needs if they had additional financial resources. The presidents of forty-one of the eighty-nine Negro colleges interviewed considered their financial condition to be the most crucial weakness in their institutions. The Negro colleges have long had to try to educate their students on a disproportionately small share of the funds spent in the enterprise of American higher education. For example, in 1959–60, the latest year for which comparable figures could be obtained, they enrolled 2.75 per cent of the nation's resident degree-credit students, but accounted for only 1.91 per cent of the total of current expenditures and only 1.68 per cent of the expenditures for plant. Even more dramatically, their expenditure per student for educational and general purposes was only $888 compared with the national average of $1,334. The Negro colleges were trying to provide a higher education for their students for just about two-thirds the money available to other institutions.

Although in the previous ten years their educational and general expenditures increased 76 per cent, they actually lost position in the nation at large because expenditures generally had risen 108 per cent in the same decade. A significant proportion of these additional funds covered contract research in which few of the Negro colleges shared.

But as Table 5 shows, even disregarding these research expenditures, the Negro colleges in 1959–60 accounted for only 2.21 per cent of the funds spent in the country at large for educational and general purposes. Moreover, as the more detailed facts exhibited in Appendix B show, the Negro colleges spent more than their part of funds for the expenses of plant operation and maintenance, nearly their share for libraries, but less than their proper proportion for all other educational purposes.

Table 5   PERCENTAGE OF COLLEGE AND UNIVERSITY EDUCATIONAL AND GENERAL EXPENDITURES SPENT BY NEGRO INSTITUTIONS, 1959–1960ᵃ

General administration and general expense	2.46%
Instruction and departmental research	2.31
Extension and public services	.37
Libraries	2.67
Plant operation and maintenance	2.95
Related activities	.96
Sales and services	.77
Educational and general expenditures, excluding organized research	2.21
Organized research	.13
Total educational and general expenditures	1.74

ᵃ Data from U.S. Office of Education. Public and private income and expenditures for 1959–60 are detailed in Appendix B, on pages 178–181.

The sources of institutional income are also significant. They not only reveal the present balance of support between public agencies and private philanthropy, but also suggest the probable slow rate of development in these institutions as a whole unless they can tap new sources of revenue. Of the $81 million the Negro colleges received in 1959–60 for current educational and general expenses, nearly $37.9 million came from state governments, over $19.5 million from student tuition and fees, $8.6 million from private gifts, $6.9 million from the Federal Government, $4.5 million from endowment earnings, and $1.0 million from local government. Of this $81 million, it is significant that outside of tuition income only $13.1 million came from private sources in the form of gifts or endowments. Moreover, the concentration of endowments in a few institutions makes this figure of $4.5 million more significant. Ten institutions hold 80 per cent of the endowment funds; five of them account for slightly more than 60 per cent; and two, Hampton and Tuskegee institutes, for almost 37 per cent.

The income of these colleges from all sources amounted to only

1.90 per cent of the national total and in several critical categories it fell markedly lower. Of funds for current expenses, the Negro institutions received 2.73 per cent of the states' support for higher education, 2.25 per cent of private gifts and grants, 2.16 per cent of endowment earnings, 1.68 per cent of tuition and fees, .69 per cent of the funds from local governments, and only .66 per cent of Federal funds. Almost all the latter went to one institution, Howard University in Washington, D.C. The latter institution is in a favored position with respect to obtaining Federal funds because since 1867 it has been directly supported by the United States Government in both capital expenditures and the costs of current operations.

These facts related to income explain in part the wide differences in per-student expenditure among the Negro institutions. In 1961–62, they spent on the average about $970 per student for educational and general purposes, but as low as this figure is compared to the national average, at least fifty of these colleges spent under $900 per student, thirty-five under $800, and twenty under $700. Other institutions outside this group could be found to match any one of them in terms of per-capita student expenditures, but they would not be among the nation's strongest, most vital colleges. *The unavoidable fact in the financial condition of the Negro institutions is that they will require large additional funds to cover current expenses and for endowment if they are to improve their present programs, and thus provide a higher education of suitable quality for their students.*

For the private institutions these additional funds must come from a variety of sources, from churches, from corporations, and from individual benefactors. If the nation's foundations want to assist in preserving the private institutions at a suitable level of service they can do so by spreading their grants more widely than they have thus far. Some foundations over the past several years have typically restricted their grants, especially those of considerable size, to a dozen or so Negro colleges commonly considered the prestige institutions. "To him who hath shall be given" seems to have been the policy. The social consequences of this practice ought to be re-examined.

No one would suggest that substantial contributions should not be made to the already well-financed Negro colleges. But with smaller investments many others could be invigorated and equipped for fuller and better service, and if such benefactions were accompanied by consultative services to improve their practices, the results would, in terms

of individual human development and social benefit, be equally rewarding. *In recent years many new foundations have come into existence,
some of them with only modest resources. Yet even with their more
limited means, they could make a significant contribution to the enhancement of the lot of Negroes by concentrating their financial aid
in one or two of the less well-known Negro colleges.* Several hundred
thousand dollars devoted annually to increasing salaries, adding scholarships, selectively expanding the library collections, and improving the
faculty could turn some of these institutions of modest quality into
first-rate colleges. They would reflect credit on a foundation of limited
national reputation, which by putting its relatively small resources into
already well-favored institutions will have little influence and gain little
satisfaction from its grants. The net effect of such limited assistance
on Negro youth could be as substantial as larger gifts to the better-
known colleges. *The opportunities for contributions of relatively small
sums to the smaller institutions are legion, and if made on an educationally discriminating basis the chances of richly rewarding results are
large.*

It is clear, however, that neither private nor corporate philanthropy alone can provide the very large additional resources required to
meet the needs of Negro youth for higher education. The only visible
sources for new funds in the required amounts are the local, state, and
Federal governments. These public bodies have the moral responsibility
to equalize the opportunities for higher education among American
youth, especially the Negroes who, since the earliest days of the Repub-
lic, through neglect and discrimination have been denied full access to
higher education.

The responsibility of the Federal Government in eradicating these
educational inequities in our national life is clear and inescapable. *The
financial contribution of the Federal Government must be large if
Negro youth and the predominantly Negro colleges are not to continue
to be disadvantaged.* In 1961–62, Federal funds comprised less than
11 per cent of the Negro colleges' income, and most of this money went
to one institution, Howard University, which enjoys a unique relationship with the Federal Government.

The indispensable role of the Federal Government is obvious in
the fact that the greatest educational inadequacies occur in the most
economically disadvantaged states, those in which in the main the
Negro's opportunity for higher education is even more restricted than

elsewhere. These commonwealths cannot be expected to provide out of their own presently limited resources the funds needed to upgrade their whole educational enterprise. Even if they make every possible effort to enhance the educational advantages of their Negro citizens, which they should do with all deliberate speed, they will fall short of the objective. Progress toward this equitable goal can only be achieved on the scale required by social justice and national well-being by large programs of assistance from the Federal Government. The passage of the Higher Education Bill of 1965 would presumably, through its provision for helping "developing colleges," be of some assistance to some Negro institutions.

The states themselves, however, cannot morally evade their own responsibilities to elevate the quality of, and extend the opportunity for, higher education among their Negro citizens. To that end they ought not to maintain two systems of higher education, one for Negroes and one for other citizens. Quite aside from the legal and moral issues involved, segregation in higher education, as well as at other levels, is an economically wasteful and debilitating practice. More than others, the economically disadvantaged states where segregation is most widely practiced cannot afford to waste their limited resources as they now do in duplicating programs, facilities, libraries, and plant in two systems of higher education, one for Negroes and one for whites. The penalty for these policies and practices is especially severe in the advanced and specialized levels of education, in the graduate schools where the numbers of students in the various specialties do not justify two or more separate establishments or curricula. The maintenance of separate, segregated systems of higher education involves economic consequences which necessarily depreciate the entire educational program. *By working toward the integration of their public colleges and universities, the states will improve the whole enterprise of higher education for all their youth and commensurately contribute to our national well-being. In view of their limited resources they should be substantially assisted by the Federal Government in their efforts to establish a full complement of higher educational services.*

In sum, recognizing the differences that exist among these institutions and the consequent limitations on generalization about them, these conclusions rest on a solid factual basis: The nation's predominantly Negro colleges are located in a wide area stretching from Pennsylvania to Texas across the border and southern states. Although most of them as yet enroll no white students, several are becoming predominantly white. These institutions are supported and controlled principally by the states and religious denominations; only a small proportion are independent of denominational or governmental support. Most of them operate only at the undergraduate level with relatively small enrollments. A number would benefit from increased interinstitutional research and planning. All these predominantly Negro institutions must have greatly increased financial support if they are adequately to serve the Negro youth who now attend them, as well as the whites who will inevitably seek their services in increasing numbers.

The following chapters present more detailed facts concerning the policies and programs of these institutions, the characteristics of their students and faculty, and the adequacy of their facilities, facts indispensable to those who wish to assist them in enhancing their services and thus raising the level of higher education for Negroes to the level required by social justice and national well-being.

Chapter 3

STUDENT COSTS AND ADMISSIONS POLICIES

IT HAS BEEN ESTIMATED THAT DURING 1963 ONE OUT OF EVERY FORTY-TWO white persons in the United States was attending a college or university, in contrast to one out of every 110 Negroes. Put another way, Negroes comprised about 10.8 per cent of the population in that year, but only 4.4 per cent of the nation's college students.[1] What accounts for such a discrepancy between the rates of college attendance among Negroes and whites?

Facts of culture, social class, discrimination, and finance all play a part in determining these differences in college attendance. For example, a greater proportion of Negroes than whites have been required to work at jobs with low status and low income, and for this type of employment they have not needed education beyond high school. Even if they had felt the need for, and had seen the advantage of, a college education, they would usually not have been able to pay for it. Moreover, like other children in lower economic families, some Negro students of considerable potential fail to go on with their formal schooling simply because they lack essential information about higher educational opportunities, the possibility of financial aid, or their ability to succeed if they tried.

---

[1] These estimates are based on the estimate of Negro enrollments described in the footnote on page 21, and an estimate that 92 per cent of the 20,311,760 non-whites in the United States in 1963 were Negro. In 1960, Negroes constituted 10.6 per cent of the nation's total population.

Other Negro youth discontinue their schooling because of a lack of motivation. The normal avenues to achievement in economic, social, and cultural life must be more widely opened before many Negro youth will be sufficiently incited to pursue higher education. To some extent the barriers are now being broken down. But until these young people become aware of the progressively unfolding opportunities and see about them examples of the rewards of effort spent in gaining a higher education, lack of hope among Negro youth will corrode their will to achieve.

The privations and restrictive circumstances of their lives have justified many in holding a devitalizing view of their vocational prospects. It is not surprising that they, their parents, and their teachers have believed that no matter how much advanced education these young people achieved they would be forced into positions of low status and compensation. Now, however, the prospects are brightening. Indeed the situation is changing so rapidly that many positions in industry and government and appointments to civic bodies go wanting because of a lack of qualified Negroes. Information about available jobs will eventually reach parents and their children through the general media of communication in the community. For the immediate future, however, the responsibility for keeping students abreast of new vocational opportunities must rest largely on specialized counselors and faculty members in the schools and colleges.

Even freer access to occupations formerly closed to them and intensified motivation will not, however, guarantee that all ambitious Negro youth will be able to gain a higher education. Two additional obstacles stand in their way: One is lack of money; the other is the inadequacy of their previous education. The deans and registrars in the eighty-nine institutions studied expressed the almost unanimous opinion that these two factors account for most of the dropouts at predominantly Negro colleges. With substantial outside help the colleges could strike down these two barriers. Hence this chapter deals extensively and intensively with the factors of students' financial resources and their previous education in relation to the fees charged and the admissions standards imposed by the colleges.

STUDENT FINANCES

In contrast to studies at other colleges and universities, which indicate that poor grades and personal reasons often play a greater role than lack of funds in causing students to discontinue their formal education, officials at predominantly Negro institutions identify inadequate finances as the primary cause for dropouts among their students.

Although carefully designed, comprehensive studies of the matter have not been made, informed persons believe that the lack of funds may also account for the fact that many Negro high school graduates do not even consider entering college. Studies have, however, established a clear relationship between the economic status of families and the educational attainment of their children. Tradition, human inertia, and the general circumstances of life doubtless restrain children and their parents from even considering the possibility of getting a higher education. But the compelling fact is that without outside help these families could not meet the costs of further schooling. Financial obstacles loom large in many Negro families, particularly in the South, the region largely served by the institutions included in this report. The figures in Table 6 indicate that the income of nonwhite families is lower than that of white families throughout the country. But more importantly in the South, where white income is approximately 20 per cent lower than elsewhere in the nation, median nonwhite income is only 46.4 per cent of that of whites.

Stated in terms of actual income available, the average nonwhite family in the South in 1960 earned $2,322 compared to $5,000 among southern white families and at least $4,371 among nonwhite families outside the South. Since many southern Negroes are unable to find jobs in other parts of the country where wages are higher, a vicious circle is passed on from one generation to the next. Many youth cannot take advantage of the opportunities for higher education because their families are unable to supply the necessary funds and, without higher education, these youths are in turn driven into low-paying jobs which prevent them from providing a higher education for *their* children.

Figures showing the general improvement in family incomes in recent years can easily lead to the false conclusion that this circle has been broken. Vivian W. Henderson has shown, however, that although the rate of growth of Negro income since 1940 has been greater than that of whites, "The absolute, or dollar difference has widened considerably [and thus] Negroes are losing ground rapidly in gaining dollar parity with whites."[2] If college fees continue to increase as sharply as they have been doing generally in the United States, Negro youth may

[2] Vivian W. Henderson, *The Economic Status of Negroes: In the Nation and in the South* (Atlanta, Ga.: Southern Regional Council, 1963), pp. 12, 13.

Table 6 MEDIAN INCOME OF FAMILIES WITH INCOME BY REGION AND COLOR, 1960[a]

REGION	WHITE	NONWHITE	DOLLAR DIFFERENCE WHITE AND NONWHITE	PERCENTAGE NONWHITE OF WHITE
Northeast	$6,318	$4,371	— $1,947	69.2
North Central	5,994	4,371	— 1,674	72.0
South[b]	5,009	2,322	— 2,687	46.4
West	6,444	4,937	— 1,507	76.6
Percentage South is of:				
Northeast	79.3	53.4		
North Central	83.6	53.8		
West	77.7	47.0		

[a] Vivian W. Henderson, *The Economic Status of Negroes: In the Nation and in the South* (Atlanta, Ga.: Southern Regional Council, 1963), p. 14, Table 12.

[b] "South" includes Delaware, District of Columbia, Maryland, Oklahoma, Texas, and West Virginia, as well as Alabama, Arkansas, Florida, Georgia, Kentucky, Louisiana, Mississippi, North Carolina, South Carolina, Tennessee, and Virginia.

SOURCE: U.S. Department of Commerce, *U.S. Census of Population 1960*, U.S. Summary, General Social and Economic Characteristics.

have an even harder time achieving equal access to higher education than they do now.

In sum, in terms of family income and hence the ability to bear the expenses, Negroes are generally less able than whites to gain a higher education. Hence the need for financial support from outside the family is commensurately larger among Negro students. If they are to achieve a higher education Negro youth will require a proportionally larger number of scholarships, fellowships, and loans than white students and on the average the stipends must be larger.

The economic privation of Negro families would not play as great a role in denying higher education to their children, nor would the need for financial assistance be so pressing, if the costs of attending a predominantly Negro institution were markedly lower than those elsewhere in higher education. Many Americans assume, in fact, that most Negro colleges are basically paupers' institutions and that they charge little or no tuition. For the whole company of these institutions, however, this assumption is false.

The United States Office of Education has recently made a study of tuition and fee charges which provides evidence on this matter. It notes that "both public and private Negro colleges have had to keep their charges at a low level because of the relatively low economic status of their clientele," and thus they have "a considerably lower ceiling on tuition-and-fee charges than public and private institutions" elsewhere in the Southeast or in other regions. But "although the ceiling rates are lower . . . , the charges of these institutions are as high, and even higher at certain [percentile] points, than those of predominantly non-Negro institutions." Juxtaposing the costs of higher education and the levels of Negro income, the authors of the study conclude that "it would appear that the charges made by predominantly Negro institutions tend to restrict college attendance more than the charges of predominantly non-Negro institutions in the Southeast restrict college opportunity."[3]

Most of the eighty-nine presidents interviewed consider tuition increases inevitable in predominantly Negro public and private colleges. In spite of this firm conviction almost all the administrators believe that

[3] Louis A. D'Amico and Maenylie M. Reed, "A Comparison of Tuition and Fees Charged in Negro Institutions with Charges in Institutions of the Southeast and of the Nation: 1962–63," *The Journal of Negro Education*, 33:2 (Spring 1964), pp. 186–190.

these increases will impose real financial hardship on most of their clientele and will completely eliminate the possibility of higher education for many prospective students unless financial aid rises faster than tuition charges. Fees paid for instruction, however, are only one part of the total cost of attending college. The costs of living away from home even with relatives interpose additional obstacles to obtaining a higher education. Unless low-tuition institutions are located within commuting distance of low-income students, higher education may still not be accessible to many.

The expenses involved in getting a college education imposed by residence away from home often exceed tuition and other fees. In the Negro public colleges in 1960–61 charges for board and room for resident students raised average costs from $140 to $562. The comparable figures for private institutions were $338 and $752.[4] To obtain information on the current cost of going to college, the Institute of Higher Education distributed a questionnaire to the students in eighty-nine of the predominantly Negro institutions. The facts gathered in this manner are, of course, subject to the errors involved in an inquiry by questionnaire. Some students may not have precise information about the total expenditures for their college education or the amount of their families' incomes. Moreover, as is always the case, some students who received the questionnaire failed to return it, thus raising a question about the validity of the sample.[5] These possible sources of error appear to be minimal, because the accuracy of the student responses appears to be documented by other information gathered from interviews with counselors and administrative officers.

The data obtained directly from students in these eighty-nine institutions reveal that in 1963–64 the average cost of attending college

[4] Board and room charges at the Negro colleges are generally lower than in most colleges, as Appendix C indicates.

[5] Because of limitations of time and money, the distribution of questionnaires was restricted to 10 per cent of the students enrolled in the eighty-nine institutions during 1963–64. Presidents were asked to transmit the questionnaires to every tenth student chosen alphabetically from their enrollment lists, but, as was to be expected, the percentage of returns varied from college to college and among types of institutions. Usable replies were received from 6,820 students, 8 per cent of the full-time degree-credit students enrolled, and varied from 7.17 per cent in the state land-grant institutions to 11.52 per cent at a unique professional school where more than every tenth student was canvassed. Students in private colleges and women are slightly over-represented in the sample, while almost no difference exists between the sample and the enrollments in two-year versus four-year colleges.

was $917. As Table 7 shows, the total expenses involved in attending junior colleges, most of which enroll only commuters, fall significantly below those for senior colleges, and students in private senior colleges pay half again as much on the average as those who attend comparable publicly supported institutions. Although the cost of attending college

Table 7   AVERAGE EXPENDITURE PER STUDENT IN EIGHTY-NINE PREDOMINANTLY NEGRO INSTITUTIONS FOR THE ACADEMIC YEAR 1963–1964

	MEN	WOMEN
Public and private junior colleges	$ 444.02	$ 478.00
Public senior colleges and universities	802.68	761.44
Private senior colleges and universities	1,240.23	1,121.70
Both sexes in all types of institutions	$917.13	

has not been determined for 1963–64 on a comprehensive national basis the figures in Table 7 unquestionably fall below the average for other institutions of higher education. If, however, the figures for 1960–61, shown in Appendix C, are used as a basis of comparison, the major charges to resident students (tuition, board, and room) in public Negro colleges averaged $562 and at all institutions $690. In the predominantly Negro private colleges, on the other hand, the average charge was $792 compared to $1,440 at all private colleges. Even when due weight is given to the lower costs in Negro colleges the generalization made earlier about the restrictive influence of tuition and other fees applies with equal force to the total costs of attending college. *The limited incomes of Negro families more often restrict college attendance than the incomes of white families.*

The facts supporting this conclusion are indisputable. In 1961, for example, fully 80 per cent of the nonwhite families in the South earned under $4,000 a year, compared to less than 40 per cent of the white families.[6] And in 1964, while over 40 per cent of the parents of students sampled in this study earned less than $4,000, it is estimated that only 8 per cent of all students' families fall in this low-income bracket. If the figures for family income nationally are correct, parents of students at the Negro colleges earn on the average far less than

[6] Vivian W. Henderson, *op. cit.*, Table 21, p. 22. It should be pointed out that the comparisons on the total costs of higher education and the family incomes here discussed have risen among the population at large, and hence the figures for 1960 or 1961 could today be too low.

parents of American college students in general. Estimates indicate that over three-fourths of all families nationally with children in college may earn over $6,000 a year. Fewer than a third of the students surveyed at the Negro colleges reported a family income of that magnitude. As the figures presented in Table 8 reveal, under 10 per cent of the Negro college students come from families earning over $10,000 a year, while it is estimated that over 40 per cent of all students in the nation come from families at this income level. The Negro students whose fam-

Table 8   **FAMILY INCOME OF STUDENTS IN NEGRO COLLEGES IN 1963, AND ESTIMATED FAMILY INCOME OF ALL STUDENTS IN 1960**

	FAMILIES OF STUDENTS ATTENDING NEGRO COLLEGES	FAMILIES OF ALL COLLEGE STUDENTS
$10,000 and over	9.6%	41.1%
$ 6,000 to $9,999	22.6	36.8
$ 4,000 to $5,999	25.9	14.1
Below $4,000	41.9	8.0
	100.0%	100.0%

SOURCE: Negro college data from 6,323 completed responses to Institute of Higher Education questionnaire. National 1960 estimate from Table 5, p. 12, of Rexford G. Moon, Jr., "A Model for Determining Future Student Aid Needs in the United States for the Support of Full-time Undergraduate Education" (duplicated, 1964).

ily incomes exceed $4,000 are not much better off because the information gathered in this inquiry shows that half the families in this study earn less than $5,000 a year, and two-thirds $6,000 or less. *When the fact is added that these students have on the average between three and four brothers or sisters—the women students averaged 3.9 and the men averaged 3.7 siblings—it is clear that the income of these Negro families falls below the level at which they can be expected to contribute much, if anything, to the higher education of their children.*

The relatively high cost of attending private colleges and professional schools, whose students have on the average more family income and fewer siblings, will erect comparable barriers for the unusually able but poor Negro youth unless financial assistance in considerable amounts is provided from various sources. It is also clear that local junior colleges, whose students tend to come from families with lower incomes and also more brothers and sisters—up to 5.0 for the women and 4.5 for the men—make higher education available to many students who would otherwise be denied it. That this opportunity, which seems to be fully exploited neither by the high school graduates nor by their communities, results in great personal privation and inexcusable social waste, is undeniable. The value of the community junior college in elevating the social and economic status of Negro youth through higher education has apparently not been fully recognized. Or perhaps the matter can be summed up more accurately by saying that the junior college has not been accepted by many Negro youth and their parents as a suitable opportunity to extend their education beyond the high school. The thinking and the attitudes involved in this view are complex, but the president of a Negro junior college has this to say on the subject:

The full basis for the Negro students' general rejection of the community junior college, particularly in the South, is a subject that merits exhaustive special study. The attitudes and their implications are enmeshed with problems that extend far beyond the scope of formal education as such. To state the case briefly, the following factors seem to excite the Negro youth's spirit of rejection of the community junior college:

1. The Negro student who survives the rigors of early youth in the South and completes high school is a rarity to start with. If he finally makes it to college, he represents the fortunate one among two hundred others who fell by the wayside. Thus, to "go away" to a residential senior college, even if it is located in the South and happens to be an all-Negro institution, represents a great achievement in itself. To "go away" to college often means the culmination of the hopes and aspirations of his entire family, and often his whole community. As soon as the son or daughter "goes away" to college the parents' feeling of achievement is heightened because of their own limited opportunities. Even the best community college cannot duplicate that intangible yet vital value which the Negro youth and his parents find in attendance at a residential four-year institution away from home.

2. The great emphasis placed on the community college as being geared to meet the needs of the immediate community has virtually no appeal to restless Negro youth who see their major hopes for ultimate achievement as being by the route of escape from the southern setting that has frustrated and warped his early development. The tempo of migration of the Negro from southern communities to other areas of the United States has increased in recent years. The Negro youth is the most mobile of his race and he looks on college away from home as a means of achieving release from privation and social restrictions.

3. The community college's emphasis on vocational and technical training in its educational program carries some implications, however incorrect, that Negro students by attending community colleges might become concentrated in vocational training instead of having access to a liberal education which Negro youth associate with white students' education. As erroneous as his thinking might be, the Negro student frequently identifies vocational training as preparation for subservience in the caste system.

The complicated problems which these attitudes toward the junior college in the Negro population create cannot be easily or quickly resolved. That this institution is one of the best and most accessible means by which thousands of Negro youth can obtain a higher education is undeniable. In fact, unless they are willing to begin their postsecondary education in these inexpensive, easily accessible two-year colleges close to their homes, as hundreds of thousands of white Americans do every year, most of them will never be able to advance to a full liberal education or to the professional schools. Two changes would surely accelerate the acceptance of the junior college among Negroes. They should be integrated as rapidly as possible to eliminate any residues of racial stigma. Their programs should, as do those of other junior colleges, offer a broad range of education preparatory for further college studies and for high-level vocational opportunities.

FINANCIAL ASSISTANCE

The facts thus far presented on the accessibility of higher education to Negro youth show that college costs and family incomes have important implications in regard to the need for financial aid among students in the predominantly Negro colleges. In view of these low incomes and burdensome costs the question naturally arises, "Where does the money come from?" In answer to a direct question on this subject, students in the survey of the Negro colleges indicated that their parents and other relatives supply a larger proportion of the funds to cover college expenses than any other source. On the average they provide 55 per cent of the total. These sums are supplemented by 13 per cent from loans, 9 per cent from savings, another 9 per cent from scholarships, and about 7 per cent from part-time work while they are in attendance. Without these loans, scholarships, and part-time jobs many would be forced to drop out. The funds from home would obviously be totally inadequate and indeed, even with an optimal combination of income from all available sources, as the presidents indicated, many nevertheless find it necessary to discontinue their higher education because of lack of money.

Since financial aids provide a major service at most of the predominantly Negro institutions in keeping students in college, a survey was made of the kinds and amounts available. Of seventy-five student personnel officers who provided information, sixty-six reported that the institution provides all three major forms of student assistance—scholarships, loans, and work opportunities. Only two, both junior colleges, do not provide loans; only five do not provide part-time work; and two do not offer scholarships. Thirty of the seventy-five institutions provide sufficient aid of these types to cover the full cost of some of their students' expenses. By various means, five—most of them public institutions —cover the full expenses of 20 per cent or more of their students. Table 9 shows the percentage of students who receive partial financial assistance in the sixty-five institutions which supplied usable information.

Table 9   **PERCENTAGE OF STUDENTS WHO RECEIVED SOME FINANCIAL SUPPORT FROM THE INSTITUTIONS THEY ATTENDED IN 1963–1964**

PERCENTAGE OF STUDENTS RECEIVING PARTIAL SUPPORT	NUMBER OF INSTITUTIONS
80–100%	3
60–79	15
40–59	20
20–39	19
1–19	8
Total	65

For all sixty-five institutions, 43 per cent of their students received some type or amount of financial aid from their own colleges, with a range of 5 per cent in one Florida public junior college to 93 per cent in a four-year private college in Mississippi.

Fortunately substantial foundation grants directly to the institutions or through the United Negro College Fund have recently bolstered the scholarship funds of many colleges. For example, Howard University and Morehouse and Spelman colleges have been able to expand scholarships through aid from the Field Foundation and the Ford Foundation.

Nine others—including the Atlanta University Center, Bennett, Bishop, Dillard, Fisk, Hampton, Knoxville, LeMoyne, and Tuskegee—will use part of their grants totaling $13 million from the Special Program in Education of the Ford Foundation for increased scholarship aid. And beyond the predominantly Negro colleges, Negro students will benefit from the $7 million Ford Foundation grant to the National Merit Scholarship Program, the Sloan Foundation grants to the National Medical Fellowships program, and Rockefeller Foundation grants to selected institutions across the nation.

Almost all the eighty-three colleges that supplied information on their part-time work programs assist students in finding jobs either on campus or elsewhere in the community, but only eleven conduct a formal work-study program where part-time work relates directly to the students' field of study. Among them, Central State College in Wilberforce, Ohio, coordinates a plan in which students spend several weeks of the academic year and the entire summer as interns in study-related jobs in Dayton industries. As part of a five-year program leading to the bachelor's degree, Tuskegee Institute's long-time "Opportunity Plan" offers a hundred students a much reduced schedule of classes together with full-time work during their first year. And several colleges have organized rewarding work-study programs with agencies of the Federal Government that provide attractive employment opportunities on graduation. In some of these Federal programs, as at Texas Southern, students alternate six months of study with six months of work. In others where the institution and agency are near each other—Alabama A & M College and NASA at Huntsville, for example—they operate on a three-day-a-week cycle. With advice and assistance from Antioch College and one of the foundations Wilberforce University expects to develop a strong work-study program over the next three years.

The work-study plan, as has been demonstrated for half a century in some American colleges, offers students opportunities to continue their education while almost wholly supporting themselves in jobs which contribute to their intellectual and social development. When properly articulated with the instructional program, the work-study enterprise has been demonstrated to enhance the total educational value of the college years.[7] *The predominantly Negro colleges should in-*

[7] A comprehensive evaluation of work-study programs appears in James W. Wilson and Edward H. Lyons, *Work-Study College Programs* (New York: Harper & Row, Publishers, Incorporated, 1961), 240 pp.

augurate additional work-study programs to permit more of their stu-dents to earn a major part of their educational expenses. Now that increased job opportunities in industry and government are being opened on the basis of equal ability these arrangements can be considerably expanded.

To encourage Negro youth to attend college and to make it eco-nomically possible for them to do so institutions should take these additional steps:

Tuition fees, especially in the tax-supported institutions, should be kept at the lowest possible level consistent with sound standards.

Loan funds should be substantially increased and liberalized for the disadvantaged, and the states which have not permitted state funds to be used to take advantage of Federal grants under the National De-fense Education Act ought to rescind these policies.

Finally, corporations, foundations, and individuals should increase scholarship grants especially for disadvantaged youth of high potential, many of whom cannot at present meet eligibility requirements because of inadequate earlier education and intellectual stimulation.

Scholarships are even more urgently needed in predominantly Negro institutions than in others, because many Negro youth fear that even advanced education will not enable them to find a job with a salary adequate to repay borrowed funds. It must also be recognized that a relatively small proportion of Negro youth would at present be eligible for scholarship funds on a competitive basis because of their inadequate earlier education. To provide financial assistance *only* on the basis of scores on national tests will in effect continue a form of discrimination by denying potentially able students what the advantaged have already achieved. *The most urgent need is for extensive grants-in-aid which would provide students of high potential ability but relatively low stand-ing on standardized tests with incentives to study and would free those who must now work to concentrate their full attention on their studies.*

The financial problems of Negro students and their need for assistance can be summed up as follows: A variety of financial aids can play a major role in breaking the vicious circle that keeps most Negroes as well as many of their white contemporaries from achieving their full educational potential. Born into families with incomes of less than $3,000 a year, and with many brothers and sisters, the social and cultural influences on their lives are narrowly limited. These and other restrictions reduce, if they do not completely stifle, their motiva-tion toward learning and social and occupational advancement. Many of their families, even with the most strenuous and self-denying efforts, cannot muster the financial resources required to provide a college education even for a single child, to say nothing of his numerous brothers and sisters. Without outside financial aid, such children can seldom avoid reliving their parents' frustrating and depressing lives, characterized by denied opportunity and consequent failure in self-realization.

Only an all-out effort on the part of the several states, foundations, and individual and corporate philanthropy to increase the financial assistance available to these young people can open college doors for the sons and daughters of substantially more Negro families. Even the best efforts of all three will not meet the full needs of poor families of the several races. A large-scale program of Federal scholarships and fellowships is indispensable to remedy the educational privation which now suppresses their sons and daughters in American society and denies the nation much needed workers in the higher-level occupations.

Because of the inadequacies in their earlier education Negro students must be allowed to qualify for this aid on bases other than national norms of educational achievement. One president of a Negro college which received substantial additional scholarship funds could not recruit enough qualified applicants for admission because of the scarcity of high school graduates able to meet the relatively high admissions standards. *Only large-scale cooperation, coordinated assistance, and a realistic understanding of past achievement and prospective potential can break the vicious circle which has confined the Negro within limited education, inferior vocational status, and second-class citizenship.*

ADMISSIONS REQUIREMENTS

If financial disabilities raise the highest barriers to students seeking a higher education in the predominantly Negro institutions, the inadequacies of their preparatory schooling interpose not much lower hurdles. The discouraging but undeniable fact is that, considered as a whole, the elementary and secondary education of Negro children as well as other disadvantaged groups is so incomplete in scope and so substandard in quality that even if they met none of the economic barriers to higher education already described many could not extend their formal schooling beyond high school.[8]

[8] The elaborate data showing the validity of this generalization which students of the problem have assembled need no detailed review. Eli Ginzberg provides an excellent summary in *The Negro Potential* (New York: Columbia University Press, 1956), pp. 42–60.

To begin with, the percentage of Negro youth who graduate from high school and thus make themselves minimally eligible for admission to college is lower than that of white youth. In 1960, for example, 78.7 per cent of the nation's nonwhites, aged twenty-five and over, had not completed four years of high school, compared to only 57.9 per cent of the whites. Fortunately, the percentages for both groups are rising; in 1940, 92.3 per cent of the nonwhites had not finished high school compared to 73.9 per cent of the whites. But despite increased rates of high school attendance, college education remains out of the reach of a far greater proportion of Negro than white youth simply because they drop out of school before receiving their high school diplomas.

The inferior elementary and secondary education of many shows forth most glaringly in the high percentage of students who, even though they graduate from high school and enter college, either drop out voluntarily because they realize their own intellectual incapacity or who are counseled to do so by their advisors. Of fifty-four institutions able to supply reliable data, two stated that they lost at least half of their incoming students for academic and other voluntary reasons before the beginning of the sophomore year, and in twelve of them over a quarter of the freshman class had left by the end of the year. Eighteen of these fifty-four colleges also reported that less than 50 per cent of all their students were making normal progress toward graduation. Although dropouts are common, their number in the Negro colleges far exceeds the average.

Figures on high school graduation can delude the uninformed. The mere fact that a young person attends school until age eighteen, or that he receives a high school diploma, or even that in some high schools he stands near the top of his graduating class, in no sense guarantees that he can meet the intellectual demands of college instruction. Evidence from tests administered to Negro students and their teachers by the military services, the United Fund for Negro Students, and the Educational Testing Service indicate, according to Eli Ginzberg, that "what schooling he [the Negro] does receive is of inferior quality and therefore has less value than the schooling received by whites. A major weakness of Negro education is the poor preparation of Negro teachers." Even after due recognition has been given to the high abilities and the unremitting dedication of many teachers in predominantly Negro schools and the demonstrable improvements being made in these schools have been taken into account, it is still true that "because of the deficiencies encountered throughout their elementary and secondary school careers, including short school terms, inadequate equipment, limited curriculum, and poorly trained and underpaid teachers, a majority of Negroes enter college unprepared to do college work of standard grade."[9]

As a result of these limitations in the earlier education of their prospective students, many of the predominantly Negro colleges are not, and until corrective measures have been applied in their earlier education cannot be, rigidly selective in their admissions policies without unjustly closing their doors to many potentially able youth. Fortunately these colleges have recognized the shortcomings in the previous education of their prospective students and have used other means than a rigid admissions process to upgrade their student bodies. Few rely heavily on standardized tests to admit or exclude applicants. Thirty-one of the seventy-five institutions that provided information on their admissions requirements use one or another of these measures of ability to help them in deciding which candidates should be admitted, but only three of the thirteen employing the Scholastic Aptitude Test (S.A.T.) of the College Entrance Examination Board have established a basic minimum score for admission—one at the fiftieth percentile, a second at the thirtieth, and a third at the raw score of 350. Five institutions using information supplied by the American College Testing program set no minimum score and the other thirteen that use a variety of other tests similarly establish no minimum score for admission.

Fifteen of the seventy-five institutions follow a common practice of selecting students in part on the basis of their standing in the upper half of their high school graduating class, and still others require a high school grade average of C. But twenty-one of the institutions, of which more than half are public junior colleges, and one a private college, admit all applicants regardless of their high school records.[10]

It should not be assumed from these figures, which typically do not compare favorably with most other institutions, that all the predominantly Negro institutions are unselective in their admissions standards.

[9] "The Education of Negroes: In the Nation and the South," p. 22. Paper presented at a meeting of the American Council on Education, held in Washington, D.C., October 18–19, 1963. (Mimeographed.)

[10] Despite these liberal admissions requirements, 49.3 per cent of the sample of students reported that they had graduated from high school in the top quarter of their classes.

For example, a comparison of the number of students who applied for admission in the fall of 1963 with the number of those accepted reveals that one of the predominantly Negro institutions rejected 138 applications for every hundred it accepted. The median institution among the private colleges and universities rejected fifty-three for every hundred accepted, the median public four-year college turned away thirty, and the median public junior college about ten. These rejections, moreover, were not caused primarily by lack of space accommodations. Of the seventy-one institutions which supplied information for the academic year 1963–64, two-thirds stated that they could have taken more students. If the applicants had been able to present qualifying credentials, in the aggregate these colleges could have accepted over 2,400 additional dormitory and 6,700 more commuting students. Until the average quality of preparatory education rises, it is clear that higher admissions standards would severely and unfairly limit the opportunities for higher education.

Some educators viewing the low admissions requirements in many of the predominantly Negro institutions contend that these colleges should either raise their standards or close. They point to the policy in many other institutions, public as well as private, of raising entrance requirements and thus improving the academic quality of the student body. They believe firmly that the Negro institutions must do the same if they are to achieve defensible academic status and provide a suitable higher education for their students. Since the proposal to close a number of these institutions has already been critically appraised it need not be reconsidered here. But the raising of admissions requirements at the Negro institutions does demand a critical assessment.

It might be reasonable for these Negro colleges to attempt to elevate the standards of academic performance through more restrictive admissions policies if it were not for the fact that most of them offer the only opportunity for higher education for thousands of disadvantaged young people. Enough has already been said about the weaknesses of their previous schooling. Consider here their limited opportunities for informal education in their homes. Three-fourths of the students who responded to the Institute's questionnaire are "first generation" college students whose parents did not have the opportunity for any post–high school education. In fact, only about 56 per cent of their mothers and only 47 per cent of their fathers had even completed high school. Twenty-one per cent of their mothers and 33 per cent of their fathers had had no more than an eighth-grade education. Consider, too, the educational and cultural implications of the fact that over 46 per cent of the fathers of these students held semiskilled and unskilled jobs.

As the figures in Table 10 show, less than 20 per cent of the students' fathers and mothers in 1963 held professional or technical jobs. They also reveal that Negro colleges, like American colleges in general, attract a disproportionately high share of their students from professional families. In 1960 only 3.4 per cent of Negro men were employed as professionals or technicians, while 72.6 per cent worked at semiskilled and unskilled jobs; but about 20 per cent of the students came from professional families. The figures also show that many Negro youth come from homes in which the parents had very limited education. These colleges must, therefore, educate students who not only lack adequate schooling but who come from families unoriented to academic culture.

Table 10   **OCCUPATIONS OF FATHERS OF STUDENT RESPONDENTS IN 1963, AND OF EMPLOYED NEGRO MALES IN 1960**

	FATHERS OF STUDENTS		EMPLOYED NEGRO MALES
	MEN	WOMEN	
Professional and technical	19.8%	18.6%	3.4%
Managerial or proprietary other than farm owner or manager	5.7	5.0	1.9
Farm owner or manager	8.4	11.2	4.6
Clerical or sales persons	4.1	3.0	6.8
Skilled occupations (carpenters, plumbers, etc.)	15.6	14.4	10.7
Semiskilled and unskilled laborers	46.4	47.8	72.6
	100.0%	100.0%	100.0%

Under existing conditions of inadequate schooling and cultural influences in the home among their prospective students, most Negro colleges can take one of two positions on their admissions requirements. They can either continue to admit students with their temporary disabilities and attempt to raise them to higher levels of intellectual, vocational, social, and political competence. Or, through exclusive academic policies, they can deny these young people a higher education and *ipso facto* consign them to a personal and social life hardly less privational than the legal and social discriminations from which they are only now being freed.

To be sure, the most selective of the predominantly Negro institutions might well raise their admissions standards even higher as many other institutions are doing. It would be neither unrealistic nor academically undesirable for these few institutions as quickly as possible to limit their admissions to applicants with S.A.T. scores of 600 or higher. *But no reviewer of the purposes, programs, and prospects of predominantly Negro colleges in general can justifiably fail to observe that any sudden raising of admissions standards at most of them would for a number of years deny a higher education to many potentially able but academically underdeveloped Negro youth.* The number of these young people who should and, with added financial aid and improved instruction could, gain a college education, is rapidly expanding. They deserve a chance. But some current proposals to gain higher status in American society for the Negro college and for their students by setting high admissions standards and excessively demanding levels of performance in courses would for the present only impose new forms of exclusion and suppression.

By design this report is limited to higher education. Consequently it has not attempted to survey in detail the education Negro children receive prior to the college years. *Nevertheless, it is evident that the only satisfactory long-run efforts to improve the quality and extend the opportunity of higher education among Negro young people must begin in the first grade, or even earlier.* Until the necessary improvements occur in the elementary and secondary schools, the percentage of Negro youth who continue their formal education beyond high school will remain too small and the quality of their higher education will be lower on the average than that of their contemporaries. Only as these improvements are accomplished in the schools will the colleges be able substantially to raise their admissions standards and upgrade their educational programs. And since these colleges train the vast majority of Negro school teachers, the colleges must themselves help improve the schools through curricular reform, research, and extension. But in the meantime the opportunity for a college education cannot be postponed for twelve years while children receive adequate elementary and secondary education. For many the nation's predominantly Negro colleges must bridge the gap. Rather than limiting their admissions and their programs, these colleges must be prepared to use a variety of special educational devices, such as those to be described in the next chapter, to repair the academic deficiencies of high school graduates and prepare them to proceed apace with their higher education.

Chapter 4

ORIENTATION AND IMPROVEMENT
PROGRAMS

"THE COLLEGE HAS A RESIDUAL FUNCTION, I.E., IT MUST NOT ONLY DIS-
charge the services ordinarily assigned to it, it must also provide those
needed services which other agencies or institutions have failed to provide."[1] This conclusion of the *National Survey of Higher Education of
Negroes* in 1943 remains valid today, for the predominantly Negro colleges must not only perform the usual functions of such institutions;
they must remedy the shortcomings of their students' previous education. Some American colleges disavow this responsibility. They choose
to admit and instruct only well-prepared students, in some cases only
those who rank in the upper 5 per cent in scholastic accomplishment.
Many other colleges expect most of their students to be adequately
prepared and accordingly limit their remedial services to only a small
proportion of the freshman class who have peculiar corrective needs.
Most predominantly Negro institutions, on the other hand, face the
problem that many of their potentially superior students cannot learn
chemistry and physics because they have not yet understood equations
and cannot grasp history or poetry because they have not yet learned the
skills of efficient reading. Faced with this situation many of these institutions must spend a disproportionately large share of their limited resources on the residual task of attempting to fit five or six years of formal
education into four.

[1] Ambrose Caliver, *National Survey of the Higher Education of Negroes: A
Summary* (Washington: Government Printing Office, 1943), p. 31.

This reparative work of the Negro colleges raises more controversy, both within and outside the institutions, than almost any of their other functions. Some critics vigorously advance an easy solution to this problem. They would simply wave it aside by having these colleges exclude the poorly prepared students and accept only highly qualified applicants. This procedure has the special status-gaining feature of putting these institutions into the company of many predominantly white colleges which steadily raise their admissions standards as the demand for higher education grows. It is a policy which some faculty members in the predominantly Negro colleges would also favor because they begrudge the time and effort required for remedial work, and because they do not consider the activities involved a proper function of colleges or of their faculties. Visiting teams from accrediting agencies often indirectly endorse such restrictive practices by criticizing heavy corrective programs. And in some states, Texas and West Virginia, for example, public colleges are being instructed to stop their remedial work. It must be admitted that in terms of time, effort, and money instruction needed to build up the students' background is costly to faculties, to institutions, and to students. Many colleges at present lack adequate funds and a large enough staff to teach the courses normally offered in the regular curriculum, to say nothing of undertaking a large program of remedial instruction. And finally, the time required for corrective work often extends the student's college career into summer sessions or a fifth year, thereby imposing additional financial and other burdens.

Logically, remedial work should be the responsibility of the elementary and secondary schools. Recognition of this fact has resulted in plans recently announced, one by the Southern Association of Colleges and Schools with Ford Foundation aid, to establish centrally located clinics in urban centers to assist local schools in bringing their students up to a higher level of scholastic achievement. These activities deserve commendation and more widespread initiation. For some years, however, the predominantly Negro colleges must serve a large proportion of incoming students whose schooling has left them inadequately prepared for conventional post–secondary school instruction. *If it is socially undesirable for most of these institutions to raise their admissions requirements substantially until the elementary and secondary education of their prospective students has been materially improved, it is equally objectionable for them to admit large numbers of students and let them fail without attempting to rectify their deficiencies. Every educational institution has an obligation to assist its students, in so far as it is able, to complete the programs it offers and which students in good faith enter.*

Until now, most of the predominantly Negro colleges have attempted to meet this obligation through extra specialized instruction of various types in the freshman year. Today, however, with the help of the foundations, they are inaugurating promising innovations to identify these deficiencies in preparation and to correct them before the student arrives on campus.

ORIENTATION FOR HIGH SCHOOL STUDENTS

A number of the predominantly Negro colleges are inaugurating active preparatory programs for students still in high school. In so doing, they hope not only to motivate these students toward greater intellectual achievement and to upgrade their qualifications for admission to college, but also to provide an early opportunity for informal counseling and evaluation. A large number of Negro colleges have informally helped orient high school students toward higher education through their annual music, art, and agricultural contests and through career conferences. The latter meetings have enabled students to discuss employment prospects with representatives of government and industry and to confer with college guidance counselors.

Now, however, these colleges are beginning to launch more prolonged and systematic efforts to remedy scholastic weaknesses and to increase motivation toward learning. They are inaugurating continuing seminars and classes on Saturdays and on weekday afternoons and evenings throughout the academic year for small groups of prospective students. A full catalogue of these efforts cannot be provided here; nor is it necessary. A few examples reveal the variety of such projects already under way.

Bennett College in Greensboro, North Carolina, has a "Saturday School" for forty to fifty junior and senior high school girls from as far away as Charlotte and from towns in Virginia for instruction in reading, writing, English literature, and mathematics. LeMoyne College in Memphis conducts a three-hour, college-level humanities seminar on Saturdays for outstanding juniors from local high schools. Agricultural and Technical College of North Carolina has organized a science symposium for tenth- and eleventh-grade science students in joint sponsorship with the Army Research Office and the State Department of Public Instruction, including instruction in science, mathematics, and communications. St. Augustine's College, also in North Carolina, brings students from surrounding high schools to meet one evening a week with an outstanding scholar for a discussion of concepts ranging from philosophy and foreign affairs to high-energy physics and genetics.

From the enthusiastic testimony of teachers, students, and their parents, these in-term programs provide a rewarding type of supplementary preparation for work of college grade. In addition, they doubtless strengthen the scholastic commitment of local high schools and motivate their students toward fuller academic achievement and in some instances toward a life of scholarship.

SUMMER PRECOLLEGE PROGRAMS

Summer vacation periods also provide opportunity for intensive preparation in the basic disciplines which can obviate the need for remedial work after the student has entered college. In the past several years, a number of American institutions other than those included in this study, such as Oberlin, Dartmouth, Georgetown, Franklin and Marshall, and Princeton, have with foundation support conducted special summer programs for able, but educationally deprived, prospective college students. Similar intensive summer programs, also largely supported from foundation grants, have been developed by twenty of the predominantly Negro institutions, and more are planning to inaugurate related enterprises in the early future.

Like the programs which run through the school year, those conducted in the summer months take many forms. Some of them serve high school sophomores and juniors, others graduating seniors. Some are open only to students applying to the institution offering the summer program, others admit any college-bound youth. Some are designed for able students only, those who have already demonstrated high academic ability, others for high school graduates of promise but with low-level achievement. Some range widely across the basic disciplines, others focus on one skill, like reading or English. As an example of the latter, St. Philip's College in San Antonio offers an English enrichment program for one hour a day over a six-week period, using Science Research Associates reading materials to help any local college-bound high school junior or senior to raise his reading competence and usage level.

Education Services Incorporated, with a grant of $62,000 from the

Carnegie Corporation, is preparing and evaluating supplementary or remedial materials in English and mathematics for youth going on to college. Under the same program about two hundred high school seniors will attend Saturday programs during the second semester, 1964–65, and eight-week summer sessions in 1965 at centers in Atlanta at Morehouse College, in Houston at Texas Southern University, in Nashville at Fisk University, in New Orleans at Dillard University, in St. Louis at Webster College, and in Washington, D.C., at Howard University. This program will also train teachers in the use of the materials prepared and will operate a central coordinating office at Education Services Incorporated.

Among other projects, Kentucky State College offers a free eight-week preparatory program in college English and mathematics, open to all high school seniors in the state of Kentucky who desire to enter college. With Southern Educational Foundation aid, Albany State College in Georgia sponsors an eight-week intensive program in reading, mathematics, and English for a highly selective group of students, and combines this instruction with follow-up studies of their progress in college.

Hampton Institute in Virginia has offered summer classes for high school graduates for the past twelve years. Currently, with grants from the Carnegie Corporation and the James Foundation, it holds separate six-week specialized institutes in such fields as the humanities, social sciences, and music for students particularly interested in these subjects. Among other institutions which conduct similar summer programs with foundation support are Bennett and Knoxville colleges, Dillard University, and Hampton and Tuskeegee institutes with aid from the Carnegie Corporation; Morehouse and Spelman colleges from the Rockefeller Foundation; Texas Southern from the Fund for the Advancement of Education; Cheyney State and Jackson State colleges from the Ford Foundation; and Knoxville College from the Southern Education Foundation.

Jackson State College in Mississippi has for several years chosen forty top high school seniors from among its applicants for a summer session of intensive cultural and intellectual activities. Students from the first round of this program have now graduated. The large number of these young people who later received foundation grants or fellowships for graduate work attests to its effectiveness in both selection and instruction. With assistance from the Field Foundation, Jackson State also operates another enrichment program in which ninth-, tenth-, and eleventh-grade students and teachers come to the campus from selected high schools to participate in a six-week program of cultural and intellectual enrichment free of any charge for tuition, board, or room. By pairing teachers and their students, this unique effort not only provides a better preparation for those planning to enter college by sharpening their intellectual skills and intensifying their academic interests, but at the same time prepares teachers to provide a higher quality of instruction for other present and future students in their high school classes.

With support from the Carnegie Corporation, Tuskegee Institute in Alabama has recently inaugurated one of the most ambitious and extensive of these summer programs, designed particularly for prospective college students who score poorly on educational achievement tests. Last summer, it invited 250 high school graduates at a charge of about $50 to an eight-week, fourteen-hour-a-day summer institute with remedial courses in communication skills, mathematics, and basic study skills. To this instruction Tuskegee added work in a developmental reading and speech clinic, cultural programs, art exhibits, film and television viewing and analysis, and field trips to governmental, industrial, and other educational centers. Students from this precollege program will also attend a second eight-week summer institute following their freshman year, and this will include regular college courses. The experience of intensive and continuing educational and cultural enrichment will unquestionably bring most of these students up to a level of competence which should assure their ability to do satisfactory college work. The heartening aspect of this enterprise is the academic salvaging of many of these young people who would otherwise probably have been eliminated from formal schooling by a rigid and excessively demanding admissions policy. A similar two-summer project organized by Tougaloo Southern Christian College in Mississippi offered nine weeks of intensive work for fifty-five of its own incoming freshmen in 1964 and plans to include the same students in a follow-up program in 1965.

Bishop College in Dallas, which already schedules a voluntary six-week program in English, reading, and mathematics for its incoming freshmen, in 1965 will require all entering students who fail to score sufficiently high on entrance examinations to enroll in a twelve-week summer term. To overcome the additional financial burden on the students—the major deterrent to similar required programs elsewhere—Bishop will provide this instruction without cost and grant additional scholarship aid to needy students during their freshman year.

These intensive precollege summer sessions help to ease two major problems created by remedial work during the regular session: They relieve many faculty members of responsibility for remedial instruction during the academic year, and they enable many more students to receive and profit from instruction of genuine college grade simultaneously with their better-prepared classmates. In addition, such programs doubtless reduce the freshman dropout rate.

The evidence from these and other numerous experiments indicates that intellectual growth can be significantly improved among educationally deprived young people with intensive programs of study designed to meet their specific needs. The in-term high school and the summer programs are both devices that can be used to deal with the enormous problem of preparing potentially able but underachieving students to do satisfactory college work. *Until continuing basic improvements are made in the elementary and secondary schools that provide the early education for prospective college students, special preparatory and correctional programs appear to constitute one of the most fruitful opportunities for raising the level of academic performance among Negro college students. Hence such efforts deserve general support for student expenses and institutional costs from foundations, state and Federal governments, and all individuals and agencies wishing to equalize opportunities for higher education among our young people. More important, since these varied efforts are now still in a formative stage, the opportunity exists to coordinate them as they develop to assure the widespread adoption of demonstrably superior practices and to make certain that the needs of all deserving students everywhere are met and that any possibility of competition or duplication of effort is avoided.* Leadership in bringing together those responsible for these activities should be undertaken by some existing regional or national organization. The financial support required for the activities of coordination would be minimal in relation to the benefits to individuals, institutions, and the nation at large.

Finally, a considerable corps of the staff members for the various programs could be recruited quickly and without great expense from among undergraduate and graduate student volunteers from other colleges. The Peace Corps has demonstrated the feasibility of this type of program abroad, and it has been tried on a limited scale at home. But hundreds of interested students not now involved in Peace Corps activities would undoubtedly be willing on request to take a summer, a semester, or even a year from their studies to assist the staffs of predominantly Negro colleges in various orientation and remedial projects. These more favored young people could thus contribute markedly to the academic achievement of their contemporaries with more limited educational advantages. The spirit of dedication with which thousands of young Americans have thrown themselves into civil rights and related activities guarantees the success of this type of educational assistance to their less fortunate counterparts in the predominantly Negro colleges. The Federal Government ought to take the leadership in organizing such a program which could contribute as much to our own social and economic advancement at home as the Peace Corps has to nations overseas. Not the least of the benefits that would flow from such an enterprise would be the enhancement of the volunteers' own learning and their involvement in a social effort designed to help their fellow men.

One effort of this type was developed among Yale University law students, under whose initiative the Southern Teaching Program Inc. was organized. This organization in the summer of 1964 sent fifty-three graduate students into thirteen Negro colleges as substitute or supplementary teachers. With the support of a grant from the New World Foundation the Southern Teaching Program has opened a small office and hired an administrator to organize the program for the summer of 1965. Recruitment teams have been established in graduate schools at Columbia, Harvard, New York, Wesleyan, and Yale universities. It is expected that these efforts, under a $40,000 grant from the Carnegie Corporation, will place about 110 student instructors in twenty-five colleges.

FRESHMAN ORIENTATION

Despite the growth and the success of precollege programs, the fall of the freshman year is likely to remain the major period of orientation to higher education for most students and the time when those not yet fully prepared to undertake regular college work come to understand the demands of the college years and learn how to meet them. For years, most American colleges have required new students to take part in freshman exercises before actually beginning classes. Although the arrangements vary from college to college, the orientation period normally provides information on institutional purposes, programs, and mores, and includes placement testing, counseling on curricular options, and social activities to help students get acquainted with their classmates and to begin to feel at home on campus.

Of the seventy-five predominantly Negro institutions which responded to a questionnaire covering their student personnel programs, all have some form of orientation activities for their entering students. All but four of the colleges, three of them nonresidential junior colleges, conduct such a program before the upperclassmen return to the campus, and only nine limit it to three days or less. Forty-six use four days to a full week for orientation, and fifteen continue such activities through the first semester. Rust College in Mississippi, in fact, conducts a unique year-long orientation program, led by two faculty members with full-time responsibility for serving as class sponsors, advising the freshmen, conducting an introductory course on the use of the library, study skills, and social adjustment, arranging field trips and cultural activities, and twice a week leading freshman assembly and chapel programs.

The value of assisting incoming students in adjusting to life in a college community has long been recognized. The need for such a period of adaptation to a new academic and social environment is particularly great in colleges where many students come from high schools with limited curricula, few testing programs, and inadequate guidance services, and from homes often lacking in academic influences. It is unfortunate, therefore, that some of the predominantly Negro colleges which draw most of their students from such meager school and family backgrounds have the most limited orientation programs. *Although no statistical analysis has been attempted, information and observation gathered by correspondence, questionnaire, and visitation suggest that in most of the Negro colleges a fuller orientation program would enable their students to make the transfer from high school to college with less shock and in many instances it would make the difference between a student's remaining in college or dropping out. Each college ought to have at least one person professionally prepared to plan, organize, and direct the various activities which those who have had long experience with orientation programs consider essential to prepare incoming students to make the quickest adjustment to the academic community and to realize the maximum benefit from the very beginning of their college career.*

REMEDIAL WORK DURING THE ACADEMIC YEAR

Preparatory experiences during the high school years, in summer, and during the freshman registration period can assist students in getting a sound start and in making normal progress in their college work. In the predominantly Negro institutions, however, the most effective means for bringing them up to their maximum level of learning ability for the time being will continue to be remedial instruction through the freshman and sophomore years. The facts assembled in this study reveal that at most of these institutions from two-thirds to four-fifths of the entering students have academic inadequacies which have to be corrected before they can rise to satisfactory levels of scholastic achievement. Even at institutions where 75 per cent of the freshmen are in the upper fourth of their high school graduating classes, up to 50 per cent may require remedial instruction in some of the basic subjects such as reading, English, and mathematics. It is not surprising, therefore, that reporting on their special programs to redress scholastic deficiencies, all but four of the colleges state that they provide one or another type of such instruction during the academic year. In most instances they require students to participate in these programs until their scholastic handicaps have been removed. Of the four exceptions, two were graduate schools and the other two undergraduate institutions have very high admissions standards which eliminate much of the need for this type of special instruction.

The immediate questions facing most Negro colleges are, in fact, not how many of their students need remedial work—since a large percentage will need such help for some years to come—but rather how many of those who need it will receive it, and what type of help can most effectively and quickly raise them to their potential levels of learning. If at present these colleges assigned students to makeup courses on the basis of their placement test scores and national freshman norms, some would have to put 95 per cent of their students in such classes. Currently many colleges are unable to provide such extensive remedial service in courses which necessarily cannot be much above high school level. Hence they set the cut-off point for remedial work at a point which requires only about 50 per cent of their students to undergo this special corrective instruction. Such a concession to a practical limitation of resources may at present be unavoidable, but it should be recognized that this practice dilutes the quality of more advanced courses in the whole range of disciplines, increases the dropout rate, and makes it more difficult for graduates to compete in the work-a-day world or for scholarships and fellowships in the graduate and professional schools. They might better spend extra time in getting a sound preparatory education than to face these later frustrations and disappointments.

Most of the remedial work in the Negro institutions is concentrated in two major fields, English and mathematics. Reading, writing, and speech difficulties, limited language usage, and inadequate linguistic understanding are usually the responsibility of the English department which, in half the institutions, also conducts corrective work involving study habits and skills. At least half the institutions also offer remedial work in the other major field, mathematics. A few supplement basic programs in these two disciplines with preparatory instruction in the sciences, the social studies, and foreign languages.

To rectify the deficiencies of incoming students these colleges employ five somewhat different means which listed in order of frequency of usage are: (1) special courses, (2) intensified sections of regular courses, (3) tutoring, (4) clinical work, and (5) a reduced schedule of instruction.

SPECIAL COURSES

By far the most common type of corrective program now in use in the institutions covered by this report consists of makeup courses. Poorly prepared students are required to take such instruction or pass an equivalency examination before they can gain admission to other regular courses. Since the content of the remedial courses is considered to be of high school rather than college level, they typically do not carry academic credit. The few institutions which do grant credit for such instruction, usually in the hope of obscuring its remedial character, actually do not reduce the demands on students because they commensurately raise the credit-hour requirements for graduation. Under this policy those students who are required to take three additional hours of instruction in English and in mathematics have to accumulate 130 hours of course credits rather than the normal 124 before they are certified for graduation.

INTENSIFIED REGULAR COURSES

At least ten of the colleges require poorly prepared students to attend additional sessions of regular courses. Under this arrangement, instead of postponing the usual instruction in English or mathematics until they complete a special course, the deficient student attends the usual beginning course which meets three days a week, and then receives two additional hours of intensive supplemental instruction in which special attention is given to his observed deficiencies. A small number of institutions use this five-day-a-week plan, but keep the students needing special help in a group by themselves for all five days while their classmates attend separate and more advanced sections of the course. Another variation in the grouping arrangement involves a "three-track" system in which poorly prepared students receive supplemental work in separate sections; those with average competence pursue a course of normal difficulty; and those who at entrance have shown unusual knowledge and aptitude enter advanced sections and receive additional enriched assignments.

TUTORIAL ARRANGEMENTS

Like many other colleges thirty of these institutions offer some type of tutorial instruction. Most American colleges which have tutorial programs make such individualized instruction available only to superior students. This is also the general practice in the Negro institutions. It is obvious, however, that poorly prepared students can profit as much, if not more, from personalized instruction, and some of these colleges, recognizing its potential, have established a tutorial system predominantly for students who need special help. This instruction is given by both faculty members and especially able advanced students. *The predominantly Negro institutions should make individualized or tutorial instruction available to their best students and also to their able but academically deficient students in order to bring them up to the highest potential levels of achievement.*

CLINICAL WORK

Clinical or laboratory work employing mechanical devices such as programmed instruction and tape recorders is offered by sixteen institutions to enable students to correct their particular academic weaknesses on an individual basis. The communications skills of speech and reading receive special attention in these programs. Most of these clinical and laboratory experiences are used both by students required to undergo remedial instruction and by others who, though not seriously deficient, nevertheless voluntarily undertake the improvement of their skills in the tool subjects. Although clinical instruction is more costly than the usual remedial courses, it has sometimes proved more effective because of its flexible adaptability to the student's particular individual needs and time schedule. Such arrangements are also more attractive to students because less stigma attaches to clinical work which they and their classmates view more as an effort to improve themselves than as evidence that they are academically inferior and of unproved capacity to profit from college instruction.

REDUCED LOADS

A few institutions employ an indirect method of aiding poorly prepared students by allowing or requiring them to enroll in fewer courses than the normal fifteen hours of class work until they demonstrate their capacity to carry a full schedule. This arrangement allows students to concentrate on fewer tasks, and thus move satisfactorily at their own individual pace. It has the disadvantage, however, of slowing down their academic progress without providing the necessary supplemental work to enable them to move at an accelerated rate of learning in accordance with their potentially greater ability.

Intensive study needs to be made of these various types of remedial instruction to determine their effectiveness in terms of more rapid learning, more intensive motivation, and more lasting persistence in schooling. The Negro colleges could benefit most from moving their remedial work out of the freshman year into precollege programs. But until concentrated preparatory programs during the high school years and the summer immediately prior to admission are possible, two types of freshman remediation appear to offer highest promise: clinical work outside the regular classes, and the three-track program where normal course work is supplemented for the disadvantaged students by further preparation and for the advanced students by additional work.

Until suitable preparatory education is generally available considerable financial support should be provided for remedial instruction in the Negro colleges. One of the quickest methods of increasing assistance to poorly prepared students would be to expand tutorial programs through the help of student volunteers under the domestic Peace Corps. Students in such a program could live in the colleges, work under the direction of the local staff, and continue their own education informally while helping their fellow contemporaries to overcome their scholastic deficiencies. Many of the other needed improvements among the predominantly Negro colleges in curriculum, instruction, and facilities will require substantial financial support, but aid in orienting students to college work and assisting them through specialized individual treatment once they are in college can be made possible through the humanitarian dedication of American college students who are now more than ever moved to help the disadvantaged members of their generation.

Chapter 5

THE CURRICULUM

THE KIND, QUANTITY, AND QUALITY OF THE EDUCATION THE NEGRO RECEIVES will decisively condition his own welfare as well as that of the entire American society. What each individual is able to achieve in the realization of self, in the level of his accomplishments, in civic responsibility, and in economic efficiency is the human capital he brings to society at large.

An examination of the appropriateness of the kinds of higher education now available to American Negroes in these institutions must focus on two things: (1) the opportunities accessible to them for the exploitation of their talents in cultural, social, and civic efforts, and in the economic enterprise;[1] and (2) the suitability of the kinds of courses and curricula now open to them in terms of their personal ambitions and abilities and their right as American citizens to develop themselves to the fullest. The first of these factors is basic to the individual's motivation and to the maximization of his contribution to society; the second has to do with the means of developing himself as a person for his own

---

[1] Participation in the American economic enterprise is competitive. Worker selection takes into account the applicant's knowledge, skills, habits, and attitudes as important aspects of job competence. The comparisons of the economic and social status of the American Negro sometimes made with that of groups in other lands are irrelevant and misleading, for the American Negro is not in direct competition with such groups. He must live and compete in this society. His social life, his exercise of citizenship, and the conduct of his work are *here*. He has no alternative, nor should he be required to choose any other, but to strive for achievement on the basis of full equality with all citizens of this nation, and the educational system must offer him full opportunity to do so.

good and satisfaction. This chapter reviews the courses of study available in the predominantly Negro colleges to enable students to achieve these two goals of self-enlargement and social contribution.

In most times, and in most countries, only students who could afford to be unconcerned about their eventual employment and its economic rewards have been able to enjoy an exclusively cultural or nonutilitarian higher education. Students from lower and middle economic levels are, therefore, normally seriously interested in getting an education that will rather quickly lead to a specific job and to enhanced economic status as well as to cultural advancement. Negro youth do not differ in this respect from their contemporaries. Because of the depressed social, financial, and occupational position of a large proportion of Negro youth, it is not surprising that the curricula of most predominantly Negro colleges have a decidedly occupational orientation. But, the range of vocational options is generally limited. This fact is impressively revealed in the large percentage of students enrolled in programs preparing teachers for the elementary and secondary schools, until recently the only major occupational programs which have offered enhanced social status and relative economic security.

Before analyzing the specialized academic and vocational curricula available in the predominantly Negro institutions it should be observed that they have not been completely indifferent to the general education of their students. Even in the programs with the heaviest vocational orientation the purposes and courses of study reveal that they, like their sister institutions, have designed programs combining cultural growth and job preparation. The balance between liberal or general education and the vocational component, however, varies widely.

GENERAL EDUCATION

Virtually all these institutions offer and generally require their students to pursue some form of general education program, a liberal arts sequence normally but not always completed in the first two college years. Although policies differ from one institution to another, the great majority of the private colleges attempt to assure breadth of learning through a required set of broad survey courses in the three major divisions of knowledge—the natural sciences, the social sciences, and the humanities. The majority of public institutions, on the other hand, more commonly prescribe selected elementary courses in the various liberal arts disciplines to achieve similar broad educational goals.

In both types of institutions, however, the humanities bulk larger in the total curriculum than other disciplines, a condition which commensurately limits the education of their students in other fields, especially the natural sciences. The publicly supported colleges, however, tend to maintain a better balance among the disciplines than do the private schools. The primary difference between public and private colleges in respect to the breadth of their undergraduate programs lies in the heavy concentration in the major found in the former. This high degree of specialization stems from the fact that in these institutions vocational objectives dominate the total undergraduate program. In fact, a third of these colleges permit students to begin to specialize as early as the freshman year.

Compared with other colleges some of these institutions provide a broad general education for all students, but the purposes of others are narrowly limited. In their eagerness to prepare their clientele for the higher-level positions so rapidly becoming accessible to them, the colleges which serve these thousands of Negroes, as well as the white youth who will increasingly enter their classrooms, will have to be constantly aware of the fact that social status, full acceptance in the civic body, and the discharge of the responsibilities of enlightened citizenship depend as much on one's general education as on his vocational competence and the economic advantages it provides. All their curricula should, therefore, include a broad range of instruction in the liberal arts disciplines to complement the various programs of occupationally oriented studies.

Since the objectives and the offerings of the three different types of institutions of higher education included in this report vary somewhat from one another they will be considered separately.

THE JUNIOR COLLEGES

The junior or community colleges in the country at large provide programs with a wide variety of combinations and proportions of general and specialized studies. Few, if any, of the institutions of this type limit their offerings to terminal job training. Like most American junior colleges, the Negro institutions offer some terminal programs leading directly to work, but more often their curricula prepare students for further education in a program leading to a bachelor's, or graduate, or professional degree. Hence the Negro junior colleges differ somewhat from others in the percentage of their students who go on for further formal schooling. An intensive analysis of fourteen of these two-year colleges reveals that in ten of the fourteen over half their students transfer to other institutions for more advanced instruction, and in two of the remaining four between 40 and 50 per cent of their graduates continue their formal education elsewhere. These figures contrast sharply with those for the clientele of junior colleges generally for in the latter two-thirds or more of their students do not transfer to a four-year institution.

This relatively large percentage of graduates who continue their formal schooling is the result in part of a peculiar situation in the state of Florida where many of the predominantly Negro junior colleges are located. In some counties of this state the state educational authorities assign the responsibility for vocational-technical education and adult-continuing education to other educational establishments. It is questionable whether this separation in Florida of post–secondary school technical education from the institutions which provide terminal and preparatory academic programs at the junior college level is educationally sound. For the Negro junior colleges at large it is patently unsound. The junior college presidents seem to accept this view because in personal interviews they stated that technical education was already substantial and growing. They also recognized the community college as the institution ideally designed to provide such instruction but observed that at present the allocation of responsibility, limited financial resources, inadequate physical facilities, and the unavailability of suitably prepared faculty members prevented them from establishing adequate two-year programs of technical education.

They advanced the following three compelling reasons for making terminal occupational programs prominent elements in the curricula of these junior colleges.

1. Terminal programs are needed to prepare young people for specific local jobs. In many communities in the North and South, Negroes now have access to occupations formerly closed to them. The traditional purposes of junior colleges make them more aware of the wide range of local vocational opportunities than the four-year degree-granting institutions and more inclined to cooperate with local industries and businesses in preparing young people for them.

2. Terminal programs are needed to meet the demands of a geographically and occupationally mobile population. A technical terminal education will enhance a Negro youth's ability to move more

freely within a family of occupations, to find a better job, to step onto the first rung of a particular vocational ladder from which he can rise beyond any level to which he could normally aspire with only a high school education.

3. Terminal programs are needed in the predominantly Negro junior colleges for the present to equalize educational opportunities. A number of southern communities maintain junior colleges open only to white students. While integration moves forward terminal programs offered in a nearby predominantly Negro junior college will place Negro youth in a position to compete for job opportunities now closed to them. Negro junior colleges now tend to emphasize curricula preparing for occupations in cosmetology, carpentry, brick masonry, barbering, secretarial training, and auto mechanics, while the white two-year institutions offer technical training involving the skills required in semiprofessional occupations. These institutional differences constitute an inexcusable denial of the Negro's right for suitable education and the benefits which flow from it. While the institutions now serving each race separately are being integrated the present predominantly Negro junior college ought to provide a broader range of terminal programs.

In summary, the junior colleges now attended predominantly by Negroes generally need to be strengthened by increasing the range of their occupationally oriented curricula, so that young people can begin to advance themselves into higher occupational and social status in their own communities and elsewhere. They should also provide broader programs of preparatory academic instruction for the increasing numbers of youth who will continue their formal higher education through four or more college years. It has already been shown that financial disabilities deprive many potentially able Negro youth of a college education, and that these privations imposed by economic factors can be almost as restrictive on self-realization as the barriers of segregation. The junior college, with its low tuition and other costs, and its nearness to the student's home, can provide a higher education for thousands of Negro youth who will then be qualified to enter gainful employment or to go on to further higher education. This study detected a reluctance on the part of Negro students to attend a junior college. The reasons for this attitude are complex, but these young people will be making a serious mistake if they do not seize the advantages which the local college offers in extending their formal schooling, in preparing for better and more lucrative jobs, and in elevating themselves in American society generally.

Local communities, with the help of the states and the Federal Govern-ment, should expand the opportunity for a junior college education among Negro youth with the provision that these institutions should be open to all members of the community without regard to race.

THE FOUR-YEAR COLLEGES

At present the vast majority of Negro youth are served by four-year colleges. The kinds and the scope of education offered in these institu-tions will, for many, set the limits on their personal advancement. Hence this study made an intensive analysis of the curricular offerings of twenty-six public and thirty-seven private colleges which together enroll over 80 per cent of all students in the predominantly Negro four-year colleges. Table 11 presents comprehensive information on the number and types of curricula offered in these sixty-three institutions which altogether now schedule a total of 1,198 undergraduate majors, an average of nineteen each. Approximately 16 per cent of these depart-mental concentrations are in the natural sciences, 18 per cent in the social sciences, and 20 per cent in the humanities. The most noteworthy figure, however, relates to the professional or vocational programs which account for 46 per cent of the total of 1,198 independent majors.

In the liberal arts departments these figures reveal some striking contrasts with the usual offerings in other undergraduate institutions. For example, although students in fifty or more of these sixty-three colleges can major in biology, chemistry, English, history, music, or sociology, at more than half the colleges students cannot major in economics, political science, or art; and in less than a third can they major in physics, psychology, or speech and drama. Virtually all these subjects can be elected as a major in other liberal arts colleges of the country, and the vocational outlets in several of these fields are numerous.

The curricular disbalances in the liberal arts disciplines in these sixty-three colleges can be matched in the professional fields. Although forty, or 63.5 per cent, of the colleges have majors in elementary educa-tion and thirty-five in business management, other occupations in which there are large national shortages—nursing and social work, to use only two examples—are poorly represented. Only eight institutions offer majors in nursing and only one in social work.

In sum, at the undergraduate level, in both the liberal arts and professional fields, the degree programs of predominantly Negro institu-

Table 11 **UNDERGRADUATE MAJORS IN SIXTY-THREE FOUR-YEAR PREDOMINANTLY NEGRO COLLEGES, 1962–1963**

NATURAL SCIENCES	*191*	English	16
Biology	53	Agriculture	14
Chemistry	53	Art	14
Mathematics	48	Biology	14
Physics	21	Mathematics	13
Geography	5	Chemistry	12
General science	4	Music	12
Zoology	3	Secretarial science	11
Botany	3	Physics	6
Bacteriology	1	General science	5
		French	4
SOCIAL SCIENCES	*216*	History	4
History	52	Industrial arts	4
Sociology	50	Trade and industry	4
Economics	31	Social science	3
Political science	23	Sociology	3
Philosophy	22	German	2
Psychology	18	Spanish	2
Social science	17	Latin	1
Religious education and		Psychology	1
religion	2	Religious education	1
Home and family relations	1	Speech education	1
		Speech	1
HUMANITIES	*235*	*Business*	56
Music	60	Management	35
English	58	Secretarial science	11
Foreign languages	1	Accounting	7
French	32	Marketing	3
Spanish	20	*Health and Physical Education*	54
German	8	*Vocational majors*	35
Latin	2	Building construction	7
Russian	1	Electronics	7
Art	28	Carpentry and masonry	5
Speech and drama	15	Interior decorating	3
Industrial arts	8	Auto mechanics	2
Language arts	1	Cabinet making	2
Speech and hearing	1	Machine shop	2
		Mechanical draftsman	2
PROFESSIONAL AND VOCATIONAL	556	Plumbing, heating, and	
Education	282	ventilating	2
Elementary education	40	Graphic arts	1
Secondary education	15	Metal working	1
General education administration		Woodworking	1
and supervision	13	*Agriculture*	31
Nursery school education	6	Animal science	8
Teacher training:		Horticulture	7
Business management	34	Agronomy	5
Home economics	26		

Table 11   UNDERGRADUATE MAJORS IN SIXTY-THREE FOUR-YEAR PREDOMINANTLY NEGRO COLLEGES, 1962–1963, Continued

Agriculture, cont.		*Preprofessional*	7
Agricultural economics	4	Social work	3
Poultry	3	Law	1
Microbiology	2	Medical biology	1
Agricultural engineering	1	Medical chemistry	1
Dairy	1	Theology	1
Home economics	26	*Library science*	5
Food and nutrition	17	*Architecture*	4
Textiles and clothing	7	*Medical technician*	4
Institution management	2	*Journalism*	2
Engineering	25	*Law*	2
Electrical	8	*Aviation*	1
Mechanical	7	*Chemistry, professional*	1
Architectural	5	*Physical therapy*	1
Civil	5	*Social work*	1
Pharmacy	11		
Nursing	8	Grand Total	1,198

tions tend to be concentrated in a limited number of curricula or majors. These limitations place obstacles in the way of those Negro youth who want, and are prepared to profit from, education in other fields. Some significant contrasts appear, however, when the public and the private institutions are compared with respect to the percentage of the major programs they provide in the liberal arts and in the professional fields. The majors of private colleges tend to be more heavily concentrated in the liberal arts departments, while their public counterparts stress professional specialization. Table 12 shows that almost two-thirds, or 65.5 per cent, of the hours of instruction scheduled by twenty-five four-year private Negro colleges was in the liberal arts departments while the comparable figure for eighteen public colleges was only 52.7 per cent. In the latter institutions 46.1 per cent of the curricular offerings were in professional curricula, while in the former the corresponding figure was only 34.1.

In spite of this difference in curricular structure, however, the dominant vocational orientation of even the private colleges is evident in the smaller proportion of their offerings in the liberal arts fields than is common among private colleges generally. Hampton and Tuskegee institutes are eliminated because their broader orientation makes comparison inappropriate. In the remaining twenty-three Negro private liberal

**Table 12   CREDIT HOURS OF INSTRUCTION OFFERED FIRST SEMESTER
1962–1963 BY FORTY-THREE PREDOMINANTLY NEGRO COLLEGES**

DEPARTMENTAL MAJORS	18 PUBLIC COLLEGES	25 PRIVATE COLLEGES
Physical sciences	16.8%	19.3%
Social sciences	13.9	18.4
Humanities	22.0	27.8
Professional	42.7	32.4
Vocational	3.4	1.7
Other and unclassified	1.2	.4
	100.0%	100.0%

arts colleges, 29.8 per cent of their curricular offerings are in professional and vocational subjects while in contrast, in twenty-five selected eastern and midwestern liberal arts colleges, all predominantly white, the corresponding figure is 22.7.[2]

Disregarding for the moment the heavy weighting in professional subjects and focusing only on the range of liberal arts instruction, the figures reveal that the predominantly Negro colleges differ in another significant respect from the other twenty-five colleges. The Negro colleges, both the two-year and four-year institutions, offer a considerably wider range of courses in the humanities and a much narrower body of instruction in the natural and social sciences than do their counterparts. Nearly 40 per cent of the liberal arts offerings in Negro junior colleges, and 42 per cent in Negro four-year colleges, are in the humanities, compared to 25.9 per cent in the predominantly white colleges. As Table 13 shows, the Negro junior colleges offer a somewhat greater proportion of instruction in the natural sciences than do the Negro four-year colleges, but neither the natural sciences nor the social sciences are as extensively represented in either type as in other institutions.

There is an even greater disbalance in the curricula of the Negro colleges than the figures in Table 13 reveal because a disproportionate share of the courses in the humanities is found in English, accompanied in some institutions with relatively strong programs in foreign languages and fine arts. This emphasis on the humanities at the expense of the natural and social sciences may be characteristic in general of southern

[2] Earl J. McGrath (ed.), *Cooperative Long-Range Planning in Liberal Arts Colleges* (New York: Bureau of Publications, Teachers College, Columbia University, 1964), p. 14.

Table 13   **PERCENTAGE OF COURSE CREDIT HOURS IN THE THREE MAJOR LIBERAL ARTS FIELDS**

	12 PREDOMINANTLY NEGRO JUNIOR COLLEGES	43 PREDOMINANTLY NEGRO FOUR-YEAR COLLEGES	25 OTHER FOUR-YEAR COLLEGES
Natural sciences	36.3%	30.8%	41.6%
Social sciences	23.8	27.2	32.5
Humanities	39.9	42.0	25.9
	100.0%	100.0%	100.0%

higher education, but it is more likely the result of long years of primary orientation toward teacher training with an attendant predominance of women students, more of whom normally concentrate in the humanities than in the sciences. This imbalance may in part be due to the somewhat slower speed at which the curriculum has been changing in these institutions than in others. Facts revealed earlier suggest that predominantly Negro colleges have not generally kept abreast of the rapid expansion in the sciences.

The foregoing figures related to the undergraduate liberal arts offerings in the Negro institutions show that, especially in the natural and social sciences, they are inadequate to meet the needs of many young people whose major intellectual interests and potential or demonstrated abilities lie in these disciplines. The most disturbing disclosure is the complete lack in many colleges of majors in such fields as physics, mathematics, and economics, without which many young people will be denied employment in a number of select occupations or opportunity for graduate study leading to other forms of occupational preferment.

The professional programs listed in Table 11 and in Appendix B indicate the dominant position occupied by programs for the preparation of elementary and secondary school teachers. Of the professional and vocational undergraduate majors in sixty-three Negro colleges, 282, or 56 per cent, were in education. At the graduate level this professional concentration is even greater. Fifty-two of the eighty-nine professional master's degrees offered in the twenty-one Negro institutions relate to teaching. The professional divisions listed in Table 14 further document the disproportionate emphasis on the preparation of teachers. Sixty-five schools of education account for 40 per cent of the 163 separately organized professional units in the eighty-nine predominantly Negro four-year colleges and universities.

Table 14   TYPES OF PROFESSIONAL SCHOOLS OR DIVISIONS IN PREDOMINANTLY NEGRO COLLEGES AND UNIVERSITIES, 1962–1963

Education	65	Health, physical education	3
Agriculture	17	Dentistry	2
Business	9	Medicine	2
Home economics	9	Social work	2
Nursing	8	Field services	2
Theology	7	Art	1
Engineering	6	Architecture	1
Law	6	Drama	1
Music	6	Food administration	1
Industrial education	5	Medical technology	1
Technical education	4	Public health education	1
Pharmacy	4	Veterinary medicine	1
Library science	3	Total	163

These facts about the curricular specializations which the predominantly Negro colleges now offer will surprise no one acquainted with the employment opportunities traditionally open to members of that race. School teaching has been nearly the only white-collar profession open to most Negro graduates. In the years ahead it is likely to remain the career of many. In view of the need for well-prepared teachers throughout the country, but especially in the schools which until now have been segregated, this career interest should not be discouraged if it is a genuine vocational choice. But now other vocations are accessible. *The curricular options in the predominantly Negro colleges must be expanded if many Negroes are not to be kept in low economic and social status by narrow curricular options.*

In view of the increasing requirement for postbaccalaureate study in many of the professions it is significant that this pattern of limited curricular options also obtains at the graduate level. Eight of the twenty-two Negro colleges that award the master's degree limit it to the field of education, a ninth offers such a degree only in religious education, and a tenth only in education and home economics.[3] Similar restrictions exist at the doctoral level. Three institutions award doctorates: Meharry Medical College in medicine and dentistry, Atlanta University in biol-

[3] The master's degree programs offered by predominantly Negro institutions are listed in Appendix D.

ogy, and counseling and guidance, and Howard University in chemistry, English, government, history, pharmacology, physics, physiology, and zoology.

Most presidents of the predominantly Negro institutions keenly appreciate the need for greater curricular diversification. In interviews with staff members of the Institute of Higher Education, eighty-five presidents identified thirty-nine programs that their institutions should add to existing curricula, twenty-four of them directly related to professions and vocations. For example, six propose to add computer analysis, five see the need for curricula in business administration, another five consider instruction in electronic technology essential, and many recognize the indispensability of expanded and improved programs in physics and mathematics. These curricular options should be established as rapidly as qualified faculty members and appropriate facilities become available.

Indeed one of the most difficult problems facing these institutions as they attempt to expand their offerings stems from the dearth of qualified teachers in science and technology. Although this is a general problem in American higher education, it is peculiarly acute in these institutions. Nearly every four-year Negro institution properly hopes to offer a major in physics. At present, industry, research institutes, and government agencies command a large percentage of the new Ph.D.'s in this field. Few of the persons now receiving the doctor's degree are willing to accept appointments in academic institutions like those included in this study which provide only limited or no opportunity for advanced instruction and research. While the administrative officers in these institutions were being interviewed one new Ph.D. in physics was discovered who had the opportunity to visit fifteen Negro colleges to be considered for a teaching position. The difficulty of securing faculty members in the sciences, and in some of the other subjects such as accounting, is further compounded for some Negro colleges which by law are prohibited from hiring non-Negro faculty members.

Even those graduates of predominantly Negro colleges who desire to go on to secure the doctor's degree and then return to teach are sometimes barred from integrated graduate schools by admissions standards and accreditation practices which set the level of preparatory accomplishment beyond their reach. Others after they are admitted often find that their earlier education has inadequately prepared them for the rigors of graduate instruction and consequently they drop out.

In order to give Negro youth of real academic promise, but inadequate earlier education, the opportunity to enter the advanced levels of instruction in the graduate schools, the latter institutions and the accrediting associations should devise programs which might require a somewhat longer than normal graduate training, but which would include elements of advanced undergraduate work to correct their deficiencies. This arrangement would be far sounder and fairer than the not uncommon practice of allowing Negro candidates to qualify for graduate degrees on lower standards of achievement than those applied to white students. This practice is in the long run of no advantage either to the individual or to society. In time the elevation of standards in the schools and the colleges attended predominantly by Negroes will make special treatment at the graduate level unnecessary, but for the next ten or fifteen years, unless special arrangements are made, many Negro youth will be unfairly penalized and the academic and industrial worlds denied their much needed services.

In the meantime, many Negro colleges should expand their specialized undergraduate majors in the liberal arts and in occupationally related fields. The demands in several of these fields far exceed the supply of qualified personnel. Negro men graduating in 1964 with a major in physics, engineering, or mathematics could choose from a number of alternative positions in teaching, in industry, and in the government. Comparable opportunities already exist in some other professional areas, but Negro youth will not be able to prepare themselves for occupations now accessible to them until the colleges offer the appropriate programs. *The data in this survey show that for many Negro youth the lack of suitable curricular options now bars the doors to educational advancement and vocational opportunities almost as tightly as earlier segregation.* These colleges need more financial aid to engage the necessary personnel and acquire the additional facilities to increase the range of their programs. They should exercise care, however, in not adding many highly specialized advanced courses, especially in the liberal arts disciplines which have been shown to be extremely costly and not needed to prepare students for advanced work in a graduate or professional school.[4]

The curricular offerings are too restricted in some departments in these institutions not only because of the lack of funds and faculty but

[4] See Earl J. McGrath's *Memo to a College Faculty Member* (New York: Bureau of Publications, Teachers College, Columbia University, 1961).

because of the dominant demands of entrenched disciplines. Many one-man departments in new fields, found especially in the private institutions, may be impressive in the catalogue, but they are not large enough to offer the range of courses required for a suitable major. Their very weakness makes it impossible for them to compete for additional support with larger, better-established departments with a reputation for placing graduates. Many of the education departments which have provided the best job opportunities in the past are now the largest departments and command a disproportionate share of the institutional resources.

Further evidence of curricular inadequacy can be found by examining the number of programs approved by the appropriate accrediting agencies. All the professional schools listed on page 75 offering programs in architecture, dentistry, law, medicine, music, pharmacy, social work, and veterinary medicine are accredited by their related professional organizations. In contrast, however, only a small proportion of the programs in business, engineering, and nursing in Negro colleges are accredited, and even in the field of teacher education, the most common and oldest professional program in these institutions, the proportion of accredited curricula is below the national average.[5]

Educational institutions have a tendency to prepare their students for yesterday's job, but because of their dominant concern with the preparation of elementary and secondary school teachers this is now more true of Negro colleges than of others. For this reason, to the extent that the predominantly Negro colleges emphasize professional preparation rather than liberal education, as many of them do, they need even more than others to keep their programs up to date. The revolutionary changes in the preparation of teachers now occurring in many colleges and universities have affected only a few of the predominantly Negro colleges. If the curricula of these institutions are to be expanded to prepare for positions in the technical fields and in the social and natural sciences, and if the professional programs are to be kept abreast of the most advanced developments, the related departments of instruction will have to be enlarged and manned by persons in touch with the latest developments in their fields. This will require

[5] Of the 123 predominantly Negro institutions thirty-one are not accredited by a regional accrediting association. Of these, twenty-one are junior colleges, nine are four-year colleges, and one is a master's degree–granting institution, Alabama State College. See Appendix A for further breakdown.

substantially larger financial support. The administrators and boards of trustees in these institutions will have to exercise unusual leadership in obtaining and allocating additional funds to new programs and to the enrichment of old programs. Moreover, educational programs with greater curricular specialization must be inaugurated if these colleges are to provide equal opportunity for employment in the various branches and levels of the American economy and social structure.

STUDENT ENROLLMENTS AND PLANS

Thus far this chapter has supplied information about the curricula presently offered or needed in the predominantly Negro colleges. The mere existence of courses of study does not, however, assure that they will be chosen by students who could profit from them. Hence, this investigation sought information on the actual curricular choices of students, for their elections shed additional light on their probable opportunities for further advanced education, or for vocational placement and progress. Table 15 lists all the fields in which more than 1 per cent of either the men or women in this sample were majoring in 1963–64, and indicates the percentage of the 2,880 men and 3,592 women enrolled in each. In this group of students in the predominantly Negro colleges majors in teaching and business administration account for a large percentage of the enrollments in the professional fields. The 24 per cent of the women and 6 per cent of the men majoring in elementary education are not surprising in view of the traditional occupational opportunities in teaching. The more than 10 per cent of both men and women enrolled in business and secretarial programs indicates the increasing opportunities for Negroes in commerce and industry. In the liberal arts disciplines the natural sciences attract more men than any other major division of knowledge and the women major more frequently in the humanities, a not uncommon distribution in other comparable institutions.

These figures related to the curricular choices of Negro students gain significance when juxtaposed with comparable data for students attending similar institutions when the United States Office of Education made its study nearly twenty-eight years ago. The comparisons exhibited in Table 16 reveal the significant shifts in students' curricular choices since 1940. When the majors of the graduating seniors in the present study are compared with the subject choices of seniors in forty-nine

Table 15   PROPORTION OF STUDENTS MAJORING IN SELECTED FIELDS, 1963–1964

	MEN	WOMEN
NATURAL SCIENCES		
Biological sciences	10.4%	5.8%
Mathematics and statistics	7.6	3.8
Physical sciences	3.2	a
SOCIAL SCIENCES		
Social science	14.1	11.9
HUMANITIES		
English	2.3	8.2
Fine arts	4.8	3.8
Foreign languages	1.0	2.8
Industrial arts	3.0	a
PROFESSIONAL AND VOCATIONAL		
Agriculture	2.2	a
Architecture	1.5	a
Business administration and related		
Education	10.7	9.9
Administration	a	1.1
Elementary education	6.4	24.4
Secondary education	2.8	1.7
Physical and health education	7.2	3.7
Engineering	4.8	a
Home economics	a	5.5
Law	1.3	a
Medicine	1.2	a
Nursing	a	2.0
Pharmacy	1.2	a
Secretarial	a	1.8
OTHER (specified)	6.7	5.8
UNDECIDED	a	1.0
NOT INDICATED	3.3	2.8

a Less than 1 per cent.

**Table 16   MAJOR FIELDS OF SENIORS IN PREDOMINANTLY NEGRO COLLEGES
IN 1940 AND IN 1963**

	1940	1963
Agriculture, industrial arts, and home economics	23.0	6.1
Business	4.8	11.7
Education	22.3	28.3
Arts	1.8	4.8
Humanities	22.6	10.2
Physical sciences	8.4	8.1
Health	9.2	13.3
Social sciences	11.7	17.0

1940 SOURCE: Table 31, page 55, "General Studies of Colleges for Negroes," *National Survey of the Higher Education of Negroes,* Volume 2 (Washington: Government Printing Office, 1942).

predominantly Negro colleges included in the 1940 *National Survey of the Higher Education of Negroes,* two notable changes stand out. The proportion of seniors majoring in the traditional crafts of agriculture and industrial arts, and in home economics has shrunk by almost three-fourths, from 23.0 per cent, the largest category in 1940, to 6.1 per cent, the second smallest in 1963. The number of students majoring in business, on the other hand, has increased by 143 per cent. In spite of the relatively heavy offerings in the humanities those fields now account for less than half the proportion of the 1940 majors. Although the numbers involved have risen significantly, the physical sciences have not changed their relative position with respect to the percentage of students who concentrate in these fields.

A further check was made on the curricular interests of students by interrogating them about their career plans. Over a fourth of those who replied had either not decided on a field of work or did not reveal their decision. Those who had at least tentatively made up their minds about an occupation named seven principal fields of employment. These seven occupational groupings accounted for the following percentages: high school teaching, 13.8 per cent, and elementary school teaching, 11.6 per cent—a total of 25.4 per cent intending to teach; business, 8.9 per cent; social science and service, 8.1 per cent; medicine, dentistry, nursing, or other health fields, 7.7 per cent; mathematics and statistics, 3.9 per cent; and the biological sciences, 3.7 per cent.

The career goals of the students going into teaching, the business fields, and the social sciences, roughly match their previously reported chosen fields of study. Like the figures related to the majors, the career choices of Negro youth show a major shift in the past two decades away from agriculture and industrial arts. A nationwide study of college seniors cosponsored by the United States Department of Labor, National Institutes of Health, and National Science Foundation, to be completed in the near future, will provide more detailed information on career plans of students at a variety of institutions. The present sample of students in the predominantly Negro institutions is sufficient, however, to show conclusively that there has been a decided shift in their occupational choices away from the traditionally rural crafts and vocations toward the emerging opportunities in urban business and the sciences in the urban centers. The economic, social, and political changes now occurring so rapidly justify the conclusion that these present occupational trends among Negro youth will continue and doubtless accelerate.

DEGREES GRANTED

An analysis of the level and types of degrees awarded by the predominantly Negro colleges affords still another body of evidence on the kinds of higher education they now provide for their students. In some respects information about the degrees they award reveal more about their purposes and services than the figures presented on course offerings, enrollments, and career plans, for degrees indicate the number of students who were actually successful in completing a full college program. Since all those who drop out of college are eliminated from the figures on the number and kinds of degrees awarded the latter serve as a corrective on misleading inferences which might be drawn from figures on enrollments and course credits. The data on degrees awarded in Negro colleges have particular significance because of the higher-than-average academic mortality rates among their students. Hence the number of degrees awarded is a more valid measure of the students' job prospects than their own career plans which may be at variance with their abilities, motivation, or financial resources.

Table 17 presents this information taken from the annual survey of earned degrees issued by the United States Office of Education showing the fields of study in which eighty-five predominantly Negro

Table 17   BACHELOR'S DEGREES AWARDED BY EIGHTY-FIVE PREDOMINANTLY
NEGRO COLLEGES IN 1962–1963

	NUMBER	PERCENTAGE OF NEGRO COLLEGE DEGREES	NEGRO COLLEGE DEGREES AS PERCENTAGE OF NATIONAL TOTAL
NATURAL SCIENCES			
Biological sciences	828	6.5%	4.3%
Mathematics	619	4.9	3.8
Physical sciences	348	2.8	2.1
Geography	12	.1	1.1
SOCIAL SCIENCES			2.8^a
Sociology	613	4.9	
History	347	2.7	
Psychology	211	1.7	
Economics	64	.5	
Political science	150	1.2	
Religion	44	.3	1.1
Philosophy	3	x^b	.7
Other social sciences	701	5.6	
HUMANITIES			
English and journalism	676	5.4	2.2
Foreign languages	147	1.2	1.5
Fine and applied arts	106	.8	.7
PROFESSIONAL AND VOCATIONAL			
Education	6,436	50.9	6.3
Business and commerce	462	3.7	.9
Health professions	205	1.6	1.7
Engineering	200	1.6	.6
Home economics	156	1.2	3.5
Trade and industry	114	.9	6.8
Agriculture	43	.7	.9
Library science	23	.2	5.0
Architecture	6	x^b	1.1
Law	5	x^b	2.1
OTHER	120	.9	
Total	12,697	100.0%	3.1%

^{a} All social science degrees were grouped.
^{b} x = less than .05 of 1 per cent.

institutions awarded 12,697 four-year degrees in 1962–63. The most impressive fact revealed in Table 17 is the preponderance of degrees awarded to those who expected to become teachers. Indeed, more than half of all the four-year degrees granted by these institutions in 1962–63 went to graduates with this occupational goal. Of the 38 per cent of the degrees awarded in the natural sciences, the social sciences, and the humanities, a considerable proportion were undoubtedly earned by students who also expected to enter high school teaching. Significantly, only about 10 per cent of all these 12,697 degrees were related to other professions and vocations, the largest business, and even this field of swiftly increasing opportunities accounted for less than 4 per cent of the total.

The right-hand column of Table 17 shows the proportion of the nation's undergraduate degrees awarded by the Negro colleges. These figures clearly confirm the fact alluded to earlier that the Negro colleges graduate a disproportionately high percentage of their students in education, trades and industry, home economics, library science, mathematics, and the biological sciences. Even though the first three categories include a much smaller percentage of students than they did in 1940, they still occupy the top position in the list. On the other hand, these colleges fall considerably below the national proportions in the number of degrees granted in the arts, philosophy, English, business, and engineering fields.

These figures on degrees granted reflect the fact that the offerings in the liberal arts disciplines in these predominantly Negro colleges are too narrow. An analysis of the range of different courses offered shows that the average for these colleges is 301.4 credit hours for those with less than five hundred students to 773.2 in colleges with more than two thousand. By contrast, in twenty-five independent liberal arts colleges[6] the liberal arts offerings ranged from 671.7 in those with enrollments below 850 to 949.6 in those with enrollments of more than twelve hundred. Although some American colleges schedule too many specialized programs and courses, this is not true of most of the colleges in this study. If Negro youth, and white students who will increasingly attend these institutions, are not going to be barred from entering a life of scholarship or employment in the professional and other high-level

[6] Earl J. McGrath (ed.), *Cooperative Long-Range Planning in Liberal Arts Colleges* (New York: Bureau of Publications, Teachers College, Columbia University, 1964), p. 13.

occupations they must have access to programs of study not now offered.

These figures related to the number of majors in various curricula, the stated vocational objectives of Negro students, and the degrees they earned in part reflect a distinctive characteristic of the student composition in predominantly Negro colleges. In contrast to most other colleges and universities, the Negro colleges and universities are attended preponderately by women. Not only do women outnumber men; their ratio is twice as high as in the nation's colleges at large. Over 122 women attend the predominantly Negro institutions for every one hundred men, compared to sixty women for every one hundred men in higher education generally. Seventy-three, or 87 per cent, of the eighty-four coeducational Negro institutions from which information was obtained enroll a majority of women. Only three of the remaining eleven —the Agricultural and Technical College of North Carolina, Howard University, and Lincoln University in Pennsylvania—because the types of curricula they offer normally attract men rather than women, show a heavy preponderance of male enrollments. This atypical proportion of men attending most of these colleges is not characteristic of the non-white enrollments in other regions of the country. There males account for from about 56 to 61 per cent of nonwhite enrollments in higher education and for about 64 to 66 per cent of white enrollments. These racial differences may be a result of larger migrations of Negro men than women from their Southern home communities to colleges and universities in other sections of the country. Yet, the fact that even outside the South women form a sizable proportion of nonwhite enrollments suggests that migration is not the only factor at work.

The significantly low ratio of Negro males enrolled in the predominantly Negro institutions deserves a more intensive and exhaustive analysis than time and resources permitted in this study. Information obtained in interviews with staffs and students, however, suggests that the availability of certain types of job opportunities accounts in considerable part for the disproportionately large enrollment of Negro college women, particularly in the South. Teaching has provided the primary vocational outlet for the graduates of these institutions. Moreover, through the years the heaviest demand for teachers has been in the elementary schools, since the number of Negro youth attending high school has been relatively small. Since women have usually taught elementary classes in the United States, it is natural that state teachers colleges for Negroes should have been attended largely by women and that the private liberal arts colleges with few other professional offerings would also preponderantly attract members of this sex.

Whatever the validity of present explanations for the preponderance of women among Negro college students, it is essential that steps be taken to increase male attendance. Efforts to this end will have to be initiated in the earlier stages of formal schooling, that is, in the elementary schools where children are psychologically conditioned and educationally prepared for higher education. Indeed, community adult education programs and counseling facilities for Negro parents could, over the next decade, have a profound influence not only on the percentage of their male offspring who continue their education beyond high school, but on the motivation of all their children toward the goals of higher education. Undoubtedly the level of scholastic achievement would also be raised and persistence in college encouraged by the resultant family understanding and encouragement. Without such early parental influences on motivation and career choices the efforts of the colleges to attract more male as well as female students will be at best reparative and halting exercises.

For the time being, however, the Negro colleges can take two major steps to attract and to hold a larger percentage of Negro young men. First, they can help spread reliable information about emerging vocational opportunities for Negro men more widely among their families and their teachers in the elementary and secondary schools. The fact that in many fields the bars of vocational discrimination are being broken down still remains unknown to many Negro youth, or because of past experiences with discrimination, they consider such reports false or at least inapplicable to them personally. To overcome this negative mental set the schools can supplement their own efforts in informing young people about emerging opportunities by calling on successful Negroes in various walks of life to describe in person the vocational and other status-improving opportunities now available to those who will prepare themselves. Because of their own publicly recognized success such persons could lend reality to statements which from others, especially whites, might have a Micawber-like fictitious ring.

Second, the predominantly Negro colleges must offer the types of instruction attractive to male students and directly preparatory for positions which with satisfactory academic records they can have reasonable assurance of obtaining. The facts already presented prove that present curricular limitations in these institutions make the achievement of these new occupational goals impossible for many Negro youth. Not all colleges should, nor could they defensibly, offer every possible course of study for which some demand exists. But certain privational curricular lacks are obvious. For example, only one in three of the Negro colleges whose undergraduate departments were surveyed offers a major in physics. Yet this field can open a direct avenue for men to excellent positions in teaching, in scientific research, and in industrial and government employment. Similar curricular inadequacies have already been exhibited in the list of major fields of study which could if available lead to lucrative employment and enhanced social status.

Nothing said here urging the establishment of additional curricular choices for men should be interpreted as proposing a reduction of comparable, although in some cases different, opportunities for women in the predominantly Negro colleges. On the contrary, more women should be enabled by earlier education, financial aid, and expanded counseling facilities to attend college, and the curricular options now generally open to them should be appropriately broadened and strengthened. But since the general status of the Negro in American society will in considerable measure be determined by enlarged educational opportunity for Negro men, it is even more important at the moment that the accessibility, the variety, and the quality of their higher education be enhanced.

These facts related to enrollments, curricular offerings, majors elected, career choices, and degrees granted show unmistakably that the predominantly Negro colleges ought to offer a considerably more diversified range of curricular options. To this end, it is essential that the presently Negro public colleges, like most other former normal schools and teachers colleges, become multipurpose institutions in fact as well as in name. The several state governments have an obligation to provide the necessary resources to enrich the curricular offerings of these state colleges and to strengthen their instructional programs. Many of the private colleges will not be able to diversify and expand their curricula to the same extent as the public institutions because of their inability to raise the additional necessary funds, but each such institution can enlarge its program in selected fields, such as physics, psychology, nursing, social work, or the complex of instruction in the allied medical services. The various states should make over-all master plans for curricular development and the essential supporting faculties and facilities, including all their institutions without regard to the present racial composition of their students. Further, public and private institutions should cooperate in regional planning in order to guarantee maximum educational opportunity for all their citizens at the least expense.

Expanded offerings in the predominantly Negro institutions must go hand in hand with expanded enrollments. Indeed, the speed with which new curricular options are established and maintained on a solid instructional basis will, to a considerable extent, determine the number of students who will want and be able to take advantage of such instruction. As long as these colleges continue to form the major source of opportunity for the higher education of the Negro population in the southern states, which constitutes over 6 per cent of the nation's total population, to say nothing of the white citizens who will increasingly attend them, they should equip themselves to educate more than the 3 per cent of the nation's undergraduates that they presently graduate.

Diversification and expansion are also urgently needed at the graduate level, where in 1962 the predominantly Negro institutions granted only 1.4 per cent of the nation's fifth-year degrees and less than one-twentieth of 1 per cent of the nation's research doctorates. At the graduate level, the expansion and diversification of degree programs must for the years immediately ahead be limited to a few major institutions. The graduate programs at qualified private institutions—Atlanta, Fisk, Hampton, Howard, Xavier, the Interdenominational Center, and Meharry Medical College, for example—require rapid expansion. In selected fields, graduate programs should be instituted at a few other strong private institutions in order to invigorate their whole academic enterprise. Investigators working at the frontiers of knowledge would enliven their entire campus life, attract more students of high intellectual promise, and gain status for the institution among the company of scholars. But it is highly questionable whether most of the others can inaugurate and sustain high-quality graduate work for some years without impairing their undergraduate offerings which are at present in need of large additional support for teachers, facilities, libraries, laboratories, and administrative leadership. These institutions ought to concentrate on strengthening the undergraduate majors they now have and on others that are needed, leaving the further education of their graduates to other better-equipped predominantly Negro institutions and the other great centers of learning throughout the country.

What the future of graduate education in many of the public col-

leges should be is debatable. The states have two major options open
to them in providing more and better graduate opportunities to their
Negro citizens. They can continue to organize more varied graduate
programs of higher quality in the predominantly Negro institutions even
though adequate programs and facilities now exist in the other state institutions serving solely or predominantly white students. If they choose
this alternative they will tend to perpetuate a dual system of graduate
education for white and Negro students and at punitive if not prohibitive cost. Under the other alternative they would concentrate graduate programs in a few highly qualified institutions, some of which at
present are attended predominantly by Negroes, and encourage students,
regardless of race, to attend them. Quite aside from the advancement
of integration this second option has obvious economic and educational
advantages. The excessive cost of any dual system of education is accentuated at the graduate level where adequate facilities and equipment for professional training are prohibitively expensive unless used
by a suitable number of qualified students. *Consequently, although the
graduate programs in some Negro public colleges can be strengthened
and expanded, greater emphasis should be given to developing graduate
opportunities for Negro students at predominantly white public institutions which already have strong graduate departments. Where such
opportunities exist or are developed, the graduate programs of many
of the Negro colleges, which, as has been shown, are concentrated in
teacher education, should be gradually discontinued. In the few cases
where public Negro colleges already have strong graduate programs,
these should be strengthened, opened to students of all races, and not
duplicated elsewhere except where economic, social, and educational
considerations justify such duplication.*

In sum, the curricula of the predominantly Negro colleges, although
varying widely from institution to institution, are heavily weighted in
favor of the humanities and reciprocally reduced in the natural and
social sciences. This curricular imbalance accentuates—and if allowed
to persist, will perpetuate—academic and vocational deprivation among
Negro youth. The predominantly Negro colleges need to strengthen
their programs, in part by enriching existing courses, in part by adding
completely new instruction. These additions and expansions are needed
at once to extend educational opportunity for the individual Negro student and to make his full potential services available to American society

as a whole. The necessary developments should, however, in spite of their urgency, be made judicially in terms of currently available resources and a realistic appraisal of prospective additional assets.

The whole range of curricular options in both the liberal arts and the professional fields should be open to Negro youth but not all institutions should attempt to provide the full complement of services. To the degree that they overextend their efforts they will adulterate the quality of their entire program and thus handicap rather than benefit their students. Systematic and continuing institutional, state, and regional planning is urgently needed so that the complete range of such requirements as faculty, physical facilities, libraries, and administrative personnel can be envisaged from the outset and the costs predicted with maximum exactness. To achieve the most effective expansion and improvement of services, all institutional programs should rest on the most reliable analysis of prospective need, the existing offerings in other institutions, the speed of *de facto* integration in all sections of the country, the availability of potential resources from individuals, organizations, and government, and consultation with national accrediting bodies and other agencies which can provide informed advice on proved educational policies and practices.

Chapter 6

COUNSELING AND INSTRUCTION

MORE VARIED AND EXTENSIVE CURRICULAR OFFERINGS IN THE PREDOM-
inantly Negro colleges will provide the substance of a more complete
and suitable education for their students. But whether these students
get into programs appropriate to their interests and abilities and
whether they will be able to master the subjects they pursue will depend
to a considerable extent on the institution's appraisal of their aptitudes
and previous accomplishments, the counseling services made available
to them, and the quality of instruction they receive. Before the institution of their choice can assist them in selecting appropriate courses of
study and counsel them as they advance in their chosen programs it
must know much more about students than their previous academic
records reveal. Hence this inquiry sought information about the testing
programs administered to students at the time of admission and the
uses to which the resulting information was put in the student personnel services.

TESTING AND COUNSELING

Seventy-three of the predominantly Negro colleges supplied detailed information on various aspects of their student personnel services, including such matters as the number and types of measuring
instruments used to determine the scholastic and personality characteristics, and the aptitudes and vocational interests, of their students.
All seventy-three reported that they administered some type of instrument which they used in connection with their student personnel serv-

ices, particularly in academic counseling and placement. As reported earlier, the majority did not use standardized tests as selective devices in their admissions process, but all administered at least one such instrument after students have arrived on campus. In fact, all but one of the seventy-three require their students to take at least two such tests, and twenty administer four or more.

The testing instruments used cover a variety of intellectual, personality, and vocational characteristics. Sixty-five of the colleges use tests which evaluate academic achievement, fifty-eight measure college aptitude, twenty-nine assess vocational interests, and twenty-five analyze personality attributes. The scores which students make on achievement and aptitude tests administered during the freshman orientation period are used extensively in placing them in appropriate courses and sections. Faculty members and professional counselors use the vocational and personality measures along with scores on achievement and aptitude tests in advising students concerning their educational and vocational plans and problems.[1] All these seventy-three institutions make some type of counseling service available to their students, but four provide no personal and ten no vocational counseling.

Even those which do furnish some form of academic and vocational counseling cannot offer a professionalized service, because many of their faculties do not include specialists in the behavioral sciences and the related disciplines. Under these staff limitations regular faculty members and administrators assume a much larger than normal responsibility for counseling activities. In fact, only forty-three, about 60 per cent, of these seventy-three institutions employ any professionally qualified staff members to perform the important services associated with academic counseling. Only twenty-six have full-time counselors to deal with the personal problems of students, and eight of these twenty-six are deans of men or women who of necessity bear a host of other administrative and social responsibilities.

ACADEMIC COUNSELING

Considering the counseling program as a whole, even though only

[1] Half the institutions report that they routinely interpret test scores to students; another third disclose scores on request; only six do not inform students about their standing on the tests taken.

60 per cent of these institutions have professionally qualified personnel to provide academic counseling, this type of guidance is rendered with greater skill and specialized knowledge than any of the other types. Members of the various departments, especially those in the social sciences, are used to advantage in interpreting achievement and aptitude test scores and in placing students in courses appropriate to their previous achievements, their potential abilities, and their academic goals. Every institution has some form of academic counseling at least of modest effectiveness, but only a few provide a fully rounded and professionally sound service to fit student aptitudes and abilities to the types and levels of instruction from which they can most fully profit. *Until more of these institutions can provide fuller academic counseling services the percentage of voluntary withdrawals and academic failures will remain abnormally and unnecessarily high.*

VOCATIONAL COUNSELING

In view of the rapidly changing occupational opportunities and patterns it is fortunate that none of the predominantly Negro institutions fails to aid students in making vocational choices and in finding suitable employment. Over 90 per cent of the seventy-three institutions hold campus career meetings at which members of the staff and outsiders, particularly those representing industry, business, and government agencies, describe various vocational opportunities open to graduates and the kinds of education required to qualify for these positions. Eighty-four per cent operate a placement service, and over 50 per cent maintain collections of relevant occupational library materials. Thus it would seem that students should be able easily to obtain the kinds of information needed to decide which types of jobs suit their own particular abilities and interests. Yet even though 86 per cent provide some form of vocational counseling, only five colleges, all private institutions, employ full-time vocational counselors, and only sixteen engage professionally prepared persons on a part-time basis. Experience elsewhere has shown that even diligent and sincere counseling, when provided by persons untrained in vocational guidance, often lacks relevance and objectivity. These facts are of special importance now when up-to-date vocational guidance is urgently needed and occupational opportunities are opening up for Negroes with increasing speed.

PERSONAL COUNSELING

The services which many of these institutions provide for their students who have temporary or persistent personal problems are severely limited. Of all seventy-three institutions only fourteen at present have arrangements for direct psychiatric treatment for students who suffer emotional maladjustments or mental illnesses. Others handle such personal problems by sending students either to the counseling staff, chaplains, and clergymen, or to physicians and members of the health service who are not psychiatrists. In recent years health services in colleges and universities generally have been substantially expanded. Recognizing the close relationship between physical and mental health and academic success colleges today generally make appropriate provision for counseling to alleviate personal problems and thus maximize intellectual and personal growth. In this respect all but a few of these seventy-three colleges are ill-prepared to serve their students, many of whom, like their contemporaries elsewhere, need sound advice and often systematic treatment.

The strategic significance of educational, personal, and vocational testing and counseling in the social, economic, and vocational advancement of Negro youth imperatively requires that these colleges and universities expand and professionalize such services as rapidly as possible. This proposal does not rest on the assumption that some faculty members and administrators cannot be effectively involved in comprehensive counseling, but those whose temperament and experience have especially equipped them for such assignments will, with the impending unprecedented increase in students, have to carry a particularly heavy burden of conscientious academic advising. Moreover, the range of counseling activities, especially those not solely concerned with such matters as subject-matter requirements and course sequences, is becoming so wide and the related knowledge so esoteric that amateur counselors acting without professional assistance and supervision may sometimes do more harm than good. *The absolute minimum counseling staff for any institution should be one highly trained professional person familiar with all facets of testing and advisory services and capable of organizing and administering a comprehensive program of this sort under the office of the president or, in a large institution, under the dean of students.* Such a person should be able not only to function within the broad range of student personnel services. He should also be able to assume responsibility for acquainting other members of the faculty with essential basic information about the characteristics of the students they teach and the recent developments in the counseling field. *In order to prepare them to assist more actively in the counseling program selected faculty members should receive specialized training during the summer or during the regular session at institutions offering courses or workshops in student personnel services.*

If Negro colleges are to be able to engage these urgently needed individuals with the proper professional qualifications the graduate schools must make a special effort to develop programs of professional training to which currently employed, as well as potential, counselors may be sent. *Graduate study in advanced personnel work, in-service courses and workshops, foundation and government fellowships, and extensive recruitment among Negro college graduates must all be utilized to the fullest if an adequate corps of various types of counselors is to be produced to handle the swiftly growing need for their services.*

INSTRUCTION

The quality of teaching, the work of the faculty, largely determines the quality of any educational program. And the quality of the faculty is determined to a large extent, although not entirely, by the financial resources an institution has to spend for instruction. It is significant, therefore, that the predominantly Negro colleges as a group have through the years consistently spent far less per student than other institutions for teaching and related research—and comparatively the situation has not improved in recent years. In 1949–50 they spent on the average $275 per student, $19 less than other American colleges. By 1959–60, although the Negro colleges were spending much more per student on teaching and research, $470, this sum was still $60 below the national average. Thus, even though they had raised their instructional expenditures 71 per cent in this ten-year period they had fallen 5 per cent further behind the national average. In the interim their situation has deteriorated further with the intensified competition for teachers.

Without an unprecedented rise in the $50 million a year they currently spend on instruction, many of the Negro colleges will fall still further behind their sister institutions in the quality of their teaching.

Those already relatively well-financed will doubtless obtain the necessary additional resources to continue to enlarge, diversify, and improve their present programs, while also recruiting faculty members of the highest achievements. But unless drastic steps are taken immediately the economically weak institutions will be even less able than they are at present to provide the type and quality of instruction their students need and deserve. Students who come from homes of limited intellectual and social stimulation, who have had an inadequate secondary education, and whose communities often offer narrow cultural and vocational opportunities, as earlier sections on admissions standards and remedial work have shown, ought to have above rather than below standard instructional service.

As impressive as they are statistics do not convey the detrimental effect that the lack of funds has on instruction in most predominantly Negro colleges. For example, although the Negro colleges tend to enroll somewhat more students per professor than other institutions, their professors do not spend an unusually large number of hours in the classroom per week nor are their classes extraordinarily large. The average ratio of students to teachers is 22.6 with a range of eighteen students in professional courses to nearly thirty in the natural sciences. If their students were better prepared for college work the numbers in their classes would be of even less significance than they actually are.[2]

In appraising this instructional situation, however, other facets of institutional life cannot be overlooked. To provide the present programs of instruction with their limited funds and without increasing their student-faculty ratios, teaching loads, or class size, most predominantly Negro colleges rely on two means of economy: They pay salaries considerably below the national average, and they impose instructional and other duties which deny faculty members the time essential in productive scholarship. Information supplied by the institutions themselves will be presented later showing that most of the predominantly Negro colleges pay their faculty considerably less than other colleges and universities. And preoccupied as most of them are

[2] According to information supplied by sixty-two predominantly Negro institutions, students on the average in four-year colleges spend 7 per cent, and in junior colleges 9 per cent, of their class time in courses with fewer than ten students. Students at public four-year colleges spend 68 per cent of their time in classes enrolling over twenty-five students; in private four-year colleges, 61 per cent; and in the junior colleges, 50 per cent in classes of this size. In six colleges, however, students spend as much as 75 per cent of their class time in classes of more than forty students.

with instructional and extensive out-of-class tasks, their teachers do not have the normal opportunities for research or for keeping up with the advances in their fields.

These two conditions place devitalizing limitations on the kind of instruction Negro colleges can provide. Like most American colleges that exhibit the same symptoms of privation, their faculties are forced to rely heavily on classroom lectures combined with textbook assignments. The lecture-textbook system is a low-cost, low-energy means of instruction. By organizing courses into lectures interspersed with blocks of required reading in standard textbooks, teachers can maintain control of the class and advance their students at steady, if not spectacular speeds. But such methods of teaching and the intellectual routines they impose do not stimulate teachers or require them to keep abreast of the scholarly advances in their fields, to say nothing of contributing to them. Moreover, since the lecture-textbook system is an essentially passive exercise for the student and authoritarian for the teacher it fails to cultivate in the former the spirit of intellectual inquiry and in the latter the quest for new knowledge. These limitations in teaching practices are particularly significant for the Negro colleges, most of whose students have grown up learning to assume passive social roles under authoritarian conditions. *For this reason the predominantly Negro college, perhaps more than most institutions, should provide a variety of educational experiences and instructional devices other than lectures and textbooks.* Teaching loads should be light enough to permit experimentation and the exploration of new teaching techniques. Some of these institutions do provide various forms of individualized instruction for their weaker students and others have seminars and tutorial arrangements for the more able and advanced, but the number offering such opportunities is limited. These practices deserve wider adoption. To that end the following practices now in use in some of the Negro colleges are described.

OUTSIDE READING

One of the important outcomes of a higher education should be the habit of reading—reading the world's best literature, old and new, as well as magazines, newspapers, and other published materials which keep the individual informed about current issues and problems and the trend of events in the world at large. Unless college graduates acquire the habit of continual self-enlargement through reading, their college education, however good otherwise, soon becomes outmoded. Some of the predominantly Negro institutions use various devices to cultivate the practice of reading outside required class assignments. Kentucky State College and Mississippi Vocational College, for example, encourage nonassigned reading by placing newspapers, magazines, and paperback books in dormitories and the student union. Bennett College expects all its students to subscribe to at least one local or nationally known newspaper. Knoxville College encourages students to develop their own personal libraries by purchasing second-hand books at a book fair conducted by the college at which volumes can be bought for a nickel or dime a piece. A few colleges either purchase paperback books and give them to students or sell them at low cost. Bethune-Cookman provides an opportunity for each student to select three books other than those assigned in his regular courses each semester during his four years of college and requires him to write critical analyses of these works. All LeMoyne College students each semester study one special book not included in their regular course assignments and discuss it in their classes and in chapel meetings.

PROGRAMS FOR SUPERIOR STUDENTS

Various types of individualized instruction for the superior student have become common in American colleges and universities. These teaching procedures can be of special value in the predominantly Negro colleges, many of whose students are more diversified than others in ability and previous academic achievement. All have some students of exceptionally high aptitude and intense academic interests who should be encouraged to move forward in their intellectual development at an above-average pace. It is encouraging to observe that thirty-three of the eighty-nine institutions visited report special programs of instruction for such superior students. In a few institutions as many as 10 or 15 per cent of the student body may be the beneficiaries of individualized instruction, but typically only a few receive such personal treatment. Some Negro colleges have planned an honors program, but have delayed launching it until a larger number of highly qualified students have enrolled or until their financial resources have increased sufficiently to meet the additional instructional costs.

The lack of students prepared to undertake accelerated or additional study appears to have been the chief limiting factor in the extension of honors programs among the Negro colleges, but many are not economically able to provide the additional faculty time and effort required to conduct seminars or individual tutorial instruction. Another factor of indeterminable significance is faculty members' lack of experience with this kind of teaching which requires skills quite different from those used in lecture-recitation procedures. Yet this type of special treatment is especially important in these Negro colleges because each has some students of high ability who must inevitably languish under the slow pace, the routine procedures, and the lack of direct contact with superior minds which characterize many of their classroom experiences.

The thirty-three institutions which do offer some type of honors work organize such programs in various ways. At St. Augustine's College in Raleigh, North Carolina, honors students attend selected courses in their major fields and participate in related independent study and honors seminars. In contrast, superior students at Southern University in Baton Rouge work with professors in an informal relationship but continue to meet in regular courses with their classmates. Rather than selecting students for special honors work, Texas Southern in its "Astro-program" encourages them to make a personal commitment to do more than the usual amount of course work, and with aid from the Fund for the Advancement of Education it assigns special faculty advisors to help them discharge these self-imposed additional responsibilities. Tougaloo Southern Christian College, with Field Foundation funds, provides two full-time tutors who supervise independent study programs for superior students.

To acquaint students with the relation of the various disciplines to each other and to the most pressing contemporary issues, Fisk University organizes its honors program around both departmental honors seminars and four interdisciplinary colloquia in the social sciences, natural sciences, and humanities. "The Good Society" is designed for freshmen, "Science and the Modern World" for sophomores, "Twentieth Century Images of Man" for juniors, and "Great Issues" for seniors. North Carolina College at Durham is now conducting a special program involving study skills, critical writing, and propaganda analysis for a small proportion of students on an experimental basis with the possibility of adopting it eventually for all students. Unlike most such experiments this project includes a built-in plan for evaluation. Honors students and a control group who have been paired on the basis of entrance examinations will be tested during their four years to determine the effects of the special program.

Several other institutions emphasize different forms of independent study. Talladega and Huston-Tillotson colleges, for example, expect honors students to prepare a research paper or senior thesis as part of their final year's work, while Lane College permits the abler students to undertake action projects, such as teaching their major subject to local school children. And Central State College in Ohio allows selected students to pursue some of their courses through study on their own, but evaluates their independent work by requiring them to take the final examination along with those who have regularly attended class.

PROGRAMMED INSTRUCTION AND LANGUAGE LABORATORIES

Few Negro institutions have inaugurated programmed instruction in which students use mechanical aids to learn at their own rate. Morgan State College in Maryland, however, has recently received a large grant to develop programmed learning in a variety of fields. Knoxville College has established a Technical Teaching Center that is preparing programmed remedial material for use at the secondary school level and with their own college students. The demonstrated success of programmed instruction under proper supervision indicates that it should be more widely used especially in remedial work in the basic disciplines in which many Negro students exhibit serious weaknesses. One teaching device widely used since the Second World War has been adopted by one-third of the Negro colleges visited. These institutions have established laboratories in connection with the teaching of English and foreign languages. Such laboratories are also being used intensively at some institutions like Mississippi Vocational College to prepare foreign language teachers for the elementary and secondary schools.

TELEVISION AND TELEPHONE

About twenty-five Negro colleges use closed-circuit television as part of their instructional programs. Delaware State College employs this teaching device in its own educational program and it also prepares elementary teachers to use it in connection with the television teaching programs recently introduced into the Delaware elementary schools. Hampton Institute uses television as a laboratory for training speech and drama students, and Virginia State College employs it to bring visiting scholars to all those on the campus. With support from the Fund for the Advancement of Education ten colleges participate in a telephone course originating at Stephens College.

COMMUNITY EDUCATION

Most predominantly Negro colleges attempt to provide extensive educational services for their local communities, including adult education courses, Great Books discussion groups, workshops, lecture series, conferences, and musical and dramatic productions.

In terms of scope the largest of these special community services in the Negro colleges encompasses the broad evening instructional programs. Some institutions like Delaware State College, Central State College in Ohio, and Kentucky State College actually offer regular freshman and sophomore courses, as well as specialized vocational courses, for those who cannot, or prefer not to, attend classes in the daytime. Bluefield College in West Virginia and St. Philip's College in Texas conduct specialized adult education courses under the Manpower Retraining Program for workers who need to learn new job skills. Tuskegee Institute is undertaking an experimental pilot project to educate functionally illiterate families, and students at St. Philip's College are being trained as tutors of illiterates in the San Antonio area.

Most of the colleges also encourage their students to engage in teaching and service in the community as part of their college experience. Under the leadership of the dean of students Tuskegee has helped students organize their own volunteer "Domestic Peace Corps" in which they spend weekday afternoons and Saturdays and Sundays on community projects ranging from the tutoring of high school students to helping local families with budget and home planning, renovating and painting homes and schools, and operating a bookmobile throughout Montgomery County.

STUDENT EXCHANGE

None of the above formal and informal instructional devices is unique to the predominantly Negro colleges. Some are found on many American campuses. But one device for expanding the range of educative experiences of the predominantly Negro college is quite distinctive if not unique within American higher education, the formal exchange of students between predominantly Negro and predominantly white institutions. This form of student exchange differs from the usual formal transfer of students from one institution to another. It involves official arrangements between institutions for the interchange of students for specified periods of time and it has a definite cultural objective supplementary to the education normally received in the classroom.

A special inquiry was made in this study into the kinds and numbers of student exchange programs in operation in the spring of 1964. The replies received from 1,400 colleges and universities, indicated that in the academic year 1963–64 twenty-seven predominantly Negro colleges had established arrangements for the exchange of their students with sixty-four predominantly white institutions. In addition, twenty predominantly white institutions declared their intention to begin exchanges during 1964–65 or 1965–66.

The privately supported colleges and universities seem to have been especially enterprising in establishing working relationships of this type for they conduct almost all the current student exchange programs. In fact, only two of the twenty-seven Negro institutions and only two of the sixty-four predominantly white institutions having such arrangements are publicly supported. As the figures indicate, the participating Negro colleges have established exchange relationships with more than one other college, in some cases quite a number. For example, Tougaloo Southern Christian College has recently expanded its exchange arrangements to include twenty other institutions; Fisk exchanges students with seventeen, Spelman with thirteen, Morehouse with nine, and Hampton Institute and Bennett College with six institutions, respectively. During 1963–64, some 320 students were moving from one campus to another, 180 remaining in attendance at the host institution for a full semester or more, and the other 140 students staying for varying periods from a few days to several weeks.

The purposes of these exchange programs include the fostering of better understanding among students from different regions, backgrounds, and ethnic groups, the broadening and intensification of the educational and social experiences of the participants, and the facilitation of movement of students from one campus to another to observe at first hand different cultural and institutional settings.[3]

The organization of the student exchange programs can be classi-

---

[3] For a brief statement on new programs offered by a number of universities to expand educational opportunities for Negro students and to raise academic levels at Negro institutions, see *Circular Number 67* of the Association of State Universities and Land-Grant Colleges, Office of Institutional Research, Washington, D.C., January 14, 1965. Student and faculty exchanges are also discussed.

fied under four main types, the first of which involves neighboring colleges and universities, those situated within commuting distance of one another. Catawba and Livingstone colleges in North Carolina, for example, have established such relationships. This arrangement, although it does have the advantage of bringing two different racial groups together, springs primarily from the need to make instruction, especially in advanced courses, available to students who could not pursue such courses at their home institutions. Only rarely, as at Hampton Institute and Washington and Lee University, does it include social activities.

The second type of exchange moves a small number of students to another institution, sometimes quite remote from their own campuses, for a few days or a week. They live in the dormitories, visit classes, take part in social activities, and participate in discussions, often under the sponsorship of student government or other local student organizations. While the formal educational benefits from these short-term visits are obviously small, under proper circumstances the visits can have a considerable effect on the students' social attitudes and concepts.

A third type of exchange involves at least a semester and sometimes two of residence in another institution, commonly in the junior year. Local arrangements at both institutions are carefully planned. Through reading and discussions students receive advanced preparation, and in some programs, such as those between Macalester College in Minnesota and Knoxville and Morehouse colleges, exchangees, through their college newspapers, relay their experiences to students on their own campuses. On returning home they also provide vicarious exchange experiences for their classmates through group discussions and written reports.

In some respects, another type of exchange program is misnamed, for under this plan students from predominantly Negro colleges attend northern institutions such as Boston University, Wellesley, or Marlboro College in Vermont, but no counterpart students go to the South. The advantages of this experience in a first-class predominantly white institution to a Negro youth are obvious, but a number of the values involved in an arrangement under which two students exchange places are lost. The Negro institutions do not gain the benefits of having students from other colleges on their campuses and the white students who would otherwise be there lose the educationally valuable opportunity of living in another academic community and of learning more about Negro students, their ideas, ideals, ambitions, and background of experience. This one-sided exchange also deprives the northern institutions of the benefits of the experiences of returned students who could transmit the characteristics of another social setting to their classmates and teachers.

Institutions now considering one or another of these types of exchange should profit from the experiences of others which have encountered certain common problems. One of the most frequent difficulties for both of the institutions involved relates to the cost of sending students into another, often distant, academic community for a long period. Transportation expenses between institutions and additional living expenses, particularly at private northern institutions, prevent some students from participating in such exchange enterprises. Almost without exception special part-time work or special exchange scholarships must be arranged for students of modest means to offset added costs and loss of income from similar sources at their home institutions.

Second, different standards of academic performance among institutions must be considered and students selected in terms of their ability to compete academically without special privilege. An unprepared Negro student gains little in education, general personal development, or confidence by going to a high-quality northern college. He may fail there because of lack of background or through special concessions to his limitations on the part of his teachers he may succeed. Neither alternative will advance his education, enhance his image of himself, or improve his lot in the competitive world of later life.

Third, consideration should be given to the curricular adjustments which may be required, particularly in major fields, to prevent any interruption in either exchangee's normal progress toward his degree. Some may come from the predominantly Negro colleges in the South to an unusually demanding northern liberal arts college in which students normally advance much further into their major fields of study in four years than would be characteristic of those who normally concentrate in the same disciplines at the students' home institutions. The student who makes the reverse exchange may find himself without the advanced courses needed to complete his major in the institution of origin.

Some of the major shortcomings in existing exchange programs stem from a failure of institutions to clarify the objectives of such enterprises and to organize them systematically to achieve the envisaged goals. As experience with foreign students has too often proved the mere transporting of students to sharply different academic and social environments guarantees no positive educational or social outcome. The end result of poorly conceived or ineffectively executed programs can be and sometimes unfortunately has been an intensification of misunderstanding, prejudice, and estrangement. In the present efforts to eradicate the evils of segregation, it is important that student exchanges be skillfully and empathically designed and administered to assure maximum benefit to the individual student's personal development and social understanding. *To this end, psychologists and other social scientists in the cooperating institutions should be involved in improving exchange arrangements between the predominantly Negro institutions and others by assessing the positive and negative results of various exchange practices.*

With careful planning and continuous evaluation, student exchange programs offer a significant means to enhance the formal education of students, to nourish their social and emotional maturity, and to involve them more completely in one of the historic social movements of our national life. Under favorable conditions the experience which exchanges provide can have a deep and lasting influence on students themselves, help establish social equality, and promote genuine integration in American society.

At present, exchanges are conducted almost wholly by predominantly Negro and predominantly white institutions with national reputations, high admissions standards, and superior facilities. Several factors account for the current concentration of exchange programs in these few colleges. Their standards are more nearly comparable, their financial resources are above average, and the relationships between their faculties and administrators have been closer than is typical of the less well-known institutions. *But the need is equally great and the potential benefits even larger for student exchanges among the many other Negro and white institutions whose students are often of somewhat lower social status and academic achievement, and possibly more provincial background.* In fact Negro youth from southern colleges might feel more at home, receive more personal and genuinely interested consideration, advance more rapidly in their studies because of more nearly comparable standards, smaller classes, and individualized instruction, and gain more confidence and motivation in some of the smaller liberal arts colleges of the northern and western states than they would in the "prestige" institutions. In any event, the former ought to try to attract exchange students in the predominantly Negro colleges of modest standards and encourage their own students to transfer to the reciprocating institution.

If one of the dominant purposes of student exchange is to give young people an understanding of different cultural patterns and conditions of life in the United States, this objective may be more completely reached through exchanges among institutions in the less cosmopolitan communities of both the North and the South. Virtually all Negro colleges, even those not accredited, have some students whose abilities would make a semester's residence at a predominantly white institution a profitable experience for both the student and the institution, and many students from predominantly white colleges, especially those majoring in the social sciences, could benefit from changing places with them for a semester or a year. *In short, expansion of student exchange programs to additional Negro and white institutions is clearly indicated and to assure maximum benefit from these exchanges foundations and other private and corporate philanthropic agencies should make the substantial sums needed available to those institutions which present a clearly designed program of this type.*

Chapter 7

THE FACULTY AND ADMINISTRATION

IN 1890, FACED WITH THE PROBLEM OF COORDINATING AN UNDERGRADUATE college with the graduate and research responsibilities of a university, Harvard reached a decision which has had a profound effect on American higher education. It created its Faculty of Arts and Sciences, combining in one administrative unit the tasks of research and teaching at both the graduate and undergraduate levels. Rather than maintaining two separate faculties, one composed of undergraduate teachers and the other of graduate professors and research specialists, American colleges and universities have adopted this Harvard organization.

Accordingly, American universities now expect faculty members to be proficient at both teaching and research. And most American colleges have hoped, even if they could not expect, that their own faculties would be equally proficient at these tasks of understanding their discipline, teaching it to their students, and adding to its fund of knowledge. These diverse and in recent years increasingly conflicting responsibilities of professors cause some of the major strains and tensions in American higher education, both among institutions and within the disciplines themselves. The thinking and the actions of professors often demonstrate the extent of the polar attraction of these somewhat different academic goals. Some think of themselves as members of "the teaching profession," but in the main professors in American colleges and universities do not consider themselves essentially as teachers but as professional mathematicians, physicists, anthropologists, or historians. The different emphasis and value which institutions place on these several types of faculty responsibilities set the policies, albeit sometimes unconsciously, on faculty tenure, salaries, and training, and they determine the morale of the whole academic community. For this reason, the professional activities emphasized in the faculties in the predominantly Negro colleges indicate the degree to which they are in the mainstream of higher education in the United States. Before conditions of employment and the preparation of faculties are evaluated, therefore, the activities of the faculty in respect to teaching and research merit review.

TEACHING, RESEARCH, AND SCHOLARSHIP

As the earlier chapters in this report clearly reveal, all but a few of the 123 predominantly Negro institutions of higher education in the United States are essentially teaching institutions. The prime obligation of most of them is at present not the creation, but the diffusion, of knowledge. In fact, their purposes and programs show that with few exceptions their primary services are related to the teaching of undergraduate students.

Like many other American colleges, they are unable to provide their faculties with the opportunity or the resources essential to a continuing program of research. The funds devoted to research in the predominantly Negro colleges prove both the foregoing points. In 1959–60, for instance, the most recent year for which comparative figures are available, the predominantly Negro institutions spent $15 per student for organized research, while the average of all higher institutions of education in the nation was twenty times that figure, actually $301 per student. Another comparison even more dramatically exhibits the limited research activities of the Negro institutions. In 1959–60, the predominantly Negro institutions accounted for 1.91 per cent of the nation's total expenditures in higher education, but the sums spent for research formed only thirteen-hundredths of 1 per cent of the billion dollars that the nation's colleges and universities spent in research.

Even in the Negro land-grant colleges, which might be expected to be more fully oriented toward investigative work, funds for this purpose have been limited. For most of their history, these sixteen publicly supported institutions have been completely denied the usual Federal land-grant funds made available specifically for organized research. Even as late as 1962–63, when some improvement could be noted, they reported total expenditures of only $318,276 for this purpose. This figure constitutes only four-hundredths of 1 per cent of the research funds spent by the nation's eighty-seven land-grant institutions that year, institutions which because of their origins, the sources of their support, and their traditional purposes might be presumed to be a somewhat homogeneous group.

To be sure, faculty members at some predominantly Negro institutions have been given resources for investigative work. At Tuskegee Institute, for example, nearly half the faculty are involved in research projects within their fields. And the Meharry Medical College has obtained rather large resources from the Federal Government and elsewhere to enable faculty members to conduct significant research activities. But generally in these institutions neither funds nor time are plentiful for professors interested in pushing forward the frontiers of knowledge. The figures in Table 18 obtained from reports from the faculty members in eighty-three predominantly Negro institutions show that over three-fourths of their time is devoted to teaching. Administrative and other duties account for 18.2 per cent, over five times as much of their time as the 3.4 per cent which they spend in research activities. Even full professors, who surpass their colleagues in investigative work, devote less than 6 per cent of their time to such professional activities.

Table 18   PERCENTAGE OF TIME SPENT BY FACULTY MEMBERS IN EIGHTY-THREE
PREDOMINANTLY NEGRO INSTITUTIONS IN VARIOUS
PROFESSIONAL ACTIVITIES[a]

Teaching	78.4%
Administration	10.7
Research	3.4
Other	7.5
	100.0%

[a] Included are deans, department heads, three ranks of professors, and instructors. Data from 4,875 responses to a faculty questionnaire.

The paucity of investigative activities among the faculties of these institutions unquestionably affects their general intellectual vitality and their status in the world of learning. Many other liberal arts colleges face the same situation. In the essentially undergraduate colleges, however, the absence of large and vigorous research programs will not in the immediate future create their most pressing problem. To the degree possible they should extend their research efforts by adding qualified investigators to their faculties, by raising salaries to hold them, by expanding and improving laboratory and library facilities, by reducing teaching loads, and by granting paid leaves of absence to those who can profit from work at a research department in one of the great centers of learning. But few of these institutions can in the visible future expand their research programs to the point of being centers for contract research and organized investigation. Regardless of the speed with which steps can be taken to extend the scope and improve the quality of their research, these Negro colleges, like the majority of four-year colleges, must maintain their dominant concern for superior undergraduate teaching.

Even if they cannot play a major role in extending the boundaries of knowledge, all the predominantly Negro colleges need faculty members able and eager to keep their teaching in touch with the new knowledge being produced in their respective disciplines. It is a common, though unproved, view that a good teacher must be continuously engaged in the creation of new knowledge through research to keep his instruction up to date and alive. The undeniable fact is that many efficient and inspiring teachers have neither the inclination nor the ability to devote a large part of their professional lives to original investigation. They do possess the abilty, however, to comprehend the new knowledge in their specialties by keeping currently in touch with the published literature and by attending professional meetings where the results of ongoing research are presented. They should also be able to synthesize this knowledge with the vast body of existing learning so that their students will not only acquire the emerging body of relevant facts but also gain some appreciation of the intellectual methods which scholars employ in their work. The responsibility to synthesize and interpret rests on all teachers at all levels in all types of educational institutions. Here, to distinguish this responsibility from that of creating new knowledge through research, it is termed the task of scholarship. To prove adequate to their educational task, all colleges must assure that their faculties consist of men and women of scholarship, teachers who are continuing their own education and embodying new knowledge in the education of their students.

The most serious weakness of most Negro colleges in the United States stems from the inability to seek, obtain, reward, and retain faculty members rich and growing in scholarship. This is not, to be sure, true only of these institutions for many small American colleges suffer similar disabilities. Nor is it largely their own fault. American graduate education in general is inadequately organized to prepare scholars as well as they train research specialists. At the moment the resources and policies of these institutions are devoted more fully to the discharge of the latter than the former responsibility.[1] Hence the Negro colleges, like their other counterparts, encounter severe difficulty in recruiting suitable faculties. *Until the predominantly Negro colleges and universities are able to get and hold a corps of teacher scholars most of their other problems related to curricular offering, instruction, student preparation, and achievement can for the time being only be mitigated.* Programs of study and courses can best be updated, instruction diversified and individualized, and students best educated by professors who are above all competently prepared and constantly growing in their own fields of study. To make it possible and rewarding for faculty members to stay abreast of their fields and vital in their teaching will require improved faculty working conditions and enhanced faculty preparation. Consider these two requirements in turn.

CONDITIONS OF EMPLOYMENT

As pointed out in the last chapter, the teaching loads of faculty members in predominantly Negro institutions do not appear significantly out of line with other institutions. A study of fifty-seven Negro colleges showed the average teaching load of their faculties to be about twelve hours. Another survey of full professors at forty-eight Negro institutions indicated an average load of 11.1 hours. These figures fall somewhat above the median load in a number of old well-known liberal arts colleges in the East and Middle West.[2] In some Negro institutions, however, the average load is two or three hours higher than the average for all institutions, and in some individual cases over twenty hours a week. Comparative statistics are not available showing the nonclassroom responsibilities of these two groups, but collateral evidence gathered in the Negro colleges shows that faculty members bear heavier duties related to remedial work and other forms of individualized instruction necessitated by the weak preparation of many of their students. Hence

[1] See *The Flight from Teaching*, Report of The Carnegie Corporation of New York (New York: The Corporation, 1964).

[2] See Earl J. McGrath, *Memo to a College Faculty Member* (New York: Bureau of Publications, Teachers College, Columbia University, 1961).

their actual teaching loads are probably comparatively larger than these figures indicate.[3]

Certainty of continued employment is recognized as an important factor in attracting and holding the most capable faculty members. The proportion of faculty members on tenure in these predominantly Negro institutions, 54 per cent, does not vary significantly from estimated figures at other institutions. Tenure is, however, occasionally precarious in these institutions. Moreover, other features of institutional life which attract faculty members are often inadequate or completely missing. Funds for faculty travel are often limited, and even where funds are available, some professional meetings in some states have not been open to Negroes. Only about a third of the four-year institutions have an established sabbatical-leave policy or funds to put it into effect. Most of those without sabbatical privileges try to finance leaves of absence for some of their professors, either with institutional funds or outside fellowship support, but the percentage of staff members who can be away from their jobs without loss of income is small. Yet they greatly need the advanced education which such leaves make possible.

The most critical problem which these institutions have in recruiting and maintaining qualified faculty members stems from the generally low level of their salaries. Most of the presidents of the eighty-nine predominantly Negro institutions in this study, when asked to name their most pressing problems, put the need to raise salaries at or near the top of the list. Comparative data document this opinion for they show that average salaries at Negro institutions fall considerably below those paid by other colleges, either within the South or elsewhere.

The normally high competition for faculty members is intensified in the predominantly Negro colleges for they are hedged in by public school systems at the bottom which often offer higher compensation, by institutions of similar size and purposes in the region, some of which have better financial support, and at the top by northern universities which pay better than nearly all Negro colleges and some of which are now

---

[3] Faculty members at many Negro colleges devote much of their out-of-class effort to extensive aid to the primary and secondary schools through consultation, field services, clinics, and informal courses for school teachers, administrators, and college-bound students, as well as visitation and encouragement to their recent graduates in the first years of teaching. While administrators of some of the colleges are concerned about the extent of faculty time devoted to the cause of school improvement, they are restrained from limiting this work by the desperate conditions of the schools.

conducting vigorous recruiting campaigns among qualified Negro teachers. As Table 19 shows, the greatest salary differences occur in the higher ranks. In 1963–64 full professors earned an average of about $2,300 less in the predominantly Negro public and over $3,000 less in the private institutions than their counterparts nationally. Like their sister institutions the privately supported predominantly Negro colleges pay much lower salaries in all ranks than are paid by tax-supported institutions.

Table 19   **NINE/TEN MONTH SALARIES OF FACULTY MEMBERS BY TYPE OF POSITION AND INSTITUTION, 1963–1964**[a]

	NEGRO COLLEGES	SOUTHEASTERN INSTITUTIONS	UNITED STATES COLLEGES
SENIOR COLLEGES			
Professors:			
Public	$9,328	$10,582	$11,632
Private	8,113	9,389	11,158
Associate professors:			
Public	7,333	8,361	9,061
Private	6,915	7,448	8,447
Assistant professors:			
Public	6,272	7,097	7,618
Private	6,018	6,269	7,069
Instructors:			
Public	5,340	5,773	6,251
Private	4,811	5,233	5,892
JUNIOR COLLEGES			
All ranks:			
Public	6,098	6,142	7,965
Private	3,664	5,240	5,633

   [a] Data from sixty-five four-year and eighteen two-year predominantly Negro institutions from the survey by the Institute of Higher Education. Total southeastern and United States data from *Preliminary Report on 9-10 Month Faculty Salaries . . . 1963–64* (OE 52004-9) (Washington: United States Office of Education, Higher Education Business Administration Section, 1964).

Proportionately the greatest salary differences occur at the least well-paid institutions, the private junior colleges, where faculty members at predominantly Negro institutions receive an average of $3,664, less than two-thirds of the national average of $5,633 for comparable institutions. Other data indicate lower salaries on the average in Negro institutions for most administrative positions, with differences rising to between $3,000 and $4,000 in the salaries of business managers in private colleges, head librarians in public colleges, deans of women in private institutions, and deans of men in both public and private colleges.

A number of factors account for the lower average salary in Negro colleges. One is the higher-than-usual proportion of women who make up over 37 per cent of their faculties and staffs. But the dominant factor in low salaries, especially in the privately supported institutions, is doubtless the unavailability of financial resources which would be required to pay more. There is a vicious circle here which somehow has to be broken if inadequate salaries are not going to perpetuate the poor competitive position of these Negro colleges in the academic market place.

The generally lower salaries now account in part for an annual turnover rate among faculty members that ranges from 3 to 7 per cent in the stronger Negro institutions up to 15 to 35 per cent in the weaker colleges. The latter figures are excessively high and lead to institutional instabilities of a variety of types. If higher salaries could be paid the turnover rate would be reduced and faculties commensurately stabilized by longer average tenure. Those who remained would in turn be better compensated as they rose in rank. At present, however, the financial inadequacies of many of these institutions prevent them either from attracting the best-qualified candidates or from raising their salaries rapidly enough to hold them in the face of competition. This situation will grow worse rather than better as Negroes compete on equal terms for jobs in the academic world and in industry and government as they have already begun to do.

The states have begun to improve faculty salaries at the public colleges, and a variety of donors, through the United Negro College Fund as well as the nation's foundations, have helped the private colleges. Recently, for example, Miles, Morehouse, and Spelman colleges received Field Foundation grants to increase faculty salaries; the Atlanta University Center obtained similar support from the Rockefeller Foundation; Dillard University was assisted by the Stern Foundation; and salaries in nine Negro institutions will be increased under the Ford Foundation's "Special Program in Education" grants.

Some improvements can be made in salaries at the Negro institutions—even without increased financial support—through administrative economies and improved plant utilization, as the next chapter will indicate. But even significantly larger salaries and more efficient operation may not be able to raise the quality of teaching while the present faculty shortages and the student boom last. Some presidents of Negro institutions report that even their recently increased salaries have not enabled them to attract well-prepared personnel in sufficient numbers to take care of their replacements and needed expansions. Some of their former students, whom they had helped to obtain graduate degrees through financial grants in the hope of hiring them back as faculty members, now find more attractive positions open to them at other institutions, or in government or industry.

One agency that has been making laudable efforts to improve the quality of the preparation of faculty members in the predominantly Negro colleges, as well as in other institutions, is the Woodrow Wilson National Fellowship Foundation. Under its generous program for the recruitment and training of prospective teachers, this Foundation has established an internship program which enables persons who have been in graduate schools for two years to take a year off from their studies to gain teaching experience. In addition to the normal obligations of their instruction the interns, with their teaching load reduced by one-fourth, try to identify bright students who by personal tutoring might be encouraged to consider careers in college teaching. Already a number of such students have been spotted and helped on toward graduate education in their chosen fields.

One of the problems encountered by even some of their brighter students is that when they complete their bachelor's degree requirements their education has not been adequate to gain admission to a graduate school. To remedy these difficulties the Woodrow Wilson National Fellowship Foundation has inaugurated two types of programs. The first is cooperating with the Southern Educational Foundation which selects interns for an extra summer of study prior to the first year of graduate work. A more prolonged period of preparation is provided to candidates for Woodrow Wilson Fellowships who are enabled to take an extra year of college education at selected institutions before entering graduate work. During this period students take mostly undergraduate courses but they may also include one or two graduate courses in their programs.

These efforts of the Woodrow Wilson Foundation are too new to make a large-scale appraisal of their results but conferences with interns, undergraduates, and college administrators already indicate that the interns have found their teaching experiences and personal contacts with students rewarding and productive. Many undergraduates have gone on to graduate work and college administrators feel that the interns have added to the intellectual vitality of their institutions and increased the motivation of their students.

One of the real problems, and a rather new one, which these institutions serving predominantly Negro student bodies will increasingly meet in faculty recruitment and retention in the years immediately ahead, arises from the energetic efforts predominantly white colleges and universities are now making to attract well-qualified Negroes to their faculties. Northern and western colleges are seeking to hire away some of the best professors in the Negro colleges both because of their own faculty shortages and because of their desire to demonstrate equal racial opportunity and integration within their own academic communities.

The desire of predominantly white institutions in the North to show their interest in the equal-rights movement by engaging Negro faculty members is laudable. *Unless the institutions attracting a teacher away from a predominantly Negro college help the latter to find a replacement, however, the ultimate effect of this practice will inevitably be a material intellectual impoverishment of Negro college staffs and a concomitant reduction in the quality of their education.* A one- or two-year exchange of teachers rather than permanent appointment might for the time being prevent the permanent loss of a Negro teacher in these institutions and at the same time advance the racial mixture of the faculties. *In any event, before institutions consider offering a position to any professor in these colleges they ought to assume the moral responsibility of helping to find a replacement for him.*

FACULTY PREPARATION

Three observations about the faculties of predominantly Negro colleges need to be made before considering specific means for improving the preparation they receive for their demanding teaching responsibilities.

First, most of the faculties of the predominantly Negro institutions are desegregated to some degree, and at some institutions non-Negro faculty members constitute up to 40 and 50 per cent of the total. Exceptions to this statement can be found in Alabama, Louisiana,

Mississippi, and Georgia which still prohibit the employment of non-Negroes as faculty members in Negro state colleges. Even in some of these institutions, however, occasional Caucasians or Orientals are hired as "consultants" or "visiting lecturers." If, therefore, the conditions of employment in these institutions can be made sufficiently attractive, qualified members of all races will become available in larger numbers to expand and improve their faculties.

Second, the majority of faculty members received their graduate preparation outside the Negro institutions. While 63 per cent of the faculty and staff at eighty-three of the Negro colleges completed their undergraduate work at Negro colleges, only 25 per cent of those with master's degrees and less than 12 per cent of those with doctorates received these degrees at Negro institutions. It seems reasonable to assume that for the immediate future a large percentage of Negroes who seek an advanced degree will do so in the predominantly white centers of learning.

Third, caution should be exercised in using the doctor's degree as a measure of faculty competence, for it cannot be assumed that possession of the doctorate assures high-quality undergraduate teaching ability or dedication to the burdensome tasks it imposes. In fact, the products of the graduate schools increasingly prefer other employment. Ph.D. programs are oriented toward highly specialized research essential to scholarly inquiry and the production of new knowledge. This training is not necessarily an ideal form of preparation for all college professors, particularly at the undergraduate level. For a period of years the faculty members in the predominantly Negro institutions, even if they are rapidly desegregated, will have to devote themselves unreservedly to the strengthening of instruction in undergraduate courses and to the sound preparation of their students for advanced education elsewhere.

The percentage of faculty members holding the Ph.D. degree has nevertheless been used to measure faculty quality. Hence, while recognizing the limitations in this procedure, comparative figures have been assembled for predominantly Negro and other colleges and universities. The United States Office of Education has estimated that approximately 50 per cent of the faculty members at the nation's colleges and universities hold the doctor's degree while in the predominantly Negro colleges the percentage is only 30. As Table 20 shows, only in medicine and law does the proportion of doctorates among the Negro college faculty members surpass that in the nation at large.

Table 20   PERCENTAGE OF FACULTY HAVING EARNED DOCTORATES IN PREDOMINANTLY NEGRO AND IN OTHER INSTITUTIONS[a]

	NEGRO COLLEGES	NATIONAL TOTAL (*estimate*)
Agriculture	44.7%	66%
Biological sciences	47.2	78
Business and commerce	16.4	38
Education	37.2	61
Engineering	4.5	39
English and journalism	20.7	46
Fine arts	12.8	26
Foreign languages	34.1	55
Health fields	63.3	21
Home economics	13.6	19
Industrial arts	10.3	NI[b]
Law	36.0	18
Library science	5.8	NI[b]
Mathematics	20.9	48
Philosophy	62.2	69
Physical and health education	14.4	19
Physical sciences	44.9	75
Psychology	41.2	82
Religion and theology	42.3	52
Social sciences	36.5	66
Other (and not indicated)	19.9	20
Total	29.7	51

[a] Negro college data from 5,258 respondents from senior colleges surveyed by the Institute of Higher Education. National estimate from *Teaching Faculty in Universities and Four-Year Colleges, 1962–63* (Washington: U.S. Office of Education, Division of Educational Statistics, Higher Education Surveys Section, May 15, 1964), mimeographed.
[b] NI = not indicated.

As has been observed, the national average of 50 per cent should not necessarily be the norm for the predominantly Negro institutions since a greater proportion of the Negro colleges limit their major function to undergraduate teaching while some of the large universities in the Office of Education list, with their large research activities, raise the average of other institutions. In fact, the colleges and universities of the South have set as a minimum goal 30 per cent of their faculties with the Ph.D. degree. Through their regional association, the Southern Association of Colleges and Schools, these institutions have voted to require that to remain eligible for accreditation beyond December 1966 at least 30 per cent of their faculties must have earned the doctorate and 60 per cent must have gained the equivalent of three years of study beyond the bachelor's degree.

Here again the limitations in average figures should be mentioned. In some predominantly Negro institutions 50 per cent or more, in one instance 85 per cent of the faculty, holds the doctor's degree. But typically they fall below the national average and many fall well below the 30 per cent level. Hence the specific goal of accreditation, and the desire to offer better instruction, are causing many Negro institutions, especially those not now on the approved list, to attempt to raise significantly the academic preparation of their faculties. Many will do this by increasing the number of Ph.D.'s on their faculties. But this is not the sole available means of academic self-improvement and accreditation, and many institutions will have to employ other devices to achieve both objectives.

For the immediate future the greatest aid to instructional improvement will be refresher institutes, concentrated summer programs for faculty members devoted specifically to developments in each of the major disciplines. In the summer of 1964 the Carnegie Corporation and the Rockefeller Foundation financed five such institutes for professors from Negro colleges, in mathematics, biology, physics, English, and history. At Indiana University, the Ford Foundation has provided fellowships for summer programs for college teachers of business. The Federal Government, through the National Defense Education Act and the National Science Foundation, has likewise sponsored programs which have brought teachers into contact with the latest substantive and methodological developments in their fields.

The Ad Hoc Committee of the American Council on Education has initiated a number of plans for faculty improvement in the Negro institutions. In cooperation with the National Science Foundation institutes will be held in the summer of 1965—at North Carolina College at Greensboro in biology, at the University of Wisconsin in mathematics, at Fisk University in physics, and at the University of Michigan in psychology—which will accommodate thirty-five teachers in each of these fields. A similar program has been organized at Carnegie Institute in Pittsburgh under a grant from the Carnegie Corporation to serve fifty teachers of history. The Ad Hoc Committee has also requested foundation support for other institutes which, if funds become available, will enroll 550 teachers in the summer of 1965.

This type of summer program provides a form of concentrated and systematic presentation of ideas and materials, as well as sustained association with leaders in the field, which the scholarly journals and the necessarily brief annual meetings of the learned associations cannot possibly supply. Several weeks of intensive and well-directed study afford a means of keeping professors in graduate schools, undergraduate colleges, and junior colleges throughout the nation in communication with each other and in touch with the progress of their disciplines. Through short-term courses, workshops, and institutes, the colleges and universities are providing continuing occupational education for school teachers, bankers, newsmen, and farmers, among scores of other groups. The need for the continuing education of their own staffs is certainly no less pressing. *The need is so great, in fact, that these summer institutes and other short-term refresher programs should be continued indefinitely for teachers in all types of institutions who seek continued professional growth. But for the faculties of the predominantly Negro colleges these experiences can now be especially rewarding.*

Beyond these intensive summer programs, professors from predominantly Negro colleges should have greater opportunity for graduate and postdoctoral study during the academic year. In years past, the General Education Board and the Rosenwald Fund supplied much of the financial suport for these professors in the form of graduate fellowships. Now a number of foundations are doing so; among them, the Field Foundation at Morehouse, the Carnegie Corporation at Bennett College, Dillard University, and Florida A. and M.; and the Southern Education Foundation at nine southern state universities for college teachers from both predominantly Negro and white institutions. *The foundations can be of significant assistance by providing salaries and living expenses for qualified candidates either for doctoral or postdoctoral study; but this need for intensive graduate study can only be met through a variety of efforts. The state and Federal governments ought to provide similar opportunities in large numbers for qualified faculty members. And more business and industrial corporations ought to support programs of advanced training for faculty members in certain fields.*

If the institutions discussed in this report are to be benefited to the fullest the aid supplied to faculty members to advance their education ought to impose a moral if not a legal responsibility on the recipients to return for a period to the institution which grants them a leave of absence. *Without a provision that the beneficiaries of financial aid for graduate study should serve in the institutions here discussed, further extension of these programs may have the immediate effect of devitalizing the Negro colleges by draining away their most capable and enterprising staff members.* Ideally, exchange programs similar to those at the undergraduate level should also be organized among faculties through which professors, instructors, and graduate students in other institutions come to the Negro colleges to teach courses that otherwise would have to be suspended. Exchanges which involve only the opportunity for a teacher in a Negro institution to go elsewhere for graduate study or refresher programs without reciprocity may only deprive the college of a much needed teacher. Someone of equal or higher academic accomplishment should take such a person's place during his absence. In this way the strong schools with advanced studies could not only provide much-needed undergraduate teaching, but could also invigorate the local faculty by providing visiting professors able to institute seminars among their subject-matter colleagues on the staff of the host institution.

The advantages of faculty exchanges have not been widely capitalized in these institutions. According to a survey in 1963–64 only twelve predominantly Negro institutions were involved in faculty exchanges with predominantly white institutions. The most extensive exchange of teachers and consultants now occurs between Tuskegee Institute and the University of Michigan, with support from the Carnegie Corporation, but additional exchanges are being developed with the assistance of the Carnegie Corporation and the Fund for the Advancement of Education between Knoxville College and the University of Tennessee, Hampton Institute and Cornell and Yale universities, Tougaloo Southern Christian College and Brown University, and the Agricultural and Technical College of North Carolina, North Carolina College, and Texas Southern University and the University of Wisconsin. These programs, properly organized with due regard to the teaching responsibilities of the Negro faculties, should be widely extended. *Like the student exchanges, further faculty exchanges and visiting professor programs to understaffed and poorly staffed Negro colleges can be of great educational aid if certain precautions are observed.*

First, professors from other institutions must recognize the primary commitment of most Negro colleges to teaching. If morale is to be maintained they must be willing to assume teaching loads equal to those of the local staff. In addition, they must be prepared to offer extensive remedial aid, since fewer of their students in most Negro institutions will be as well prepared as their students at home. For these reasons, professors who are concerned about education in the Negro colleges and yet are most talented at specialized research might better help strengthen the faculties of Negro institutions through working with colleagues from these colleges in summer institutes and graduate programs rather than by undertaking an exchange assignment involving exclusively undergraduate teaching.

Moreover, exchange professors should be willing to remain at the Negro institutions for at least a year, and preferably two years, while the faculty members they are replacing are away for graduate study. Such a protracted period of service will enable the visiting teacher to adjust to the new institutional circumstances and to adapt their teaching to the needs of students who will probably differ from those in the institutions from which they come. Finally, such visiting teachers should be aware of the sensitive nature of their role as guests and, in particular, of the difficulty which some presidents of Negro colleges have said they experience with exchange teachers. Faculty members from northern institutions should be genuinely interested in assuming the daily burdens of devoted classroom teaching rather than accepting such appointments merely to participate in civil-rights activities, worthy as the latter may be.

The situation with regard to the exchange of faculty members may be summarized as follows: (1) It is important to persuade qualified white teachers to teach in predominantly Negro colleges and to find Negroes to teach in the institutions from which the former come; (2) white colleges which arrange an exchange program with Negro institutions have a moral responsibility to see that the interchange works to the long-range advantage of the Negro colleges; (3) both parties to such arrangements must recognize that inter-racial exchanges introduce special problems into the best conceived educational programs and into academic living; (4) teaching in the colleges which need the most help will not be the rewarding experience it should be for exchange teachers and their students alike unless the incoming teachers understand that the level of student ability and the local facilities and resources in the

Negro institutions will in most instances not match the conditions in the institutions from which they come.

The state of education in any of the nation's colleges should be the concern of all the nation's colleges. The Negro institutions themselves can take steps to strengthen their programs by improving faculty salaries, libraries, leave privileges, and other working conditions, but the other institutions of the nation, particularly the graduate schools in the major universities, have a special responsibility to help remedy existing weaknesses in the Negro colleges through programs of faculty preparation. *Programs to help strengthen the faculties in the predominantly Negro institutions, such as graduate fellowships, faculty exchanges, and summer institutes, deserve extensive additional support from foundations, corporations, individual philanthropists, and state and Federal bodies. Programs to attract more graduates of the Negro institutions into college teaching, such as those now under way at Bennett College with funds from the Danforth Foundation and through the Woodrow Wilson National Fellowship Foundation with support from the Southern Education Foundation, also deserve significant expansion.*

ADMINISTRATION

The need for improved faculty preparation applies equally to those who administer these institutions, although the means for improvement may be different. While faculty and administrative organization in the predominantly Negro institutions follow typical academic patterns, one element in the administration of many Negro colleges has long attracted attention—the dominant, if not patriarchal, role of the president. The summary of the 1942 *National Survey of the Higher Education of Negroes* stated that "the organization is authoritarian, and important decisions relative to academic affairs are made by the administrative officers" —not by the faculty.[4] Observations during this study lead to the conviction that although there are in many of these institutions numerous, often an excessive number of, faculty committees, the dominance of the chief administrative officer persists.

An increasing number of presidents appear to be delegating greater responsibility to other administrative officers and to faculty committees

[4] Ambrose Caliver, *National Survey of the Higher Education of Negroes: A Summary* (Washington: U.S. Office of Education, 1943), p. 27.

and they are encouraging wider participation in institutional governance, but in other institutions, cooperative planning involving the faculty and the administration in day-to-day policy making is nonexistent. This tradition which permits, indeed often encourages, one person to dominate the whole academic organization and the community undoubtedly has stemmed from the precarious, marginal status of many Negro colleges. Heavily dependent on the good will of influential private benefactors or local political powers, they have tended to remain "presidential" institutions. Moreover, the president at least in the past has not been *primus inter pares* because the gap between his training, ability, and strength of personality and the other members of the staff has often been so wide that he has been in fact the only person in the academic body capable of giving the leadership and making the decisions on which the very survival of the institution depended.

Yet educational considerations now require democratic administration of the predominantly Negro colleges. If these institutions expect to compete for faculty members of superior qualifications, most of whom have become accustomed to the freedom and self-determination in the great centers of learning, they will have to provide similar conditions of academic life on their own campuses. Both those faculty members who go away for advanced training and return, and those who come in as exchange professors will find authoritarian leadership uncongenial. Decentralization of authority and the introduction of accepted democratic procedures in administrative organization can improve the efficiency of management and planning and at the same time cultivate the practice of and dedication to democratic living.

Another feature of administration in these institutions deserves thoughtful consideration by all those who wish to help them achieve a higher status and the capacity for a fuller service to their clientele. Some of the presidents, like their counterparts in other colleges and universities, are fully prepared by education and earlier experiences to give inspiring and informed leadership to the academic enterprise over which they preside. They have earned the highest degrees, they have been successful teachers and sometimes able researchers, they have studied the developments in society at large and particularly in institutions of higher education, they keep abreast of these developments as they occur throughout the United States, and they have the imagination and dedication to keep their institutions in the forefront of progress. But many other administrators for a number of reasons lack these qualities essential in the direction of a vital educational enterprise. They could not in every instance put substantial additional funds to the best use in terms of modern educational developments and efficient management.

This deficiency in the administration of Negro colleges, as in many others, can be corrected by two principal procedures. Many of the present incumbents of the office could become skillful administrators and informed leaders if they had the opportunity to study the management of universities and colleges. Already, Knox College has been able with Ford Foundation help to hold two programs of management training for presidents, deans, and business managers of a number of small colleges, both predominantly white and Negro. Administrators of other colleges could serve as understudies through internships and assistantships with presidents known to be effective and successful. Or they could study at one of the centers where higher education in all its aspects has now become an accepted field of scholarship. Courses and seminars dealing with administration and organization, curricular problems, counseling and guidance techniques, and business management are available in a number of institutions both during the regular academic year and in the summer months. Boards of trustees would do well to send their presidents with vitality and ambition to these centers with full compensation while they are away. The returns on such an investment would be considerable and enduring.

The more satisfactory long-range plan to enhance the presidential position and to qualify the incumbents more fully for the able and efficient discharge of their duties is to identify promising faculty members or junior administrative officers and prepare them for the presidency by both of the foregoing methods. A foundation which would support a recruiting program of this type for a period of years could make a larger contribution to the future of these institutions by spending $100,000 a year than by other types of investment of five or ten times this magnitude. A retired president who had demonstrated his ability to direct and develop an institution of higher education, and especially to select capable deans and directors, could by leisurely visits to campuses and informal talks with local teachers and administrators identify a hundred potentially able college and university administrators and advise foundations and others concerning the type of training they would need to give effective and dynamic leadership in the years ahead. *In any event steps should be taken to identify able teachers and others and to give them a period of apprenticeship or education, or both, in preparation for the presidency in these institutions.* Other administrators below the presidential level need similar in-service training on management procedures suitable to higher education. And finally, both administrators and trustees need continuing experience in workshops and national meetings to improve their understanding of their roles and of the developments continuously taking place in American higher education.

Chapter 8

THE LIBRARY

TO RETAIN ANY VALIDITY TODAY, THE IMAGE OF HIGHER EDUCATION AS A
teacher on one end of a log and a student on the other must include a
large stack of books, journals, microfilms, and records between them. If
a library is to be of high quality, college administrators must understand
and appreciate its role in accomplishing the objectives of higher education. Faculty members must also be familiar with its collection in their
own subjects, be active in keeping the collection current, and assure its
effective use through their assignments to students. Finally, the financial
support of the library must be both adequate and free from violent
fluctuations. But funds for carefully developed collections, trained
librarians and supporting staff, and properly equipped and adequate
building space cannot assure an outstanding library if students are untrained in using these resources, faculty members are uninterested in
promoting their development, and administrators are unaware of the
library's role in the educational process.

This chapter reports on four major features of the Negro college
libraries: their material resources of facilities and collections; their human
resources of trained staff members; the use of these resources by students
and faculty; and the administrative and financial support sustaining
them.

The quality of any college library is determined first by the extent
and nature of its material and human resources. When its holdings are
insufficient, outdated, or inadequately housed, or when its staff and
services are unreliable, unimaginative, or ineffective, the library cannot

actively accomplish its functions of augmenting the talents of the faculty (and partially offsetting their shortcomings) and exploiting the capacity of students to learn. The resources and services of Negro college libraries run the gamut from excellent to poor, but unfortunately the curve of quality is heavily skewed toward the lower end. Their problems are the problems of most small college libraries, but they are more prominent and more intense. The need for library resources and services is accentuated in most predominantly Negro colleges by their lack of sufficiently trained faculty members and their larger than normal proportion of poorly prepared students.

MATERIAL RESOURCES

Although the buildings which house libraries are less important than their holdings, the age and structure of the physical facilities influence their accessibility and hence their efficient use. Of the sixty-nine predominantly Negro institutions which supplied information about their library buildings, 39 per cent of these structures were erected before 1945, 26 per cent between 1945 and 1954, and 35 per cent since 1955. Thus a number of these buildings are relatively new and might be expected to exemplify recent developments in efficient library facilities and usage. Few of them, however, embody such accepted ideas as facilities for group study, typing, and the use of audio-visual materials, and inadequate design of some of the newest buildings has resulted in observable inefficiencies in service as well as extravagance in operating cost. Ratings of the predominantly Negro institutions by the Association of College and Research Libraries would indicate that the physical facilities of only 50 to 60 per cent meet the set standards of the American Library Association in terms of seating capacity, book capacity, and general suitability, with the private four-year colleges making the poorest showing. *As increases in enrollments require renovating or rebuilding of library facilities, the Negro colleges, and particularly state architects responsible for the design of public college libraries, could profitably examine the methods of library planning and the resulting innovations in construction found in other colleges which have recently erected new library buildings.*

The three most important measures of the adequacy of library resources are the total number of volumes in the collection, the annual additions of volumes, and the number of journals and periodicals currently acquired. It is generally agreed that to be adequate, a small to medium-sized four-year liberal arts college should have a minimum basic collection of fifty thousand volumes and a junior college should have twenty thousand volumes. Several of these institutions have excellent library holdings, but data supplied by the cooperating institutions indicate that the average Negro college library does not have the necessary basic collection. In fact, it is likely to have only between 30 and 60 per cent of the titles on any given subject list of basic books.

Despite extensive improvements and additions to their libraries, of the sixty senior colleges and universities which supplied information on their collections, only twenty-two, or 36.6 per cent, had over fifty thousand volumes, five had even fewer than the twenty thousand expected of junior colleges, and the smallest had 10,096 volumes. The collections of most of the junior college libraries are markedly inferior. Only one out of nineteen public and private junior colleges comes up to the accepted twenty-thousand-volume standard, only one other has over ten thousand, and nine contain fewer than five thousand volumes. What is worse, minimum standards and requirements for accreditation have had a tendency to induce additions sheerly for the sake of increasing the size of the collections. Several of the institutions have added worthless material to their collections in large quantities, diluting both the quality of the collection and the effectiveness of staff work.

Data on the number of volumes added each year and on subscriptions to periodicals are not much more encouraging. Forty-six of the colleges increased their collections in 1962–63 by at least 5 per cent, but this generally accepted rate of increase is inadequate for many of them if they are to remedy the deficiencies that have resulted from years of substandard support.

In sum, when all types and sizes of institutions of higher education are thrown together, most Negro college library collections are generally inferior to those of other American colleges. Negro colleges on the average are substantially below the others in library collection size, rate of growth, and budgetary resources, and as a group they lack their share of distinctive or exceptional libraries.

This appraisal of Negro college libraries is confirmed by the assessments of over seven hundred faculty members from predominantly Negro institutions who responded to a questionnaire from the Institute of Higher Education. The majority of respondents from fifty-one of the sixty-three four-year colleges judged their libraries to be adequate to support the teaching of beginning students. In only nineteen of the sixty-three four-year colleges did a majority of the faculty consider the library resources adequate for the needs of advanced classes. Moreover, faculties in the junior colleges reported significant deficiencies in books published before 1945, back files of journals, government documents, and audio-visual materials. Many faculty members also pointed to a specific lack of key titles and landmark books for students in major subject fields, as well as a deficiency of journals, reference materials, and source documents which they needed to keep abreast of scholarly developments in their own disciplines.

Finally, many faculty members in various disciplines expressed the need for films and records and for the equipment to use them. Every college library should have collections of recorded music, poetry, and drama, as well as guides to available films and funds for renting them. The whole range of audio-visual materials offers an especially effective means to help broaden the knowledge and stimulate the intellectual interests of students of limited backgrounds, and the evidence from this survey indicates that professors and their students in the predominantly Negro colleges would make much use of these materials if they were available.

In short, most predominantly Negro college libraries are adequate in books required for beginning courses, but they are desperately inadequate in books and journals for use of upperclassmen and the faculty and in their audio-visual materials. *The colleges need to increase their own rate of support for library collections. They could attract useful contributions to their collections while warding off useless gifts which only impose wasteful burdens on already limited resources by distributing to their alumni and patrons a carefully worded statement outlining in general terms the kinds of books most needed in their libraries. But drastic outside action should also be launched to strengthen the collections of Negro college libraries.* A start on this task has been made in selected institutions by several of the foundations. For example, seventeen of the Negro colleges have received W. K. Kellogg Foundation funds for books in teacher education; the Rockefeller Foundation is helping develop the joint Atlanta University Center library; and the Stern Foundation is aiding the Dillard University library. Books in print can now be supplied, fully processed and with prepared catalogue cards, at a cost per volume about equal to list price. *Most Negro colleges deserve grants averaging at least five dollars a volume to bring their basic collections up to date and to provide strong foundations for the major elements of their programs.*

Certain institutions should be granted additional funds in the subject fields of their especially able faculty members, whose own development and that of their students is now handicapped by inadequate library holdings.

To produce the maximum benefit from this additional financial support, however, a pool of consultants should be available to aid librarians of the institutions which receive substantial supplementary funds. Four or five consultants competent in the major areas of building planning, collection development, collection weeding, and staff utilization could bolster the efforts of these institutions and enhance the effect of the grants. Indeed, foundations and other prospective donors might well make their grants contingent on the use of such advisory services.

HUMAN RESOURCES

Given adequate facilities and collections, the number and professional qualifications of staff determine the scope and effectiveness of library services. Discussions, correspondence, and reports from the Negro colleges indicate that the number of librarians of reasonable professional competence is far too small to meet their staffing requirements. Two-thirds of their professional staff had earned the fifth-year professional degree, but a large number of them received their training from nonaccredited schools. More important, these professional librarians are in most cases handicapped by a lack of strong supporting personnel. Each professional person in the library should normally be matched in smaller institutions by one clerical person, and in larger libraries, by two. Yet with the exception of the largest libraries, professional personnel in the Negro colleges actually outnumber clerical staff. As a result they perform routine functions and are unable to undertake many of the professional responsibilities characteristic of librarians. Only 35 per cent of the college libraries included in this study meet American Library Association standards for the number and training of their personnel. Twenty-two per cent were judged marginal, and 43 per cent were judged deficient. The public four-year colleges rank somewhat higher on the average than the private in number and quality of staff members, almost certainly because their salary schedules tend to be higher.

This serious shortage of adequately prepared librarians handicaps the Negro college libraries in two respects. First, only skilled librarians can make fully effective use of funds, whether they are spent on mateterials, staff, plant, or equipment. Second, many of the students enrolled in predominantly Negro colleges need more rather than less imaginative assistance and guidance in putting the resources of a library to use. As one professor from Dillard University stated:

> The Negro student in the deep south lacks sufficient experience with good libraries and abundant reading; he therefore does not use what he has well, nor does he respect a library and understand responsibility for returning and handling books. *We therefore need more trained librarians than the ordinary school.*

Only the best librarians are capable of meeting the demanding challenges of this phase of their work.

There is no easy and quick way to overcome staff weaknesses and shortages in the predominantly Negro colleges. Some inroads will doubtless be made on this problem through the recent large grant of the Rockefeller Foundation to the Atlanta University Library School calculated to increase the number and improve the quality of librarians. *But in addition a correspondence course for individual use or for staff training programs would increase the professional competence of many present librarians. Funds are also needed for regional workshops to provide these librarians with ideas and devices to improve and to evaluate their library services.* Such workshops might be more valuable for this purpose than state and national library conventions, which few Negro college librarians are presently able to attend.

Training grants, correspondence courses, and workshops are part of the substantial effort needed to bring the staff services of most Negro college libraries up to average quality. In addition to these devices to improve library services there is one indirect method which could be used. As stated earlier in another connection, the size of the student body could be increased with little additional cost in terms of some types of services and facilities. The significance of size may not at first be apparent, yet in most of the Negro colleges each dollar available for the library could be better used by an increased number of students. For example, the same basic book collection can serve nine hundred students almost as well as three hundred. Essentially the same staff at the circulation desk can control a library entrance whether one hundred or five hundred students pass through it daily. Most existing card catalogues could be used by an increased number of students.

In short, a library serving a small institution is inefficient simply because the same basic operating structure is required in a small as in a large college to order books, to catalogue books, to pay bills, to control circulation, to type catalogue cards, and to carry out other routine tasks. Hence one obvious way to reduce the inefficiency of the small college library would be to increase enrollments.

The demand for higher education generally, and among Negroes specifically, and an increased percentage of attendance in the appropriate age group, will in the years ahead expand the average institutional size and thus make better use of the library facilities. A more direct approach, however, would be to improve the efficiency of present purchasing and cataloguing practices. The creation and operation of a college library service center to act as the purchasing and cataloguing agent for a number of small colleges in a given region would effect material savings and increase efficiency. A comprehensive but uncomplicated plan for such a service center could be prepared with little difficulty by drawing on the experience of any of the several existing technical service centers in public library systems. Reasonably accurate estimates of operating costs and of potential savings could be projected for libraries of varying sizes. With this information in hand, the merits of the service center concept could be presented to college administrators and librarians in a geographical region.

The success of such a project would hinge on the care with which its goals were defined and on the skill with which the system was designed and presented to prospective users. Individual libraries, whether Negro or not, could send to the center a check list of books indicating desired titles. They would then receive fully catalogued and processed volumes ready to be put into their collections, together with full sets of cards for their catalogues. Financed on the basis of a combination of subscription fees and service charges, the center would submit monthly itemized bills to the colleges. At the outset, private colleges would doubtless be the principal users of such a center, but the efficiency and economy of its service might eventually overcome the restrictive purchasing procedures in public institutions and open the way to contracts with them.

Large research libraries have already recognized the need for cooperative cataloguing and coordinated collecting. The staffs of small libraries no less need to be relieved of the burdens of many operating routines to enable them to get on with the educational aspects of librarianship. A service agency of the type proposed would give small libraries the operating advantages of large ones. As volume dictated, data-processing or copying equipment could produce catalogue cards in volume at low unit costs as a byproduct of the order routine. Maximum discount rates could be obtained on purchases, billing procedures could be automated, and the time-consuming, essentially clerical, routines of technical activities would be largely eliminated from individual libraries. Thus the staff would be freed for the more important work of reference service, collection development, and student instruction. In the long run, this increased emphasis on the professional aspects of librarianship would attract more promising and much-needed young people to the profession than any other steps these libraries could presently take.

Until such a service center is available, every Negro college library should be assured a subscription to Choice, *a recently established reviewing journal prepared specifically for college librarians and faculty members.* Choice currently reviews the vast majority of titles which liberal arts colleges are likely to purchase. Its cost of $20 a year may be beyond the reach of some of these libraries, but a subscription could provide a selection aid of major inportance, especially to small institutions. Later, marked copies of Choice could serve as a standard request form which individual colleges could transmit to the proposed service center. A foundation could find in Choice a relatively inexpensive way to help the Negro colleges since a year's subscription for all of them would cost only about $2,500.

LIBRARY USE

Most American colleges record and report figures on the circulation and use of their collections in such diverse fashions that no attempt has been made here to establish an average per-student circulation figure for the predominantly Negro institutions. Information concerning library usage from annual reports, conversations with the cooperating librarians, and random sampling of book circulation cards indicates, however, that with notable exceptions, neither the faculty nor the students in most Negro colleges are heavy users of the library.

A few examples will document these observations. In his annual report for 1962–63, the librarian in one Negro land-grant institution indicated an annual average of 19.4 loans per student for home use. The faculty in this institution accounted for an average of nine loans a year in comparison with 31.7 for faculty members of North Central Association institutions. At another state college the faculty averaged only seven loans in the academic year 1962–63. At five other institutions, the faculty average ranged from two to seven books, and at these institutions it was estimated that faculty members check out less than one of every twenty-five new books acquired by the library and in general do not know what books the library contains in their own fields.

Exceptions exist, of course, to these examples of low usage. At Bennett College, for example, the faculty borrowed over two thousand volumes during 1962–63, and at St. Augustine's College the average student withdrew twenty-two volumes from the general collection and forty volumes from the reserve stacks. But on the whole the libraries in most Negro colleges do not appear to be used extensively, either within the academic program or for outside reading.

The misuse of collections must also be recorded. Most of the college libraries are plagued with major book-loss problems, but these problems are magnified in the poorly financed institutions. One of the larger institutions in this study has had to replace a multivolume encyclopedia more than once in a single year, and others report annual losses of books worth several thousand dollars. The home environment and high school experiences of many students do not cultivate an interest in the habit of using, or a respect for books. *Hence the colleges must establish stronger programs orienting their students to the use of libraries. Their students require more instruction regarding the use of library resources than others who have had broader experience with substantial collections of books either in their homes or in their earlier schooling.*

FINANCIAL SUPPORT

The basic factor in providing library resources adequate to an institution's educational program is the amount of money available for these resources. One of the most striking contrasts among Negro college libraries is the wide variation in the size of their budgets. Among Negro liberal arts colleges enrolling over five hundred students, for example, the gross funds available for library use vary by as much as 400 per cent, and by as much as 500 per cent in terms of expenditures per student. In some Negro junior colleges, total library expenditures are fifteen times as large as in others.

There is evidence, however, that the Negro colleges are aware of the necessity to budget more adequate funds for their library services. Thus in the decade from 1950 to 1960, they increased the per-student expenditures for their libraries by 116 per cent—the largest incease of any of their educational and general expenditures. By 1960, in fact, they were spending $41 per student on their libraries in contrast to the $40 average being spent by all American colleges, and they were allocating a larger proportion of their educational expenditures to this purpose than the average American college. In other words, the Negro colleges are making a considerable effort by themselves to overcome the deficiencies of their libraries. As they increasingly use a greater variety of teaching techniques than textbooks and lectures, and as their faculty members increasingly attempt to keep up with the advances in their fields, the Negro college libraries will need even more extensive support to remedy their deficiencies.

The present condition of the library services in most of the predominantly Negro colleges can be summed up in the statement that the physical facilities are in general more adequate than the books, journals, films, and records they contain, or the number and training of the library staff. Their collections and staff need extensive strengthening to rectify a history of insufficient support and to help lift teaching and learning out of ritual and routine.

Chapter 9

FACILITIES

STATISTICAL DATA ABOUT THE PHYSICAL FACILITIES USED FOR VARIOUS purposes by institutions of higher education are less satisfactory than any other type of information about their characteristics because the quality of buildings cannot be even roughly inferred from such facts as the age of structures, the floor space they provide, and their adaptability to particular use. No appraisal of its adequacy in teaching chemistry can be inferred from a statement that a college has a chemistry laboratory with thirty student stations. Some very old buldings erected at small cost in terms of the current value of the dollar may be more satisfactory for some educational purposes than others constructed half a century later. On the other hand, a newly erected but poorly designed library or laboratory may not be as functionally useful as a skillfully renovated older building. Moreover, the aesthetic features of the latter may indirectly contribute more to the informal education of students than the former which may be a mere pile of bricks, mortar, and glass. An on-the-spot appraisal of the physical and educational value of the plant in these institutions would have provided information not obtained through the use of questionnaires. Lack of personnel, time, and money precluded such visits. And local observations would in any event have involved subjective judgments. The data obtained by questionnaire and by observation on some campuses, however, provide a reliable picture of some features of the physical facilities in these colleges and universities.

On the basis of such information, which was voluminous, it can be said that the facilities of many of the predominantly Negro colleges present a more favorable picture than some other features of their institutional life. The facts presented thus far have shown that many of the predominantly Negro colleges urgently need substantially increased student financial aid, new curricula, more diversified instruction, strengthened facilities, and enlarged library resources and services, but the physical facilities of the Negro colleges come closer to meeting their needs. In some respects—in accommodating their present enrollments, for example—their buildings and other facilities are more nearly adequate than in many other institutions. It it true, of course, that most of the Negro institutions, particularly the private colleges, could greatly benefit from modernized equipment, additional buildings, and the renovation of existing facilities. But in many their existing plant and equipment offer considerable opportunity for expanded use without large expenditures for additional structures. Physical facilities can be treated under these headings: first, the location of the Negro colleges; second, their investment in the present plant; third, the need for additional accommodations; and fourth, their student housing capacity, present and potential.

LOCATION OF INSTITUTIONS

Administrative officers were asked to express an opinion concerning the locations of their institutions in terms of their potential clienteles, the supporting constituencies, and the social, economic, and demographic character of the surrounding areas. In the main they expressed satisfaction with their present locations, but three types of objections were raised by some institutions.

Some junior college officers believed that their location within or immediately adjacent to high school buildings created special problems. When the junior college occupies the same plant which serves high school students, students and faculty often move freely from one institution to the other. Some college and some high school courses are taught interchangeably by the same teachers and attended by both types of students. The possible maladjustments in the level and intensity of instruction are obvious. But a more important factor relates to the attitudes of Negro youth toward attending a junior college. Evidence has been cited elsewhere showing that some students who leave one of these joint high school–junior college institutions at the end of the twelfth grade do not wish to continue their education locally because they feel that they are only receiving additional high school instruction for another two years with the same teachers, under the same schedules, and in the same classrooms. Even those who do go on feel that motivation is lessened and the opportunity for independent creative work of college grade is materially reduced.

Some junior colleges now occupying the facilities and using the staffs of high schools could be improved by moving to new locations. This separate establishment can only be justified, however, as the number of students increases to a point which will enable the institution to offer a richer curriculum with appropriate programs of general, preparatory, and vocational education. And the increased enrollments will depend on a changed image of the junior college among Negro youth. Junior college presidents generally strongly favor the establishment of separate junior college campuses and plants with their own faculties, students, and academic policies and programs. In view of the argument presented earlier for a larger attendance of Negro youth at junior colleges with a greater diversity of academic and vocational programs, the judgment of these presidents on the location of their buildings seems sound.

Some of the senior colleges seem to be poorly situated in terms of using their resources to provide the fullest service for the largest number of students. In some instances they are needlessly and wastefully close to one another. The establishment of two colleges in the same neighborhood has sometimes occurred when a state has discontinued an earlier practice of supporting a church-related college and established its own nearby. The institutions on adjoining campuses at Wilberforce and Central State in Ohio and at Claflin and South Carolina State came into existence in this manner. Other institutions like Rust and Mississippi Industrial College in Holly Springs were placed in geographic proximity because a church wanted to preserve its denominational identity. Both practices have resulted in uneconomic operations and less adequate education than they could have provided in different locations or through cooperative efforts after establishment. Like other institutions, predominantly Negro colleges have tended not to eliminate unnecessary duplication of services and facilities through cooperative efforts. In fact they often compete. The matching of activities, facilities, and programs causes excessive capital as well as current operating expense. By spreading their limited resources thinly they individually deprive themselves of the opportunity of offering a stronger program in a narrower range of disciplines and subjects while in concert they could actually extend the scope of their curricula.

What has been said about the waste in a duplication of services in nearby institutions applies with particular force to segregated units of the same state systems of higher education. In some towns like Tallahassee, Florida, two universities maintained at public expense have for years offered similar instruction to two student bodies which in many subjects could have received instruction in the same classes without increasing the size of the instructional staff. Fortunately, at some instructional levels at least, in some neighboring institutions students of both races are now being intermixed.

The third type of faulty location is found where a predominantly Negro college has been set in a rural region inaccessible to the residents of any community other than the small group of local citizens. Sometimes this undesirable situation is aggravated by the development of a Negro ghetto around the college which entrenches segregation on campus and off. Institutions in thinly populated regions generally suffer economic, social, and educational privations. They cannot draw enough students to create economically viable establishments because their potential clienteles cannot afford to live away from home. Second, their rural locations deprive them of many of the rich educational advantages of the urban centers with their varied population, diversified industry and commerce, and rich artistic and other cultural activities. Third, since opportunity for part-time employment outside the college is almost completely lacking many youth of limited financial resources cannot attend rural colleges.

It has been said that it is as difficult to move a college as a graveyard. Nevertheless, the problems created by location could be alleviated by several types of cooperative arrangements. Two small colleges providing essentially the same services for the same types of students could combine their efforts either through merger or a division of labor. Two or more church-related colleges in the same area could unite and still maintain their special religious functions by retaining appropriate denominational instruction and other exercises for the youth of their own particular churches. Such mergers are made difficult by entrenched denominational interests and officers but often the alternative to joining the efforts of several church-related colleges will inevitably be low-quality education for their young people or eventual extinction.

Where two or more institutions cannot be organically joined, as in the case of privately supported and publicly supported neighboring institutions, arrangements can still be made for the common appointment of faculty members, exchange of students (especially in advanced specialized courses), joint use of library buildings and collections, and cooperative extraclass cultural programs including lectures, concerts, and artistic exhibits. Budgetary arrangements can be made for suitable payments for these services from one institution to another and the expenses of each commensurately reduced. Some such arrangements could lead to substantial improvements in educational programs through more economic management.

INVESTMENT IN PLANT

A visitor to many campuses cannot help but be struck by the impressive facilities of several of the predominantly Negro institutions, especially some of the state colleges and universities. They include some of the most handsome, attractively landscaped, and well-kept campuses in America. This impression is borne out by statistical data which indicate that by and large the Negro colleges have spent a higher proportion of their total funds for facilities than for most other categories of expense. For example, the figures in Appendix F indicate that while the Negro colleges' proportion of national current fund income and expenditures in 1959–60 was less than 70 per cent of their proportion of national enrollments—approximately 1.90 compared with 2.75 per cent—their proportion of the value of college physical plants was almost identical with their enrollment—2.76 compared with 2.75 per cent.[1] And although they were not spending proportionally as much as all colleges to expand their facilities, they were spending a rather high proportion of funds to operate and maintain their facilities—2.95 per cent of the national total, or $158 a year per student in comparison to the national average of $139 per student. These above-average expenditures for operation and maintenance unquestionably occur because of the need to renovate older poorly constructed buildings which for many years have not been kept in top condition. Accordingly, it would be a mistake to assume that funds have been used extravagantly for plant upkeep.

The plant facilities in the Negro colleges have been notably improved

[1] It should be noted that the proportion of property value was ahead of enrollment at public institutions but behind at private. The Negro public colleges in 1959–60 enrolled 2.89 per cent of all public college students and their property value for plant came to 3.03 per cent of the national total. But the private colleges, with 2.55 per cent of private college enrollments, held only 2.40 per cent of all property value for private college plant.

in recent years. In the twelve years from 1949–50 to 1961–62, the value of the Negro colleges' facilities increased from $156 million to $418 million. By 1961–62 it was estimated that the replacement costs of these facilities come to over $700 million. By the latter year they had spent approximately $4,038 on their facilities for each student enrolled, an amount only 9 per cent below the national average of $4,431. Moreover, thirty-five of the eighty-three Negro institutions for which data were available exceeded the national average. Since building costs in the South, where the vast majority of Negro colleges are located, tend to be considerably lower than in the rest of the nation these institutions proportionately get more for each dollar spent than the majority of white colleges elsewhere. Thus the funds expended per student on facilities actually come even closer to being equal to the average expenditure for the rest of higher education.

As the figures in Table 21 show, the range of investment in their plants varied greatly, in fact from over $10,000 per student in two of the colleges down to $789 per student in one junior college which shares facilities with a high school. However, most of the colleges fell close to the norm of the country at large. Of the forty-three institutions listed in Table 21 having an investment in all facilities of from $2,500 to $5,000 for each student enrolled, twenty-five of them had over $4,000 invested in plant alone.

Table 21   INVESTMENT IN PLANT AND EQUIPMENT PER STUDENT IN
EIGHTY-THREE NEGRO COLLEGES, 1961–1962

	PUBLIC SENIOR COLLEGES	PUBLIC JUNIOR COLLEGES	PRIVATE SENIOR COLLEGES	PRIVATE JUNIOR COLLEGES	TOTAL
Over $10,000	2				2
$7,500–$9,999	2		1	1	4
$5,000–$7,499	3		9		12
$2,500–$4,999	17	2	21	3	43
Under $2,500	3	8	10	1	22
Total	27	10	41	5	83

The low standing in plant investment of several of the public junior colleges results in part from the practice of using local high school buildings, while the relatively high standing of several public state colleges stems in some part from significantly increased legislative appropriations for construction during the past decade to bring their facilities more in line with those of state colleges for white students. In fact, the sudden efforts of some states to provide equal but separate facilities of higher education for the different races has caused a few of the Negro state colleges to suffer from an abundance of new but unsystematically planned construction. Some have been provided with new buildings which are empty because no funds were appropriated for equipment, and occasionally they have received expensive equipment, such as astronomical apparatus, without the funds needed to employ faculty members qualified to use it.

The question arises whether the kinds of construction in which the predominantly Negro colleges have invested is appropriate to their needs and programs. As might be expected from the review of curricular offerings and faculty assignments only a small percentage of the funds spent for construction covered facilities related to research. Table 22 shows that only three-tenths of 1 per cent of the value of the physical plant in the public Negro colleges is in buildings used for research. Moreover, even these small funds are concentrated in a few institutions. Of the 7 per cent invested by the private Negro colleges in such plant facilities, over three-fourths is accounted for by two private universities.

Table 22   PERCENTAGE OF BOOK VALUE OF PLANT IN BUILDINGS OF
VARIOUS TYPES IN PREDOMINANTLY NEGRO AND OTHER
INSTITUTIONS OF HIGHER EDUCATION

| | PUBLIC INSTITUTIONS | | PRIVATE INSTITUTIONS | |
	NEGRO	ALL U.S.	NEGRO	ALL U.S.
Instructional	49.6%	47.4%	31.2%	42.6%
Research	.3	12.9	7.0	8.6
General[a]	9.1	7.4	14.5	7.1
Auxiliary[b]	8.1	6.3	6.8	4.7
Residential	32.9	26.0	40.5	37.0

[a] *General* includes administration, auditoriums, chapels, heating and maintenance, faculty clubs, etc.

[b] *Auxiliary* includes dining halls, book stores, student unions, infirmaries, etc.

SOURCE: United States data from unpublished report of the United States Office of Education. Negro college data cover 1,341 buildings at seventy-four Negro colleges surveyed by the Institute of Higher Education in 1963–64.

The major difference among the predominantly Negro and white institutions, the value of research facilities, will doubtless become less pronounced in the years ahead.

Few of the predominantly Negro institutions are at present research-oriented, and although few of these can in the visible future become large centers of organized research as more of their faculty members receive advanced degrees and continue their interest in research and scholarship, the institutions will have to devote more of their resources to research facilities than they have spent for this purpose in the past. Hence their investments in research will have to form a larger share of their total expenditures and if it is agreed that the proportion of the facilities devoted to student housing should not be lessened, the proportion of general and auxiliary facilities is likely to decline toward the national average.

Table 22 shows that the percentage of the book value of plant facilities used for instructional purposes in the *private* Negro colleges falls considerably below the comparable figures for *all* institutions of higher education, 31.2 and 42.6 per cent, respectively. The value of general purpose buildings, such as auditoriums, chapels, and offices is proportionately far lower in the latter than in the former, 7.1 and 14.5 per cent, and the value of residence halls is also proportionately lower in the other institutions, 37.0 per cent compared to 40.5 per cent in the Negro colleges.

NEEDED FACILITIES

In spite of the proportionately large investment of the Negro colleges in buildings and equipment, fifty-three of the eighty-eight presidents interviewed for this report stated that inadequate facilities of one type or another constituted a major problem. Available space is already inadequate for present instructional purposes and will soon cause a more critical problem as enrollments increase with unprecedented speed. Officials at the public institutions report that at least 34 per cent of their buildings are antiquated, obsolescent, or otherwise unsatisfactory for modern educational purposes, and 37 per cent of the officials at the private institutions express the same view. One private college dean, stating an opinion common among the administrative officers interviewed, said that entering students who come from soundly constructed and well-equipped high schools are often deeply disappointed when they see the dirty, old, run-down, crammed-together campus buildings in which they may have to live and learn for four years. He added that because of their poor plants and the lack of modern equipment many of the predominantly Negro colleges are doing yesterday's teaching job.

This impression gains support from the fact that 27 per cent of the buildings in Negro colleges were constructed before 1930. Seventeen per cent of the gross area in public institutions and 23 per cent in private institutions need rehabilitation. In spite of high expenditures for maintenance over one-third of their buildings continue to be in poor condition compared to the physical facilities on other campuses. They need major renovation and repair to achieve standards of health and safety as well as educational suitability in terms of the improvements in teaching and campus living in the recent years.

Table 23 shows some significant comparative facts about the condition and suitability of buildings on Negro college and other campuses. When the public and private Negro institutions are compared the latter have fewer buildings built before 1900 which local officials feel should be completely replaced, 50 and 30 per cent respectively, but of those erected since 1950 the public institutions seem to have put up sounder and better-designed structures than the private. As noted previously, some southern states have in the past decade made larger appropriations to their segregated Negro institutions to raise them to a level comparable to others that are publicly supported.

The most arresting facts in Table 23, however, are the differences between the Negro and the other colleges. Fifteen per cent less of the buildings on the private Negro college campuses are considered satisfactory for continued use than on the campuses of their predominantly white counterparts. And in both public and private Negro colleges the officials consider a much larger percentage of the buildings erected before 1900 unsatisfactory than the administrators of other colleges and universities. The percentage of buildings considered in need of rehabilitation is twice as large in both public and private Negro colleges as in other institutions of higher education. The small percentage, only 1 per cent actually, of the public Negro college buildings erected from 1950 to 1957 which need to be replaced shows again the effort of many southern states to make these institutions comparable in physical facilities to others under public control. Apparently the private institutions have not been able to build as well for 6 per cent of their structures erected in the same period need to be replaced.

As might be expected, Table 24 reveals a positive relationship between the age of buildings and the frequency of rehabilitation. Approximately two-thirds of the buildings constructed before 1920 and half of those constructed between 1920 and 1929 that are in use in 1964 have been reconstructed. Direct observation of the present condition of some of these buildings and the statements of the presidents reveal that if the necessary funds had been available even more of the buildings erected before 1930 would have been renovated. When the figures in Table 24 showing the percentage of structures already renovated are added to those currently in need of rehabilitation, as indicated in Table 23, it is patent that the condition of the facilities, especially among the private Negro colleges, is less satisfactory than mere figures on size, floor space, and the number of students accommodated might suggest.

Table 23   CONDITION OF BUILDINGS CONSTRUCTED THROUGH 1957
IN SEVENTY-FOUR NEGRO COLLEGES AND IN ALL COLLEGES
CLASSIFIED BY PERIOD OF CONSTRUCTION AND BY CONTROL

PERIOD	SATISFACTORY FOR CONTINUED USE		SHOULD BE REHABILITATED		SHOULD BE REPLACED	
	NEGRO	ALL U.S.	NEGRO	ALL U.S.	NEGRO	ALL U.S.
PUBLIC						
Before 1900	25%	54%	25%	18%	50%	28%
1900–1919	33	60	40	19	27	21
1920–1929	54	74	27	14	19	12
1930–1939	69	82	24	8	7	10
1940–1949[a]	53	43	15	8	32	49
1950–1957	92	90	7	3	1	7
Total public	66	63	19	9	15	28
PRIVATE						
Before 1900	44	67	25	18	31	15
1900–1919	59	74	26	15	15	11
1920–1929	61	83	26	10	13	7
1930–1939	74	89	11	6	15	5
1940–1949[a]	61	65	21	5	18	30
1950–1957	88	94	6	3	6	3
Total private	63	78	20	9	17	13

[a] With the exception of the 1940's the percentage of the structures that are still considered satisfactory increases for each decade until the present. The exception of the 1940's undoubtedly stems from the fact that following the Second World War, many colleges and universities obtained discarded military buildings which they planned to use only as long as necessary to accommodate the returning veterans, but which they have been forced to continue to use because of continued high enrollments and lack of funds.

Table 24 NUMBER AND PERCENTAGE OF BUILDINGS AT SEVENTY-FOUR NEGRO COLLEGES REHABILITATED ACCORDING TO THE DATE OF CONSTRUCTION

PERIOD OF CONSTRUCTION	NUMBER OF BUILDINGS	NUMBER REHABILITATED	PERCENTAGE REHABILITATED
Before 1900	81	55	67.9%
1900–1919	146	98	67.1
1920–1929	139	72	51.8
1930–1939	189	80	42.3
1940–1949	231	80	34.6
1950–1959	329	53	16.1
1960–1964	168	4	2.4

Presidents were asked to indicate which types of buildings their institutions now most urgently needed. Most frequently they placed the library at the top of the list. In addition, sixteen indicated a need for new dormitories, twelve for additional science buildings and general classrooms, eight for humanities buildings with space for the communication arts, music, and fine arts, eight also for language, scientific, and technological laboratories, five for gymnasiums, four for student unions, three for faculty offices, and three for dining halls.

But in the opinion of the officers of many of these institutions, even if they had all these additional buildings, they would still not be fully prepared to offer a suitable education in some fields. For example, nearly every one lacks some of the modern type of teaching equipment typically used today in science, language, reading, and other laboratories. The unavailability of computers, typewriters, dictating machines, and other equipment has prevented many Negro colleges from offering up-to-date programs of technical education. In fact, in some institutions new equipment is more urgently needed than new construction.

Space studies and direct observation show that in some of these institutions a good deal of valuable space is virtually standing idle or is used only during a small percentage of the hours in a work week. *Space utilization studies and more careful scheduling of classes and other activities would, as in virtually all other colleges and universities in the nation, increase the efficiency of usage and thus reduce current operating expenses as well as capital costs for new construction.*

Facts gathered for 1962 and presented in Table 25 show that these predominantly Negro colleges could in their present facilities accommodate a considerably higher proportion of new students than most colleges.

In that year the Negro colleges reported that 30 per cent more students could be accommodated in their classrooms than they then enrolled. Moreover, they calculated that they could provide laboratory stations for nearly 40 per cent and reading-room space for nearly 25 per cent of their students at one time. These latter figures compare favorably with the situation in other institutions.

Table 25   ROOM CAPACITIES OF SEVENTY-FOUR PREDOMINANTLY
           NEGRO COLLEGES, 1961–1962

	PUBLIC INSTITUTIONS	PRIVATE INSTITUTIONS	TOTAL
Enrollment	59,575	33,946	93,521
Lecture classroom capacity	66,800	54,970	121,770
Laboratory stations	26,110	11,231	37,341
Library and reading rooms	11,776	11,439	23,215

The relative adequacy of teaching, and other, space in institutions of higher education can be determined by comparing the number of places available in relation to total enrollments. Table 26 presents such data for the predominantly Negro and other colleges. These figures show that in terms of their ability to accommodate additional students, the Negro institutions are on the average in a somewhat better position than their counterparts. The total lecture-classroom capacity is 112 per cent of the enrollments in public Negro colleges while the comparable figure for other public institutions is only 86 per cent. Private Negro college capacity is 162 per cent of enrollment compared to 102 for other comparable institutions. Stated in another way, the *public* Negro colleges could have seated all their students at one time in classrooms and still had room for 12 per cent more students, while the *private* Negro colleges could have seated 62 per cent more students than they enrolled. In contrast, all *public* institutions in the United States could have accommodated only 86 per cent of their students at once, and *private* institutions only 1 per cent more students in lecture classrooms than their total enrollment.

Although the difference was not as great as in lecture classrooms, the seventy-four Negro institutions also had a greater relative capacity in laboratory stations. The laboratories of Negro colleges could have accommodated 44 per cent of their total student enrollments compared with 37 per cent for all institutions, while the comparable percentages were 33 and 32 in private institutions. Similar advantages exist in available library space. The *public* Negro colleges could have accommodated one-fifth of their total student enrollment at one time in reading rooms compared to one-seventh for all public institutions, and *private* Negro colleges could have seated one-third of their student bodies at one time compared to one-sixth for all similar institutions.

Table 26   STUDENT STATIONS AVAILABLE FOR ONE HUNDRED STUDENTS ENROLLED IN SEVENTY-FOUR NEGRO AND IN ALL COLLEGES

	PUBLIC INSTITUTIONS		PRIVATE INSTITUTIONS	
	NEGRO	ALL U.S.	NEGRO	ALL U.S.
Lecture classrooms	112%	86%	162%	101%
Laboratory stations	44	37	33	32
Library and reading rooms	20	14	34	17

In short, as of 1962, the Negro colleges were more capable of accommodating additional students with their existing academic facilities than the average college. These facts on availability of space suggest that before large expansions in physical plant are undertaken careful utilization studies should be made of the types of facilities which are now available and the manner in which they are being used. Such studies could be beneficial in several respects. They could reveal the buildings and the rooms which with modest expenditures for repairs and renovation would for a period of years be entirely satisfactory for any prospective curricular offerings. They could also undermine the costly practice common in institutions of higher education throughout the United States of reserving certain rooms or buildings for only one department or one teacher even though such a policy might mean that these facilities would stand idle many hours each week while new construction was being urgently demanded. Regardless of the large additional funds which these institutions in the early future should receive for improving and expanding their physical plants these wasteful space-utilization practices will have to be eliminated if prospective student bodies are to be suitably accommodated and efficiently instructed.

Space studies are also needed to provide a sound factual basis for the planning of future buildings. Costly mistakes in design are obvious in buildings recently erected in which walls, lighting, and electrical outlets have not been properly located and in which entrances, exits, halls, and walkways have been constructed with inadequate regard for student traffic patterns. Space and related studies can also provide information indispensable in the economic erection of the kinds of buildings, the acquisition of the proper equipment, and the provision of the other physical facilities which these institutions will need if they are to inaugurate the types of instructional programs required to prepare their students to take advantage of the new vocational opportunities for Negroes. Finally, space studies will be essential in the comprehensive campus planning which needs to be done on a systematic and continuing basis in all institutions of higher education in the years immediately ahead.

The consultation center which was proposed in Chapter 2 to serve the institutional research needs of these and other colleges could provide the most effective means of instituting space-utilization studies in the Negro colleges. With consultation available at low cost from this center, institutions could begin to undertake space and time studies, analyses of present and forecasts of future needs for equipment, comprehensive planning of campus layout and building location, and the preparation of long-term budget figures related to physical facilities.

STUDENT RESIDENCES

The potential benefits available to the predominantly Negro colleges through improved space utilization are matched by the enhanced educational opportunities which could be realized by capitalizing on their heavy investment in residential facilities. For a variety of reasons, the Negro colleges tend to be atypically residential. Fewer than 30 per cent of their students live at home and commute to the campus; over 30 per cent actually come from outside of the state. Off-campus housing is common at most Negro colleges. In a few institutions, because of the lack of college residence facilities, more students live in rented rooms in private homes than on the campus itself, and at three institutions over half the students whose families do not reside nearby live off campus. Two facts about these privately owned facilities are of particular significance. First, although fifty of the sixty Negro senior colleges have social fraternities or sororities, with the exception of one at Meharry Medical College none of these organizations maintains its own residence as is common elsewhere. Second, less than half the Negro institutions inspect or approve off-campus housing for their students, an almost universal practice in other institutions.

In spite of notable exceptions, the Negro colleges generally house far more students in their own facilities than live off campus. Among the twenty-four *public* senior colleges and universities which supplied relevant information, only five reported that fewer than half their students resided in college-owned buildings. The percentage of students housed on campus ranged from 40 to 98. The *private* senior colleges and universities do not differ materially from their public counterparts. All but one is basically residential, and twenty-five of the thirty-five house more than 50 per cent of their students in their own halls. The three private junior colleges house from 70 to 90 percent of their enrollment on campus. As is understandable from their declared community purpose, only the public junior colleges serve local students predominantly, but even here, one of the twelve has some housing for its students.

As Table 27 shows, the Negro institutions have a significant advantage over the average college in the capacity of their dormitories to house their students, an advantage almost double that of other colleges either public (43.1 to 21.4 per cent) or private (53.6 to 27.9 per cent). Their capacity in dining halls is relatively close to the national average among public institutions, but sharply higher among private colleges.

Table 27   **CAPACITIES OF DORMITORIES AND DINING HALLS IN RELATION TO TOTAL ENROLLMENT IN NEGRO AND IN OTHER INSTITUTIONS**

	PUBLIC INSTITUTIONS		PRIVATE INSTITUTIONS	
	NEGRO	ALL U.S.	NEGRO	ALL U.S.
Dormitories	43.1%	21.4%	53.6%	27.9%
Dining halls	29.4	25.1	81.0	31.7

Only in providing housing for married students do the Negro colleges fall below the national average. The public Negro colleges now provide only 2.1 housing units for married students for each one thousand students enrolled, while for all other public institutions the comparable figure is sixteen. The difference between private Negro institutions and all other private colleges is much smaller, but nonetheless substantial, 4.4 and 8.7 per thousand, respectively.

The heavy investment of Negro institutions in student residences can be either a liability or a major educational asset, for college housing can either reinforce and contribute to the exercises of the classroom, or it can negate and invalidate educational purposes. The major advantage of the residential college, indeed its unique opportunity in comparison to the commuter college, is its capability of providing an environment with an educative impact on its students twenty-four hours a day. These incessant environmental influences can be especially beneficial to Negro students, many of whom have been shown to lack opportunity at home for study, reflection, and cultural stimulation. The salutary effects of dormitory life and other campus situations can, however, only become instrumental when the college deliberately and systematically plans to make the out-of-class features of campus residence contribute to the educational, social, and cultural development of the student.

In the main the Negro colleges have recognized the need for cultural enrichment among their students and have attempted to use their residential facilities to complement the formal educational programs. Typically their dormitories are staffed by full-time personnel who not only maintain order but also counsel students. Normally, however, there is only about one residence staff member for every hundred students, and an overcrowding of some dormitories has been unavoidable. Moreover, although some Negro colleges use the dormitories to provide informal education through newspapers, magazines, and books, as mentioned in Chapter 6, few have attempted to integrate dormitory life and classroom activities by involving the residence staff in teaching or the faculty in residence staffing.

As other institutions throughout the country are demonstrating, residence halls offer rich opportunities for broadening the educational influence of the college and relating classroom learning to out-of-class life. In this respect the predominantly Negro colleges have an advantage over their sister institutions for their dormitories house a significantly larger proportion of their students. *If the full value of campus residence is to be realized additional buildings will be needed to relieve present overcrowding in some dormitories and social centers. Furthermore, more vigorous leadership will be required if the Negro colleges are to take advantage of the unique opportunities offered by the relatively large percentage of their students who live in the academic community.*

The facts with respect to the facilities of Negro colleges can be summed up as follows. Generally they have more space available per student than other institutions. Many could, therefore, enlarge their enrollments without erecting more classroom buildings. Some of the physical plants are in excellent condition. They include structures of attractive and functional design. Many others, although providing enough space, are old, run-down, unattractive, and poorly equipped and maintained. Massive financial resources will be needed to bring these physical facilities up to efficient levels of operation, and to enhance their comfort and attractiveness. Many institutions could economize in current expense and in capital outlay by merging their facilities, or by using them jointly. *Detailed studies are needed in all these institutions of the present utilization of space, the probable future need for new buildings of various types, and the relation between educational goals and plant facilities.* Long-range plans on these bases should effect substantial economies and result in better education for Negro youth. To some extent other young people will be drawn to these institutions in the degree to which their buildings, facilities, and equipment more nearly match similar features of institutional life elsewhere.

Chapter 10

SUMMARY

AS RECENTLY AS TEN OR FIFTEEN YEARS AGO, A VISITOR TO MANY OF THE small liberal arts and teachers colleges of America would have wondered how long many of them could survive, and indeed whether they should. Financial impoverishment appeared to doom them to mediocrity; the curricula of many needed reform; with rare exceptions their faculty members were poorly paid; they lacked the tools and techniques to operate efficiently and effectively. One would not have believed that in the intervening years they could have made such progress as they have. Yet, with dedicated leadership, increased corporate support, more substantial alumni-giving, larger foundation grants, government assistance, and with augmented fees, the majority have succeeded in providing a higher education more nearly adequate to the demands of the times and the needs of their students.

Many of the nation's predominantly Negro colleges are now handicapped by the same conditions that restricted developments in these other small colleges fifteen years ago. The curricula, faculties, students, and facilities of the Negro colleges have the same potential for improvement. These institutions now face the same problems which lay before the others some years ago. Moreover, their difficulties are deepened by the inadequate educational background of their students and the limitations imposed on Negroes by a society that has prevented their full participation in many areas of the national life.

Hence, although these predominantly Negro colleges, along with their sister institutions, have been struggling to increase their educational effectiveness, they have been less successful. Now the welfare of the nation, as well as social justice, demands that they be given the resources and the moral support to expand their purposes, their programs, and their capacity to serve far more rapidly than other colleges. In the past, in responding to emerging needs, American higher education has moved forward with the speed of the DC 3. Today the jet propulsion of the DC 8 has been harnessed to meet our transportation requirements. But many of our educational policies, practices, and facilities have reached only the DC 4 stage. Now a whole series of social changes are breaking upon the colleges—among them, the civil-rights movement, an occupational revolution and technological unemployment, increased migration and urbanization, the wave of students from the postwar baby boom, and severe shortages of qualified teachers. Together they make rapid change imperative throughout our system of higher education, but among the Negro institutions the rate of adaptation must be accelerated far beyond that in other institutions which in the main are already further advanced.

In the earlier chapters of this report information has been assembled from a variety of sources to describe these Negro colleges. Questionnaires filled out by a sample of their students and their faculty members, detailed reports prepared by their administrators, visits and interviews by experienced observers to nearly three-fourths of their campuses, data from other published and unpublished studies, the opinions of a host of persons familiar for years with their internal operations—all these have provided reliable facts. A vast body of information from these varied sources has been used in an attempt to gain a comprehensive and objective picture of the conditions in the predominantly Negro higher education establishments and to make recommendations to expand and improve their services in the shortest possible time.

Thousands of persons and organizations, public and private, have already begun to provide a great variety of assistance to these institutions. All public-spirited and thoughtful Americans will applaud and many will join in these efforts. The millions of dollars already appropriated by the branches of government or contributed by philanthropy will help relieve their present privations and correct the most obvious inadequacies, but they will not go far enough. Several hundred million dollars in addition to the usual support will be needed in the years immediately ahead. But if these added resources are to be put to the best use they must be distributed and applied with perception, deliberation, and wisdom.

No one can possibly possess all the reliable facts and the judicious judgment needed to remake the former Negro establishment of higher education if these institutions are to serve fully the needs and fulfill the rights of Negro youth and of their white contemporaries who will increasingly attend them. This report, however, presents a great mass of relevant information, offers a number of carefully considered although not necessarily incontestable suggestions, and raises some basic questions to which only the passage of time and trial-and-error experience will supply answers.

CONCLUSIONS

Anyone who sincerely wants to understand the condition and potential of the nation's 123 predominantly Negro colleges and universities must recognize the basic fact that they vary as widely in quality and in character as the other institutions which constitute the American higher education enterprise. On any measure of faculty preparation, student abilities, library facilities, buildings, and curriculum, some would rank high and some low. Piney Woods Country Life School in Mississippi no more epitomizes them than Slippery Rock State College in Pennsylvania, despite the stereotype of its name, epitomizes the one-time normal schools. Thus any generalizations about the predominantly Negro colleges and universities, including those that follow, cannot be interpreted as an affirmation that they do not differ considerably one from another. Actually each of them could be matched with another American college and university. Nevertheless, if all the institutions of higher education were ranked on the various features which characterize an academic institution, more of the Negro institutions would fall in the lower than in the upper 50 per cent.

Second, of the two college and university functions, teaching and research, all but a few of the predominantly Negro institutions are manifestly preoccupied with the former rather than the latter. Their teachers spend on the average over 75 per cent of their time on instruction and less than 4 per cent on investigation. Within the liberal arts disciplines their curricula exhibit a stronger emphasis in the humanities than in the social sciences and the natural sciences. Even the curricula of the liberal arts colleges themselves, however, are obviously weighted with instruction designed to prepare teachers for the elementary and secondary schools, until recently the principal white-collar occupation open to Negroes in the South.

The predominantly Negro institutions are chiefly four-year under-graduate colleges, augmented with a scattering of junior colleges typically with small enrollments, a few graduate schools, only three of which offer the doctor's degree, two of them only in selected fields. Their origins lie in the missionary movement of the northern churches in the mid-nineteenth century and in the land-grant legislation of the Federal Government first enacted in 1862. Nearly half continue to be sponsored and in part supported by religious denominations, but the publicly sup-ported institutions, as in the case of other institutions, account for an increasing proportion of their total enrollments. Many enroll an eco-nomically wasteful and an educationally debilitating small number of students.

Most Negro institutions, unlike American colleges generally, enroll a preponderance of women rather than men. Their entering students are on the average less well prepared for college work than those in other colleges, and because of lack of money they have difficulty in completing their education, with the result that the percentage of forced or voluntary dropouts is larger than normal. Negro families have generally been less able than white families to pay the costs of higher education and in spite of the advances in family income in recent years they are now relatively more, rather than less, handicapped in this respect. Hence, among Negro students the need for financial aid from outside the family, in the form of scholarships, fellowships, part-time and summer employment, and loans, is commensurately larger in Negro colleges. The elementary and secondary education of many Negro students is so inadequate that some Negro colleges must attempt the almost impossible task of compressing as much as six years of instruction into the normal four college years. The common practice of elevating the scholastic performance of their students through programs of remedial instruction during the freshman year has now been expanded and intensified with the addition of pre-admission corrective work in the regular high school years and in the summer vacation, and enrichment programs in the summer between the college years and during term.

Most of these institutions suffer from serious shortages of funds even to sustain their established programs at adequate levels, to say nothing of the needed expansions into new fields. Their income and their expenditures fall far below the proportion of the nation's students they serve. The salaries of their faculty members are on the average over a thousand dollars below those in other institutions of higher education and some pay as much as several thousand dollars less on the average than their sister institutions in other sections of the country. Yet, except at certain selected institutions, mostly in the East, the tuition fees charged in the predominantly Negro colleges are not materially below those at other institutions. Faculty members in these institutions devote a much higher proportion of their time to teaching and assisting students in various other ways than is typical of other institutions. Most of them, therefore, have little time or opportunity to continue their own education at the graduate level or to do research.

As a whole, in terms of number of buildings and area of floor space, their campuses and physical plants are more adequate to their needs than those of most colleges. But many of their structures are old, inadequate to the needs of modern higher education, and poorly equipped. In their library holdings, rate of growth, and budgetary resources these institutions generally fall below average, and they lack their proper proportion of distinctive or exceptional libraries.

The majority of these Negro institutions are in fact if not in law still segregated. A number have a scattering of white and other students and in several of the forty-eight colleges that enrolled non-Negroes last year integration is well advanced. Several are, in fact, well on the way to becoming predominantly white institutions.

In spite of their growing student bodies the predominantly Negro colleges now account for less than 3 per cent of the nation's college students and their share of total national enrollments is slowly declining. Nevertheless, they still provide a higher education for more than half of all Negro college students in the United States. Any reasonable estimate of the speed of desegregation suggests that these institutions for the foreseeable future are likely to provide the major source of educational opportunity for Negroes who continue their education beyond high school.

The demands for an expanded and more diversified higher education which these institutions will inevitably be called on to meet in the next decade cannot be satisfactorily satisfied without massive additional financial support from a great variety of sources, public and private, corporate and individual, denominational and secular. Without this greatly magnified support much of the present heartening public concern about the inequities the Negro has suffered in American society and efforts to eradicate them will regrettably be abortive. For as a number of economists, sociologists, and generally well-informed persons have observed, economic well-being, job opportunities, social status, and general public acceptance today depend on the amount and kind of education the individual has. This will be increasingly true, regardless of race.

Opening the doors to higher education for the Negro is an indispensable step, indeed the sine qua non *in his personal and social advancement.* The right to vote, the right to work, the right to live where he chooses, the right to move freely anywhere in American society— these rights are all dear to the man who knows what freedom is and wants it. But the right to education is no less precious than these, and to a growing degree it is the single right without which a man cannot fully obtain the others. Negroes and all citizens who want to gain for them the full benefits and privileges of living in this society ought to pour their energies into efforts to expand the opportunities for higher education among Negroes and to improve its quality.

RECOMMENDATIONS

Thus far this report has treated a variety of aspects of education in the predominantly Negro colleges and universities and under each topic some recommendations have been made, including those related to the organization and financing of the Negro colleges, their admissions policies and financial aid to students, their orientation and remedial programs, their curricula and their counseling and instructional services, their faculties and their administrative staffs, and their libraries and physical plants and equipment. Some of these recommendations concern matters of overriding importance demanding immediate action. Others are of lower priority, or in fact must be delayed until precedent steps have been taken. Still others must be carried out at different paces in different institutions, and a few have no relevance to the purposes of some institutions—for example, the establishment of graduate programs which obviously should not be the concern of junior colleges. At this point these suggestions for action have been rearranged, sharpened up, and brought within smaller compass.

1. *Maintain and Strengthen Most Existing Institutions.* The view that many of the predominantly Negro colleges ought to be closed or allowed through inadequate support to languish, should be abandoned. This point of view springs from a false notion of academic excellence and supports a policy in conflict not only with the rights of many

disadvantaged youth, but also with the public interest. None of the predominantly Negro colleges should be allowed to die until their present and prospective students can be fully assured of better educational opportunities elsewhere. In this day when for the first time the nation has really awakened to the indispensable value of higher education and consequently needs every existing institution to accommodate the irresistible legion of oncoming students, even the limited and inefficient programs in the weaker Negro institutions should be maintained while rigorous efforts are being made to strengthen them. Unless relatively inexpensive and local higher education is available, hosts of potentially eligible Negro youth will be denied any educational opportunity beyond high school.

2. *Coordinate Institutional Efforts and Establish Cooperation Among Them.* Interinstitutional cooperation and coordination should be established between Negro colleges and among Negro and predominantly white colleges. Wherever Negro youth would not be denied their proper educational opportunities, two or more struggling institutions, particularly if they are located in the same community, should be merged. At the junior college level, no more public community colleges should be established on a *de facto* segregated basis. Existing community-wide facilities should be combined or new institutions created for all students who seek post–high school education.

Greater state-wide and regional coordination resulting in specialized graduate programs in selected institutions is essential. Negro students should have the opportunity to pursue graduate study at predominantly white colleges and universities now inaccessible to them, and as these opportunities expand, graduate work at a number of Negro state colleges should be phased out. Some Negro colleges with unusual resources, or prospects for them, ought to strengthen their graduate work in a limited number of fields to which students should likewise be admitted without regard to race.

Some interinstitutional cooperation has already been accomplished among the predominantly Negro colleges, but in the interest of greater economy and more effective education this practice deserves wider adoption. Since students can often move as easily from one institution to the other as from one point to another on the home campuses, closely located institutions should use facilities, faculties, libraries, and equipment in common. Even remote institutions can use each other's services more cheaply than duplicating them and often with enhanced educational quality. One entirely new type of cooperation should be inaugurated. With outside financial aid a central college library service center should be established to act as the purchasing and cataloguing agent for a number of small college libraries, thus reducing processing expenses and commensurately enlarging the resources available for library service.

3. *Long-range Planning.* State and regional coordination through state commissions or other types of regional organization such as the Southern Regional Education Board and the Southern Association of Colleges and Schools should be promoted to enable all colleges to forecast their own potential roles and to plan their services in terms of their own resources and the services available elsewhere. Even with these coordinated planning organizations among neighboring institutions many will need outside help in making long-range plans for organizing and enriching their curricula, for recruiting and utilizing their faculties, for making maximum utilization of space and facilities, for designing and erecting new buildings, and for long-range campus and financial development.

As the predominantly Negro colleges and universities rise to the challenges of the coming years they will need advice and assistance in dealing with a great variety of problems such as their changing purposes in the light of social evolution, their educational programs, the kind and quality of their faculties, the size and character of their student bodies, the source and magnitude of their financial support, the size and character of their physical plants, and a host of other problems with which they, even more than other institutions of higher education, will be afflicted.

A center should be established in at least one of the great universities to provide counseling and field services on a voluntary basis so that these institutions as well as others needing such assistance can get informed advice from experienced persons. Such a center should also arrange cooperative activities among institutions seeking help and make available an up-to-date information service based on continuing research. This center could also serve as a clearing house for the collection and dissemination of relevant information if such services are not provided elsewhere on a continuing basis.

Its indispensable services should be counseling the participating institutions and conducting continuous research on developments in the presently Negro colleges as they enlarge and change their programs to serve more completely the Negroes who now attend them and the members of other races who will in increasing numbers seek their services. In the absence of such a center, much activity intended to advance Negro higher education could be ineffective and institutions could work at cross-purposes. With it, all concerned in the extension of better advantages for higher education to Negroes could harness their efforts in this great social enterprise.

These cooperative regional and national planning efforts will be enhanced in value and in usefulness as administrative leadership is strengthened. Many of the Negro colleges have presidents as well prepared for their responsibilities as any in the country. Others will need additional training either through long-term graduate work or through summer experiences if they are to deal effectively with the problems of institutional growth and improvement which lie ahead. Foundations should provide the substantial kind of financial assistance required by administrators at the presidential and decanal levels to pay the expenses of leave for self-enlargement. Fellowships should also be provided for promising members of the teaching staff to prepare themselves for administrative leadership positions now filled by men and women who will leave or retire. In virtually all these institutions steps should be taken by the administration to involve the trustees, the faculty, and the students more fully in the democratic practices of determining institutional policies.

4. *Faculty Development.* The faculty of every educational institution can be improved. The degree of improvement is inevitably related to a number of factors in institutional life, some material, some psychological. The Negro colleges will have to take several steps in the immediate future if they are to compete satisfactorily with other institutions in the academic market place. Most predominantly Negro colleges urgently need to raise their faculty salaries and to enhance the other perquisites of academic life if they are to be able to recruit and retain teachers capable of synthesizing new knowledge in their fields and presenting it effectively to their students. If they are to be able to compete for qualified faculty members as the present shortages become more acute, some will have to raise their salaries by several thousand dollars and increase this sum as competitive conditions raise salaries in other institutions.

Increased salaries, however, will not be enough. Other policies must provide financial assistance for those faculty members who wish to take a leave of a year or more either to complete the requirements for a doctor's degree, or to refresh themselves intellectually in a post-doctoral program. Since few of these institutions have an automatic sabbatical leave even for top-ranking faculty members, more fellowships for post-doctoral study are needed to provide relief from the routine of daily responsibilities in the classroom for their faculty members and to enable them to become acquainted with the latest developments in their fields. Most colleges will need two kinds of financial help in their efforts to provide faculty leaves, funds to cover the salary of the person being released from his regular assignments, and additional sums to secure a suitable replacement. Without such assistance in the days ahead when enrollments will increase rapidly and the demands on already limited resources will multiply geometrically, few institutions will be able to release their staff members for a full academic year. Even those who cannot be away for such a prolonged period should have the opportunity to study at a graduate center for a summer term with salary and expenses paid by the institution or an outside agency.

A limited number of faculty members will also find intellectual revitalization through an exchange of positions with teachers or research specialists in their fields in other institutions, as some are already doing. When the two exchangees can be reasonably well matched in their academic assignments this plan has real advantages, because it automatically eliminates the difficulty of finding a suitable replacement for the faculty member leaving his home institution. Even under these arrangements, however, outside support will be required because the predominantly Negro institution will normally not be able to cover the expenses of moving its own staff member to another position or to meet the differential in salary which the incoming teacher will usually require.

CURRICULUM

The curricula of the Negro colleges will need to be changed in several fundamental respects. First, some of the instruction which was peculiarly appropriate in earlier years, such as the courses in crafts, agriculture, and other vocational subjects, will now have to be minimized or completely abandoned in some institutions. Because earlier vocational outlets no longer exist this type of program no longer provides suitable preparation for work. Junior colleges can and should, however, provide terminal technical training geared to the needs of the community. On the other hand, a wide variety of new programs leading to employment in business, industry, and government, as well as to the professions, should be inaugurated in the four-year predominantly Negro colleges. Accounting, computer occupations, technician and engineering positions, assignments in the foreign and domestic government service are a few examples of vocations in which more Negroes could be placed than are now prepared to accept appointments. Every institution should not undertake to prepare students for every such possible occupational opportunity, but the number of such programs should be greatly increased, and where they already exist may need to be expanded and strengthened.

Perhaps the most pressing need in respect to the curriculum involves the strengthening of the liberal arts disciplines which prepare students for advanced education in the related graduate departments or in professional schools such as medicine, dentistry, law, or social work. The most dramatic examples of existing deficiencies can be found in the sciences. Many of these institutions offer no major in physics, for example, and others, although offering a major, have severely limited faculties, laboratories, and library collections. Negro youth, especially men, are deprived of the opportunity to major in scientific fields or receive such inadequate preparation that they cannot gain admission to a graduate department. The same conditions prevail in other fields in many institutions and they need to be improved as quickly as possible if Negro youths are to have unrestricted access to advanced educational opportunities.

These curricular improvements are also needed to increase the supply of Ph.D.'s in all the liberal arts disciplines to fill positions in teaching, in industry, and in the government. The present imbalance in the curricular offerings of most of these colleges should be offset by expanding and strengthening the offerings in the natural and the social sciences. In a number of them the excessive emphasis on elementary and secondary school teaching should be counterbalanced by more varied and strengthened offerings in the liberal arts disciplines and in the undergraduate professional fields. Education departments should be strengthened by the adoption of the newest types of teacher education courses, methods, and supervision.

REMEDIAL PROGRAMS

For the foreseeable future, most Negro colleges must be dedicated to the task of offering quality instruction to students with inadequate previous education. Among the students of even the weakest of these colleges will be found a significant percentage who would be near the top of their classes at the most selective universities if their previous education had been of even average quality. If the Negro colleges were to raise their admissions standards drastically many students would be completely cut off from higher education. Major improvements need to and will be made in elementary and secondary education, but until they are, most of these colleges should not materially raise their standards for admissions. But neither should they admit large numbers of students and let them fail without attempting to rectify their deficiencies. Widespread support should be given to efforts to improve the scholastic qualifications of prospective college students during the high school years and in special summer programs just before they enroll in college. Many special programs are now being launched to build up the academic background of those intending to enter college. These various projects ought to be intensively studied to determine which practices are most effective in removing academic inadequacies and increasing the student's motivation toward learning.

Of the various types now being used, clinical work outside of class on an individual basis and the three-track class arrangement which makes possible special treatment of the weakest and the strongest, seem now to offer peculiar promise. They deserve extensive adoption and evaluation. One program which could profit from the experience of the Peace Corps might involve a group of volunteers from other colleges who, because they had already made outstanding records in one of the disciplines, could tutor students deficient in the basic subjects. Legislation already enacted or in prospect by the Congress should provide the necessary funds to organize and support such a program the benefits of which would patently enhance the education of both the Corps member and those he tutors. An even larger number of Corpsmen should be involved in remedial programs during the summer months.

STUDENT FINANCES

Tuition fees, especially in the tax-supported institutions, must be kept at the lowest possible level consistent with educational standards. In addition, loan, scholarship, and fellowship funds should be substantially increased and eligibility standards for such assistance should be liberalized for disadvantaged youth of high potential who, because of inadequate earlier education, do not meet present requirements. Any scholarship program based on national test scores will automatically close out many Negro youth whose educational and cultural backgrounds have not adequately prepared them for such competition. Work-study programs should be extended to additional institutions to permit more students to earn a major share of their expenses at jobs related to their academic and career interests.

INSTRUCTIONAL AIDS

Instructional procedures in all institutions should be more diversified to enrich the present dominant use of lectures, recitations, and assigned readings in textbooks. The teachers in some of these institutions already employ a variety of teaching methods and materials ranging from seminars and independent study to informal reading and community action programs. They deserve wider adoption. The heavy investment of the Negro colleges in student residences, and the relatively large percentage of their students who live on campus, provides a significant untapped educational resource for informal education and cultural influence. Few now use their dormitories to integrate classroom learning with out-of-class living. Many students could be helped to adjust to an academic environment through more extensive freshman orientation.

Instruction in the use of the varied resources of the library should be provided, and library usage should be made habitual through the assignments given and through example set by faculty members themselves. Major grants are needed to rectify the historical failure to develop library resources. Such grants should include provision for expert consultation with respect to book selection, the recruitment and training of professional library personnel, and the erection of functional library buildings.

The informal instructional influences of these colleges can also be enriched through the wider organization of exchange programs involving predominantly white institutions in all sections of the country. All varieties of exchange arrangements merit experimentation from those which involve no more than a few days at a neighboring institution in which the benefits would be largely better understanding and rapport to those in which students live on a host campus for a semester or a year and continue their formal education while also gaining the benefits of living in a different cultural and social environment. These programs are now primarily limited to a few and generally to the strongest of the predominantly Negro colleges. They deserve wider adoption.

COUNSELING

Most of these institutions already provide some educational, vocational, and personal counseling and guidance. In most cases this service is rendered by faculty members and administrators who have other heavy responsibilities and who generally lack the knowledge needed for effective advising in the present complex world. These services need to be professionalized. As a minimum each institution ought to have one person on its staff who has had graduate training in the student personnel field. Selected faculty members who assist in the counseling program should be given an opportunity to acquire special training during the summer or a semester in universities which offer special programs for student personnel workers. Professional counseling is indispensable in regard to vocational opportunities and the types of training required for various occupations. The rapid opening up of new employment opportunities for Negroes makes it necessary for the colleges they attend to be prepared to provide up-to-date facts about these career possibilities. This information should be made available not only to students on their campuses, but also to prospective applicants, parents, school teachers, and community leaders so that Negro youth will know what their prospects are and be motivated to undertake the necessary education to prepare to take advantage of them.

SOURCES OF FINANCIAL SUPPORT

The proposals embodied in this report to enhance and strengthen higher education for Negro youth involve the expenditure of huge additional funds. If these resources are to be available a great variety of sources of financial support must be tapped. The nation's better-known foundations have tended to restrict their grants largely to prestigious Negro colleges. Even within the institutions which belong to the United Negro College Fund a select group have been the recipients of a large share of foundation benefactions. No one would suggest that these grants should be reduced, nor that these institutions are not deserving of even larger donations. The cold fact is, however, that a mere dozen or so of the predominantly Negro institutions will not be able to provide higher education for all the Negro youth who will have the ability to profit from it. To the degree that those institutions which do not stand in the upper 10 or 15 per cent are financially neglected, thousands of

Negro youth will be commensurately deprived of the full advantages of a higher education. Hence these colleges, too, must receive financial aid in substantial amounts.

Foundations and other benefactors can gain public acclaim by assisting the reasonably good but not superior institutions, and they can at the same time make a lasting contribution to the lot of thousands of American citizens and to the welfare of the nation. The policies of the Federal Government have favored the prestige institutions of higher education and, in the minds of some thoughtful Americans, have unfairly disadvantaged others. These policies can peculiarly discriminate against all but a few of the Negro institutions because of the relative weakness of their faculties and the inadequacy of their research facilities. Whatever justification private organizations may be able to make for their policies of selective giving, the expenditure of public money on the same basis is hardly defensible.

Government programs should take cognizance of the fact that many Negro institutions and their students may not at present be distinguished but they nevertheless deserve public assistance in their efforts to improve their lot. Even modest support of the less well-known Negro institutions by a foundation and by government can significantly increase the educational opportunities for thousands of Negro students. In recent years the states have been making significantly larger appropriations to the Negro colleges. These sums must be considerably increased if the qualitative gap between their predominantly Negro institutions and their other colleges is to be promptly closed and if they are to become integrated. These commonwealths are already spending a much larger proportion of their wealth on higher education than the economically more favored states. Yet even these unusual efforts to provide higher education for their youth leave many states wanting.

Even with the states' best efforts, therefore, the Federal Government must assume a major and inescapable role, for the Negro colleges are chiefly located in the most economically disadvantaged states of the union. As the President of the United States has made abundantly clear, education is a national problem and hence a Federal responsibility. Poor education is a reflection on our national values. The provision of equal opportunities for higher education on a national basis will require massive Federal action and support, and the institutions in this study must be its earliest and relatively largest beneficiaries if the present racial inequities are to be forever eradicated from our national life.

The predominantly Negro institutions are attempting to serve the nation as best they can under serious handicaps. Their plight is not unique, since other American colleges have had and have overcome similar problems; but notwithstanding the higher quality and the promise of a few Negro institutions of higher education the inadequacies of the group as a whole are ominously serious. Today the world measures a civilization by its treatment of all its citizens, particularly its minority groups. The United States is now being inexorably judged by its treatment of its Negro citizens. The status of these citizens in our society will in large measure be determined by their educational advantages. Equity and prudence require that the doors of educational opportunities in the predominantly Negro colleges be thrown wide open to all and that the education they provide match that available elsewhere in quality and variety.

The recommendations in this report rest on the premise that the vast majority of Americans mean what they say when they declare that all American youth should have equal access to education. The speed and the completeness with which this ideal is made a reality in the presently predominantly Negro colleges will bear testimony to the sincerity of our national commitment to this goal, unprecedented in the annals of the human enterprise.

APPENDIXES

A. Predominantly Negro Colleges and Universities in the United States, 1963–1964

B. Finances of Institutions Attended Predominantly by Negroes: Aggregate United States, 1959–1960

C. Average Charges for Tuition, Room, and Board for Predominantly Negro Colleges and for All Colleges and Universities, 1960–1961

D. Master's Degree Programs in Twenty-two Predominantly Negro Colleges, 1962–1963

E. Predominantly White Colleges in the South Which Will and Will Not Now Admit Negroes

Appendix A   PREDOMINANTLY NEGRO COLLEGES AND UNIVERSITIES IN THE UNITED STATES, 1963–1964[a]

INSTITUTION	LOCATION	TYPE	AFFILIATION	ACCREDITED[b]	USOE LIST[c]	TOTAL ENROLLMENT
ALABAMA						
*Alabama A & M College[a]	Normal	Master's	State	✓	✓	1,104
Alabama Lutheran Academy and College	Selma	Junior	Lutheran	—	—	34
*Alabama State College	Montgomery	Master's	State	—	✓	1,351
*Daniel Payne College	Birmingham	Junior	AME	✓	✓	286
Lomax-Hannon College	Greenville	Junior	Methodist	—	—	17
Miles College	Birmingham	Bachelor	CME	—	✓	774
Oakwood College	Huntsville	Bachelor	SDA	✓	✓	346
Selma University	Selma	—		—	—	184
Stillman College	Tuskaloosa	Bachelor	Presb. US	✓	✓	529
*Talladega College	Talladega	Bachelor	AMA-P	✓	✓	425
*Tuskegee Institute	Tuskegee Institute	Master's	Private	✓	✓	2,450
ARKANSAS						
Arkansas Mechanical & Normal College	Pine Bluff	Bachelor	State	✓	✓	2,242
*Philander Smith College	Little Rock	Bachelor	Methodist	✓	✓	619
*Shorter College	North Little Rock	Bachelor	AME	—	✓	204
DELAWARE						
*Delaware State College	Dover	Bachelor	State	✓	✓	563
DISTRICT OF COLUMBIA						
District of Columbia Teachers College	Washington	Bachelor	City	✓	✓	1,459
*Howard University	Washington	Doctoral	Private	✓	✓	6,288

*Bethune-Cookman College	Daytona Beach	Private	Bachelor	✓	✓	720
*Collier-Blocker College[e]	Palatka	County	Junior	✓	—	88
*Edward Waters College	Jacksonville	AME	Bachelor	✓	—	787
*Florida A & M University	Tallahassee	State	Master's	✓	✓	3,149
*Florida N & I Memorial College	St. Augustine	Private	Bachelor	✓	✓	341
*Gibbs Junior College[f]	St. Petersburg	County	Junior	✓	✓	643
*Hampton Junior College	Ocala	County	Junior	✓	—	231
*Johnson Junior College	Leesburg	County	Junior	✓	—	113
*Lincoln Junior College	Fort Pierce	County	Junior	✓	—	96
*Roosevelt Junior College	West Palm Beach	County	Junior	✓	—	231
*Rosenwald Junior College	Panama City	County	Junior	✓	—	79
*Suwanee Junior College	Madison	County	Junior	✓	—	173
*Volusia County Junior College	Daytona Beach	County	Junior	✓	—	338
*Washington Junior College	Pensacola	State	Junior	✓	—	193

GEORGIA

*Albany State College	Albany	State	Bachelor	✓	✓	1,001
*Atlanta University	Atlanta	Private	Doctoral	✓	✓	681
*Clark College	Atlanta	Methodist	Bachelor	✓	✓	770
*Fort Valley State College	Fort Valley	State	Master's	✓	✓	1,034

[a] The 123 institutions listed here were identified by the Institute of Higher Education as enrolling on a full-time equivalent basis a predominance of Negro students in 1963–64. The eighty-nine institutions which contributed detailed information about their operations for the purpose of this report are identified by asterisks before their names.

[b] "Accredited" indicates membership in the appropriate regional accrediting association in all cases except for the two identified by "P" which are accredited by the appropriate professional accrediting agency.

[c] "USOE List" indicates that the institution is listed in *Part 3* of the United States Office of Education *Education Directory, 1963–1964*.

[d] Accredited 1964.

[e] Closed 1964.

[f] Accredited September 1964.

Appendix A   PREDOMINANTLY NEGRO COLLEGES AND UNIVERSITIES IN THE UNITED STATES, 1963–1964 — Cont.

INSTITUTION	LOCATION	TYPE	AFFILIATION	ACCRED-ITED[b]	USOE LIST[c]	TOTAL ENROLLMENT
Interdenominational Theo. Center	Atlanta	Master's	Interdenom'l	P[b]	✓	105
*Morehouse College	Atlanta	Bachelor	Private	✓	✓	810
*Morris Brown College	Atlanta	Bachelor	AME	✓	✓	921
*Paine College	Augusta	Bachelor	Meth. & AME	✓	✓	430
*Savannah State College	Savannah	Bachelor	State	✓	✓	1,160
*Spelman College	Atlanta	Bachelor	Baptist	✓	✓	596
KENTUCKY						
*Kentucky State College	Frankfort	Bachelor	State	✓	✓	868
Simmons University	Louisville	Bachelor	Nat'l Baptist	—	—	134
LOUISIANA						
*Dillard University	New Orleans	Bachelor	Private	✓	✓	882
*Grambling College	Grambling	Bachelor	State	✓	✓	3,049
*Southern University A & M	Baton Rouge	Master's	State	✓	✓	5,703
*Xavier University	New Orleans	Master's	Roman Catholic	✓	✓	800
MARYLAND						
*Bowie State College	Bowie	Bachelor	State	✓	✓	365
Coppin State College	Baltimore	Bachelor	State	✓	✓	370
Maryland State College	Princess Anne	Bachelor	State	✓	✓	542
*Morgan State College	Baltimore	Bachelor	State	✓	✓	2,699
MISSISSIPPI						
*Alcorn A & M College	Lorman	Bachelor	State	✓	✓	1,423
*Coahoma Junior College	Clarksdale	Junior	State	—	✓	419
*J. P. Campbell Junior College	Jackson	Junior	AME	—	✓	171
*Jackson State College	Jackson	Master's	State	✓	✓	1,222

Institution	Location	Degree	Control			Enrollment
*Mary Holmes Junior College	West Point	Junior	Presbyterian	—	√	212
Mississippi Industrial College	Holly Springs	Bachelor	CME	—	√	497
*Mississippi Vocational College	Itta Bena	Bachelor	State	—	√	1,235
Natchez Junior College	Natchez	Junior	Baptist	—	√	187
*Okolona College	Okolona	Junior	PE	—	√	238
Piney Woods Country Life School	Piney Woods	Junior	Private	—	√	93
Prentiss N & I Institute	Prentiss	Junior	Private	—	√	195
*Rust College	Holly Springs	Bachelor	Methodist	—	√	546
Saints Junior College	Lexington	Junior	Ch. of God	—	√	17
*T. J. Harris Junior College	Meridian	Junior	City	—	√	187
*Tougaloo Southern Christian College	Tougaloo	Bachelor	AMA & UCMS	√	√	480
Utica Junior College	Utica	Junior	County	—	√	364
Missouri						
*Lincoln University	Jefferson City	Master's	State	√	√	1,483
North Carolina						
Agric. Tech. Coll. of North Carolina	Greensboro	Master's	State	√	√	2,940
*Barber-Scotia College	Concord	Bachelor	Presbyterian	√	√	311
*Bennett College	Greensboro	Bachelor	Methodist	√	√	578
Elizabeth City State College	Elizabeth City	Bachelor	State	√	√	804
*Fayetteville State College	Fayetteville	Bachelor	State	√	√	985
*Johnson C. Smith University	Charlotte	Bachelor	Presbyterian	√	√	1,027
Kittrell College	Kittrell	Junior	AME	—	—	211
*Livingstone College	Salisbury	Bachelor	AMEZ	√	√	692
Mecklenburg College[a]	Charlotte	Junior	City	—	√	186
*North Carolina College at Durham	Durham	Doctoral	State	√	√	2,483

[a] Merged with Charlotte College.

Appendix A   PREDOMINANTLY NEGRO COLLEGES AND UNIVERSITIES IN THE UNITED STATES, 1963–1964 — Cont.

INSTITUTION	LOCATION	TYPE	AFFILIATION	ACCRED-ITED[b]	USOE LIST[c]	TOTAL ENROLLMENT
*St. Augustine's College	Raleigh	Bachelor	PE	✓	✓	732
*Shaw University	Raleigh	Bachelor	Baptist	✓	✓	635
*Winston-Salem State College	Winston-Salem	Bachelor	State	✓	✓	1,212
OHIO						
*Central State College	Wilberforce	Bachelor	State	✓	✓	2,005
*Wilberforce University	Wilberforce	Bachelor	AME	✓	✓	373
OKLAHOMA						
Langston University	Langston	Bachelor	State	✓	✓	721
PENNSYLVANIA						
Cheyney State College	Cheyney	Bachelor	State	✓	✓	922
*Lincoln University	Lincoln University	Bachelor	Private	✓	✓	434
SOUTH CAROLINA						
*Allen University	Columbia	Bachelor	AME	—	✓	719
Benedict College	Columbia	Bachelor	Baptist	✓	✓	975
*Claflin College	Orangeburg	Bachelor	Methodist	✓	✓	474
Clinton College	Rock Hill	Junior	Methodist	—	—	136
Friendship Junior College	Rock Hill	Junior	Baptist	—	—	198
Mather College	Beaufort	Junior	Baptist	—	—	60
Morris College	Sumter	Bachelor	Baptist	—	✓	450
*South Carolina State College	Orangeburg	Master's	State	✓	✓	2,519
*Voorhees School and Junior College	Denmark	Junior	PE	✓	✓	208
TENNESSEE						
*Fisk University	Nashville	Master's	Private	✓	✓	955
*Knoxville College	Knoxville	Bachelor	United Presby.	✓	✓	747

College	City	Control	Degree			Enrollment
*Lane College	Jackson	CME	Bachelor	✓	✓	537
*LeMoyne College	Memphis	AMA	Bachelor	✓	✓	575
*Meharry Medical College	Nashville	Private	Doctoral	✓	P[b]	367
*Morristown College	Morristown	Methodist	Junior	✓	✓	215
*Owen College	Memphis	Baptist	Junior	✓	✓	332
*Tennessee A & I State University	Nashville	State	Master's	✓	✓	4,200
TEXAS						
*Bishop College	Dallas	Baptist	Bachelor	✓	✓	938
Butler College	Tyler	Baptist	Junior	—	—	75
*Huston-Tillotson	Austin	Private	Bachelor	✓	✓	575
*Jarvis-Christian College[a]	Hawkins	Disc. of Christ	Bachelor	✓	—	547
Mary Allen College	Crockett	Baptist	Junior	—	—	12
Paul Quinn College	Waco	AME	Bachelor	✓	—	304
*Prairie View A & M College	Prairie View	State	Master's	✓	✓	3,418
*St. Philip's College	San Antonio	Co. or Dist.	Junior	✓	✓	369
Southwestern Christian College	Terrell	Ch. of Christ	Junior	—	—	80
*Texas College	Tyler	CME	Bachelor	✓	—	387
*Texas Southern University	Houston	State	Master's	✓	✓	3,856
Tyler District College	Tyler	County	Junior	✓	✓	222
*Wiley College	Marshall	Methodist	Bachelor	✓	✓	525
VIRGINIA						
*Hampton Institute	Hampton	Private	Master's	✓	✓	1,656
*St. Paul's College	Lawrenceville	PE	Bachelor	✓	✓	406
*Virginia State College	Petersburg	State	Master's	✓	✓	3,884
*Virginia Theological Seminary	Lynchburg	Baptist	Bachelor	—	✓	197
*Virginia Union University	Richmond	Baptist	Bachelor	✓	✓	1,218
WEST VIRGINIA						
*Bluefield State College	Bluefield	State	Bachelor	✓	✓	609
West Virginia State	Institute	State	Bachelor	✓	✓	2,636

[a] Merged with Texas Christian College.

| | ALL INSTITUTIONS | | |
| | | Attended Predominantly by Negroes | |
ITEM	Total Higher Education	Number	Percent-age
NUMBER OF INSTITUTIONS	2,015	106	5.26
RESIDENT DEGREE-CREDIT ENROLLMENT, FALL 1959	3,236,197	88,859	2.75
INCOME			
CURRENT FUND INCOME	$5,812,759,325	$110,360,843	1.90
Educational and General	4,712,547,967	81,121,060	1.72
Student Tuition and Fees[a]	1,161,753,188	19,537,385	1.68
Federal Government:			
Veterans' Tuition and Fees[a]	3,483,358	87,373	2.51
Land-Grant Institutions[b]	88,296,886	485,190	.55
Research[b]	828,733,931	1,192,216	.14
Other Purposes	120,384,486	5,164,038	4.29
State Governments[c]	1,389,271,019	37,886,560	2.73
Local Governments	151,715,094	1,048,639	.69
Endowment Earnings	206,665,552	4,457,187	2.16
Private Gifts and Grants	383,186,334	8,609,278	2.25
Related Activities	244,894,351	1,856,292	.76
Sales and Services of Educational Departments	45,425,152	138,939	.31
Other Educational and General	88,738,616	657,963	.74
Auxiliary Enterprises	1,005,962,982	28,216,554	2.80
Student Aid Income[d]	94,248,376	1,023,229	1.89
PLANT FUND RECEIPTS	1,311,906,586	14,246,911	1.09
Federal Government	57,598,540	0	0.00
State Governments	320,401,229	6,502,074	2.03
Local Governments	36,304,082	103,990	.29
Private Gifts and Grants	196,464,060	1,586,792	.81
Loans From Noninstitutional Sources	363,513,511	2,525,813	.69
Loans From Institutional Sources	31,873,037	71,880	.23
Transfers from Other Funds	228,596,638	2,422,848	1.06
Miscellaneous Receipts	77,155,489	1,033,514	1.34

[a] Tuition and fees received from veterans under Public Law 550 are reported under student fees and not under income from Federal Government.

[b] Income from the Federal Government for research at agricultural experiment stations administered by land-grant institutions was reported under land-grant institutions and not under research.

[c] Includes Federal aid received through state channels and regional compacts.

[d] Specifically designated or earmarked funds.

NEGROES: AGGREGATE UNITED STATES, 1959–1960

PUBLICLY CONTROLLED INSTITUTIONS			PRIVATELY CONTROLLED INSTITUTIONS		
Total Publicly Controlled Institutions	Attended Predominantly by Negroes		Total Privately Controlled Institutions	Attended Predominantly by Negroes	
	Number	Percent-age		Number	Percent-age
704	41	5.82	1,311	65	4.96
1,847,621	53,455	2.89	1,388,576	35,404	2.55
$3,276,645,266	$64,943,821	1.98	$2,536,114,059	$45,417,022	1.79
2,689,748,884	48,108,860	1.79	2,022,799,083	33,012,200	1.63
331,955,592	7,951,783	2.40	829,797,596	11,585,602	1.40
1,135,468	31,150	2.74	2,347,890	56,223	2.39
85,768,879	485,190	.57	2,528,007	0	.00
363,513,260	403,253	.11	465,220,671	788,963	.17
96,012,070	212,053	.22	24,372,416	4,951,985	20.32
1,353,129,714	36,842,817	2.72	36,141,305	1,043,743	2.89
147,254,218	957,582	.65	4,460,876	91,057	2.04
19,684,931	34,389	.17	186,980,621	4,422,798	2.37
85,503,943	188,035	.22	297,682,391	8,421,243	2.83
130,806,239	653,320	.50	114,088,112	1,202,972	1.05
37,433,167	87,093	.23	7,991,985	51,846	.65
37,551,403	262,195	.70	51,187,213	395,768	.77
544,990,020	16,617,648	3.05	460,972,962	11,598,906	2.52
41,906,362	217,313	.52	52,342,014	805,916	1.54
831,888,048	10,230,760	1.23	480,018,538	4,016,151	.84
48,519,126	0	.00	9,079,414	0	.00
313,732,154	6,502,074	2.07	6,669,075	0	.00
36,304,082	103,990	.29	0	0	.00
19,799,664	70,358	.36	176,664,396	1,516,434	.86
238,524,139	1,668,712	.70	124,989,372	857,101	.69
9,368,995	1,994	.02	22,504,042	69,886	.31
111,349,962	1,183,396	1.06	117,246,676	1,239,452	1.06
54,289,926	700,236	1.29	22,865,563	333,278	1.46

ITEM	ALL INSTITUTIONS		
	Total Higher Education	Attended Predominantly by Negroes	
		Number	Percent-age
OTHER FUND RECEIPTS	499,005,320	6,857,383	1.37
Private Gifts and Grants	209,147,494	2,527,580	1.21
Other Sources	289,857,826	4,329,803	1.49
Net Increase in Principal of Funds	419,355,963	5,475,177	1.31
Endowment and Funds Functioning as Endowment	375,178,501	4,830,566	1.29
Annuity Funds	11,853,913	−34,643	In.ᵉ
Student Loan Funds	32,323,551	679,254	2.10
EXPENDITURES			
CURRENT FUND EXPENDITURES	5,627,961,890	107,322,034	1.91
Educational and General	4,536,056,275	78,851,835	1.74
General Administration and General Expense	587,335,719	14,471,075	2.46
Instruction and Departmental Research	1,802,871,114	41,730,198	2.31
Extension and Public Services	208,378,035	765,381	.37
Libraries	135,913,101	3,625,426	2.67
Plant Operation and Maintenance	473,681,570	13,989,597	2.95
Organized Research	1,024,398,507	1,373,987	.13
Related Activities	294,344,465	2,825,535	.96
Sales and Services Expenditures	9,133,764	70,636	.77
Auxiliary Enterprises	917,942,738	25,807,794	2.81
Student Aid Expenditures	173,962,877	2,662,405	1.53
PLANT FUND EXPENDITURES	1,195,688,859	20,085,423	1.68
Additions to Plant	1,019,650,652	18,117,202	1.78
Reduction of Capital Indebtedness	109,043,419	1,410,024	1.29
Other Deductions	66,994,788	558,197	.83
PROPERTY			
PROPERTY VALUES AT END OF YEAR	20,224,871,431	485,589,637	2.40
Physical Plant and Plant Funds	14,652,696,689	386,322,048	2.64
Physical Plant	13,588,359,819	375,642,778	2.76
Unexpended Plant Funds	1,064,336,870	10,679,270	1.00
Endowment and Other Nonexpendable Funds	5,572,174,742	99,267,589	1.78
Endowment and Funds Functioning as Endowment	5,322,970,848	96,644,236	1.82
Annuity Funds	122,757,392	868,003	.71
Student Loan Funds	126,446,502	1,755,350	1.39
Liabilities of Plant Funds	1,970,284,755	28,514,074	1.45

ᵉ In. = inapplicable.

SOURCE: Data in this table furnished by the United States Office of Education from a forthcoming publication.

PUBLICLY CONTROLLED INSTITUTIONS			PRIVATELY CONTROLLED INSTITUTIONS		
Total Publicly Controlled Institutions	Attended Predominantly by Negroes		Total Privately Controlled Institutions	Attended Predominantly by Negroes	
	Number	Percent-age		Number	Percent-age
77,025,916	454,905	.59	421,979,404	6,402,478	1.52
18,800,678	7,866	.04	190,346,816	2,519,714	1.32
58,225,238	447,039	.77	231,632,588	3,882,764	1.68
69,283,048	454,560	.66	350,072,917	5,020,617	1.43
53,810,325	23,540	.04	321,368,176	4,807,026	1.50
115,350	0	.00	11,738,563	−34,643	In.[e]
15,357,373	431,020	2.81	16,966,178	248,234	1.46
3,154,337,157	62,279,823	1.97	2,473,624,733	45,042,211	1.82
2,600,228,425	46,717,942	1.80	1,935,827,850	32,133,893	1.66
271,463,030	7,940,152	2.92	315,872,689	6,530,923	2.07
1,074,985,539	25,293,130	2.35	727,885,575	16,437,068	2.26
195,552,336	691,055	.35	12,825,699	74,326	.58
74,619,778	2,213,721	2.97	61,293,323	1,411,705	2.30
272,465,737	9,055,699	3.32	201,215,833	4,933,898	2.45
524,540,380	224,964	.04	499,858,121	1,149,023	.23
177,879,115	1,228,585	.69	116,465,350	1,596,950	1.37
8,722,504	70,636	.81	411,260	0	.00
492,557,620	14,912,279	3.03	425,385,118	10,895,515	2.56
61,551,112	649,602	1.06	112,411,765	2,012,803	1.79
739,280,977	15,661,330	2.12	456,407,882	4,424,093	.97
625,197,070	14,287,991	2.29	394,453,582	3,829,211	.97
65,394,669	897,902	1.37	43,648,750	512,122	1.17
48,689,238	475,437	.98	18,305,550	82,760	.45
9,597,526,073	247,570,960	2.58	10,627,345,358	238,018,677	2.24
8,573,947,089	245,909,011	2.87	6,078,749,600	140,413,037	2.31
7,848,415,190	237,946,459	3.03	5,739,944,629	137,696,319	2.40
725,531,899	7,962,552	1.10	338,804,971	2,716,718	.80
1,023,578,984	1,661,949	.16	4,548,595,758	97,605,640	2.15
956,051,447	742,897	.08	4,366,919,401	95,901,339	2.20
13,081,705	0	.00	109,675,687	868,003	.79
54,445,832	919,052	1.69	72,000,670	836,298	1.16
1,188,293,683	19,858,230	1.67	781,991,072	8,655,844	1.11

Appendix C

STUDENT CHARGES, 1960–1961

AVERAGE TUITION RATES FOR THE 1960–61 ACADEMIC YEAR OF TWO SEMES-
ters or three quarters were somewhat higher in public Negro colleges than
in all public colleges for both resident ($140 to $138) and nonresident
students ($372 to $338), but because of the considerably lower ceiling on
Negro private college tuition, it was less than half as much in these colleges as in all private colleges ($338 to $784).

Students attending Negro colleges had appreciable advantages in
room and board charges for the academic year. In public Negro colleges
the average charge for a dormitory room was $61 less ($122 to $183) and
in private Negro colleges $86 less ($141 to $227), while for board rates
the average was $69 less in public Negro colleges ($300 to $369) and
$156 less in private Negro colleges ($273 to $429).

It can be noted that the combined charge for tuition, room, and
board was less in Negro colleges in each category. In public institutions,
the total was $128 less for resident students ($562 to $690) and $96 less
for nonresident students ($794 to $890), while in private institutions the
total was $688 less ($752 to $1,440).

Appendix C   **AVERAGE CHARGES FOR TUITION, ROOM, AND BOARD FOR NEGRO COLLEGES AND FOR ALL COLLEGES AND UNIVERSITIES, 1960–1961**[a]

	NEGRO	ALL
TUITION		
Resident, public	140	138
Nonresident, public	372	338
Private	338	784
ROOM RATE		
Public	122	183
Private	141	227
BOARD RATE		
Public	300	369
Private	272	329
TUITION, ROOM, AND BOARD		
Resident, public	562	690
Nonresident, public	794	890
Private	752	1,440

[a] Data for this table were obtained from Office of Education studies.

ARTS AND SCIENCES	1	PROFESSIONAL AND EDUCATIONAL		89
NATURAL SCIENCES	22	*Education*		52
Biology	5	Unspecified	21	
Mathematics	5	Agricultural education	4	
Physics	3	Business education	3	
Science	3	Physical education	3	
Zoology	2	Science education	3	
Anatomy	1	Elementary education	2	
Biochemistry	1	Home economics		
Botany	1	education	2	
Physiology	1	Music education	2	
		Religious education	2	
SOCIAL SCIENCES	24	Secondary education	2	
Psychology	5	Special education	2	
Sociology	5	Supervisory and ad'n	2	
History	4	Art education	1	
American history	1	Curriculum & instr'n	1	
Economics	3	Extension education	1	
Administration	2	Industrial education	1	
African studies	1	Chemistry		9
Government	1	Home economics		5
Political science	1	Counseling and guidance		4
Social science	1	Agriculture		3
		Agricultural economics		2
HUMANITIES	21	Animal science		2
English	5	Business administration		2
Music	3	Engineering		2
Arts	2	Plant Science		2
French	2	Commerce		1
Romance languages	2	Food administration		1
American literature	1	Foods and nutrition		1
Art	1	Library science		1
German	1	Pharmacology		1
Industrial arts	1	Social work		1
Philosophy	1			
Religion and philosophy	1	Grand Total		157
Speech and drama	1			

[a] Alabama A & M, Alabama State, Tuskegee Institute, Florida A & M, Fort Valley State, Atlanta University, Interdenominational Theological, Southern University & A & M, Xavier University, Jackson State, Lincoln University (Mo.), North Carolina A & T, North Carolina State, South Carolina State, Tennessee A & I State, Fisk University, Prairie View A & M, Texas Southern University, Virginia State, Hampton Institute, and Howard University.

**PREDOMINANTLY WHITE COLLEGES IN THE SOUTH
WHICH WILL AND WILL NOT NOW ADMIT NEGROES**

INSTITUTIONS	CONTROL
ALABAMA	
DESEGREGATED	
Predominantly White	
Auburn University, Auburn	Public
Florence State College, Florence	Public
University of Alabama, Tuscaloosa	Public
includes extension centers at Birmingham, Gadsden, Mobile, Montgomery, Dothan, Selma, and Huntsville	
Sacred Heart College, Cullan	Private
Spring Hill College, Mobile	Private
DESEGREGATED IN POLICY	
All White	
Southern Union College (Jr.), Wadley	Private
St. Bernard Abbey, St. Bernard	Private
SEGREGATED[a]	
All White	
Alabama College, Montevallo	Public
Jacksonville State College, Jacksonville	Public
Livingston State College, Livingston	Public
Troy State College, Troy	Public
ARKANSAS	
DESEGREGATED	
Predominantly White	
Arkansas Agricultural and Mechanical College, College Heights	Public
Arkansas Polytechnic College, Russellville	Public
Arkansas State College, State College	Public
Arkansas State Teachers College, Conway	Public
Henderson State Teachers College, Arkadelphia	Public
Southern State College, Magnolia	Public
University of Arkansas, Fayetteville	Public
Arkansas College, Batesville	Private
College of the Ozarks, Clarksville	Private
Harding College, Searcy	Private
Ouachita Baptist College, Arkadelphia	Private
DESEGREGATED IN POLICY	
All White	
Little Rock University, Little Rock	Private

[a] Public colleges to which all students have legal basis to apply for enrollment.

INSTITUTIONS	CONTROL
FLORIDA	
DESEGREGATED	
Predominantly White	
Brevard Junior College, Cocoa	Public
Central Florida Junior College, Ocala	Public
Chipola Junior College, Marianna	Public
Daytona Beach Junior College, Daytona Beach	Public
Florida State University, Tallahassee	Public
Gulf Coast Junior College, Panama City	Public
Indian River Junior College, Fort Pierce	Public
Junior College of Broward County, Fort Lauderdale	Public
Manatee Junior College, Bradenton	Public
Miami-Dade Junior College, Miami	Public
North Florida Junior College, Madison	Public
Palm Beach Junior College, Lake Worth	Public
Pensacola Junior College, Pensacola	Public
St. Johns River Junior College, Palatka	Public
St. Petersburg Junior College, St. Petersburg	Public
University of Florida, Gainesville	Public
University of South Florida, Tampa	Public
Barry College, Miami	Private
Embry-Riddle Aeronautical Institute, Miami	Private
Jacksonville University, Jacksonville	Private
Rollins College, Winter Park	Private
St. Leo College, St. Leo	Private
Stetson University, DeLand	Private
University of Miami, Coral Gables	Private
GEORGIA	
DESEGREGATED	
Predominantly White	
Armstrong College of Savannah (Jr.), Savannah	Public
Columbus (Jr.) College, Columbus	Public
Georgia Institute of Technology, Atlanta	Public
Georgia State College of Business Administration, Atlanta	Public
University of Georgia, Athens	Public
Valdosta State College, Valdosta	Public
West Georgia College, Carrollton	Public
Woman's College of Georgia (The), Milledgeville	Public
Agnes Scott College, Decatur	Private
Columbia Theological Seminary, Decatur	Private
Emory University, Atlanta	Private
Mercer University, Macon	Private
Oglethorpe University, Atlanta	Private
Piedmont College, Demorest (NA)	Private

INSTITUTIONS	CONTROL
GEORGIA — Continued	
DESEGREGATED IN POLICY	
All White	
Abraham Baldwin Agricultural College, Tifton	Public
Augusta College, Augusta	Public
Georgia Southern College, Statesboro	Public
Georgia Southwestern College (Jr.), Americus	Public
Medical College of Georgia, Augusta	Public
Middle Georgia College (Jr.), Cochran	Public
North Georgia College, Dahlonega	Public
South Georgia College (Jr.), Douglas	Public
Southern Technical Institute, Marietta (Division of Georgia Tech)	Public
Wesleyan College, Macon	Private
SEGREGATED	
All White	
Georgia Military College (Jr.), Milledgeville	Public
LOUISIANA	
DESEGREGATED	
Predominantly White	
Francis T. Nicholls State College, Thibodaux	Public
Louisiana State University, Baton Rouge	Public
Louisiana State University in New Orleans, New Orleans	Public
Louisiana State University, Chambers Branch	Public
McNeese State College, Lake Charles	Public
Southeastern Louisiana College, Hammond	Public
University of Southwestern Louisiana, Lafayette	Public
Immaculata Minor Seminary, Lafayette	Private
Loyola University, New Orleans	Private
New Orleans Baptist Theological Seminary, New Orleans	Private
Notre Dame Seminary (Jr.), New Orleans	Private
Our Lady of Holy Cross, New Orleans	Private
St. Joseph Seminary (Jr.), St. Benedict	Private
St. Mary's Dominican College, New Orleans	Private
Tulane University, New Orleans	Private
DESEGREGATED IN POLICY	
None	
SEGREGATED	
All White	
Louisiana Polytechnic Institute, Ruston	Public
Northeast Louisiana State College	Public
Northwestern State College of Louisiana, Natchitoches	Public
Centenary College, Shreveport	Private
Louisiana College, Pineville	Private

PREDOMINANTLY WHITE COLLEGES IN THE SOUTH WHICH WILL AND WILL NOT NOW ADMIT NEGROES — Cont.

INSTITUTIONS	CONTROL
MISSISSIPPI	

DESEGREGATED

Predominantly White

University of Mississippi, Oxford	Public
Our Lady of the Snows Scholasticate, Pass Christian	Private

DESEGREGATED IN POLICY

None

SEGREGATED

All White

Copian-Lincoln Junior College, Wesson	Public[b]
East Central Junior College, Decatur	Public[b]
East Mississippi Junior College, Scooba	Public[b]
Hinds Junior College, Raymond	Public[b]
Holmes Junior College, Goodman	Public[b]
Itawamba Junior College, Fulton	Public[b]
Jones County Junior College, Ellisville	Public[b]
Meridian Municipal Junior College, Meridian	Public[b]
Northeast Mississippi Junior College, Booneville	Public[b]
Northwest Mississippi Junior College, Senatobia	Public[b]
Pearl River Junior College, Poplarville	Public[b]
Perkinston Junior College, Perkinston	Public[b]
Southwest Mississippi Junior College, Summit	Public[b]
Sunflower (Mississippi Delta) Junior College, Moorhead	Public[b]
All Saints' Junior College, Vicksburg	Private
Belhaven College, Jackson	Private
Blue Mountain College, Blue Mountain	Private
Clarke Memorial College, Newton	Private
Gulf Park (Jr.) College, Gulfport	Private
Millsaps College, Jackson	Private
Mississippi College, Clinton	Private
Natchez Junior College, Natchez	Private
Saints Junior College, Lexington	Private
Southeastern Baptist Junior College, Laurel (NA)	Private
William Carey College, Hattiesburg	Private
Wood Junior College, Mathiston	Private

NORTH CAROLINA	

DESEGREGATED

Predominantly White

Appalachian State Teachers College, Boone	Public
Asheville-Biltmore (Jr.) College, Asheville	Public
East Carolina College, Greenville	Public

[b] State-County.

INSTITUTIONS	CONTROL
NORTH CAROLINA—Continued	

DESEGREGATED—Continued

Predominantly White—Continued

Central Piedmont Community College: Elizabeth Avenue Campus (Jr.), Charlotte	Public*c*
Charlotte College, Charlotte	Public
College of the Albermarle, Elizabeth City	Public
North Carolina State of the University of North Carolina at Raleigh, Raleigh	Public
Pembroke State College, Pembroke	Public
University of North Carolina at Chapel Hill, Chapel Hill	Public
University of North Carolina at Greensboro (Woman's College), Greensboro	Public
Western Carolina College, Cullowhee	Public
Wilmington College, Wilmington	Public
Belmont-Abbey College, Belmont	Private
Brevard College (Jr.), Brevard	Private
Catawba College, Salisbury	Private
Davidson College, Davidson	Private
Duke University, Durham	Private
Elon College, Elon	Private
Gardner-Webb Junior College, Boiling Springs	Private
Greensboro College, Greensboro	Private
Guilford College, Guilford	Private
High Point College, High Point	Private
Lenior-Rhyne College, Hickory	Private
Mars Hill College, Mars Hill	Private
Meredith College, Raleigh	Private
Pfeiffer College, Misenheimer	Private
Queens College, Charlotte	Private
Sacred Heart Junior College & Academy, Belmont	Private
Southeastern Baptist Theological Seminary, Wake Forest	Private
St. Andrews College, Laurinburg	Private
Wake Forest College, Winston-Salem	Private
Warren Wilson (Jr.) College, Swannanoa	Private

DESEGREGATED IN POLICY

All White

Chowan College (Jr.), Murfreesboro	Private
SOUTH CAROLINA	

DESEGREGATED

Predominantly White

Clemson Agricultural College, Clemson	Public
University of South Carolina, Columbia	Public

c City.

INSTITUTIONS	CONTROL
SOUTH CAROLINA—Continued	
DESEGREGATED—Continued	
Predominantly White—Continued	
Lutheran Theological Southern Seminary, Columbia	Private
Our Lady of Mercy Junior College, Charleston	Private
DESEGREGATED IN POLICY	
All White	
Furman University, Greenville	Private
Lander College, Greenwood	Public & Private
SEGREGATED	
All White	
The Citadel (Military College of South Carolina), Charleston	Public
Medical College of South Carolina, Charleston	Public
Winthrop College, Rock Hill	Public
TENNESSEE	
DESEGREGATED	
Predominantly White	
Austin Peay State College, Clarksville	Public
East Tennessee State University, Johnson City	Public
Memphis State University, Memphis	Public
Middle Tennessee State College, Murfreesboro	Public
University of Tennessee (all branches desegregated: Knoxville, Martin, Memphis, Nashville)	Public
Bethel College, McKenzie	Private
Christian Brothers College, Memphis	Private
George Peabody College for Teachers, Nashville	Private
Hiwassee College, Madisonville	Private
Martin College (Jr.), Pulaski	Private
Madison College, Madison	Private
Maryville College, Maryville	Private
Scarritt College for Christian Workers, Nashville	Private
Siena College, Memphis	Private
Tennessee Wesleyan College, Athens	Private
Tusculum College, Greeneville	Private
University of Chattanooga, Chattanooga	Private
University of The South, Sewanee	Private
Vanderbilt University, Nashville	Private
William Jennings Bryan College, Dayton	Private
DESEGREGATED IN POLICY	
All White	
Tennessee Polytechnic Institute, Cookeville	Public
Carson-Newman College, Jefferson City	Private
Southern College of Optometry, Memphis	Private

189

INSTITUTIONS	CONTROL
TEXAS	

DESEGREGATED

Predominantly White

SENIOR COLLEGES

Arlington State College, Arlington	Public
Lamar State College of Technology, Beaumont	Public
Midwestern University, Wichita Falls	Public
Pan-American College, Edinburg	Public
Texas A & M University, College Station	Public
Texas College of Arts and Industries, Kingsville	Public
Texas Technological College, Lubbock	Public
Texas Western College (of University of Texas), El Paso	Public
Texas Woman's University, Denton	Public
University of Houston, Houston	Public
University of Texas, Austin	Public
West Texas State College, Canyon	Public
Southwest Texas State College, San Marcos	Public
Abilene Christian College, Abilene	Private
Austin College, Austin	Private
Austin Presbyterian Theological Seminary, Austin	Private
Baylor University, Waco	Private
Dallas Theological Seminary, Dallas	Private
De Mazenod Scholasticate, San Antonio	Private
Episcopal Theological Seminary of the Southwest, Austin	Private
Hardin-Simmons University, Abilene	Private
Incarnate Word College, San Antonio	Private
Lutheran Concordia (Jr.) College, Austin	Private
McMurry College, Abilene	Private
Our Lady of the Lake College, San Antonio	Private
Southern Methodist University, Dallas	Private
Texas Christian University, Fort Worth	Private
University of Dallas, Dallas	Private
Wayland Baptist College, Plainview	Private
St. Edward's University, Austin	Private
St. Mary's University of San Antonio, San Antonio	Private
Southwestern Baptist Theological Seminary, Fort Worth	Private
Texas Lutheran College, Seguin	Private
Trinity University, San Antonio	Private
University of Corpus Christi, Corpus Christi	Private

JUNIOR COLLEGES

Amarillo (Jr.) College, Amarillo	Public
Cisco Junior College, Cisco	Public
Cooke County Junior College, Gainesville	Public
Del Mar (Jr.) College, Corpus Christi	Public
Frank Philips (Jr.) College, Borger	Public

**PREDOMINANTLY WHITE COLLEGES IN THE SOUTH
WHICH WILL AND WILL NOT NOW ADMIT NEGROES**

INSTITUTIONS	CONTROL
TEXAS—Continued	
DESEGREGATED—Continued	
Predominantly White—Continued	
JUNIOR COLLEGES—Continued	
Henderson County Junior College, Athens	Public
Hill Junior College, Hillsboro	Public
Howard County Junior College, Big Spring	Public
Kilgore (Jr.) College, Kilgore	Public
Laredo Junior College, Laredo	Public
Lee (Jr.) College, Baytown	Public
Navarro Junior College, Corsicana	Public
Odessa (Jr.) College, Odessa	Public
Paris Junior College, Paris	Public
Ranger Junior College, Ranger	Public
San Angelo (Jr.) College, San Angelo	Public
San Antonio (Jr.) College, San Antonio	Public
San Jacinto (Jr.) College, San Jacinto	Public
South Plains (Jr.) College, Levelland	Public
Southwest Texas (Jr.) College, Uvalde	Public
Temple Junior College, Temple	Public
Texarkana (Jr.) College, Texarkana	Public
Texas Southmost (Jr.) College, Brownsville	Public
Victoria (Jr.) College, Victoria	Public
Weatherford (Jr.) College, Weatherford	Public
Wharton County (Jr.) College, Wharton	Public
DESEGREGATED IN POLICY	
All White	
Clarendon Junior College, Clarendon	Public
Mary Hardin-Baylor College, Belton	Private
SEGREGATED	
All White	
Alvin Junior College, Alvin	Public
Blinn (Jr.) College, Brenham	Public
East Texas State College, Commerce	Public
Panola County Junior College, Carthage	Public
Sam Houston State College, Huntsville	Public
Stephen F. Austin State College, Nacogdoches	Public
Sul Ross State College, Alpine	Public
Tarleton State College, Stephenville	Public
Tyler Junior College, Tyler	Public
VIRGINIA	
DESEGREGATED	
Predominantly White	
College of William and Mary, Williamsburg	Public

INSTITUTIONS	CONTROL

VIRGINIA—Continued

DESEGREGATED—Continued

Predominantly White—Contined

Medical College of Virginia, Richmond	Public
Old Dominion College, Norfolk	Public
Radford College of Virginia Poytechnic Institute, Radford	Public
Richmond Professional Institute of the College of William and Mary, Richmond	Public
University of Virginia, Charlottesville	Public
Colleges of the University of Virginia:	Public
Clinch Valley College (Jr.), Wise	
George Mason College (Jr.), Fairfax	
Lynchburg Branch of the School of General Studies, Lynchburg	
Patrick Henry College (Jr.), Martinsville	
Virginia Polytechnic Institute, Blacksburg	Public
Roanoke Technical Institute, a Division of Virginia Polytechnic Institute, Roanoke	Public
Danville Community College, a Division of Virginia Polytechnic Institute, Danville	Public
Apprentice School of the Newport News Shipbuilding and Dry Dock Company, Newport News	Private
Bridgewater College, Bridgewater	Private
Eastern Mennonite College, Harrisonburg	Private
Mary Baldwin College, Staunton	Private
Presbyterian School of Christian Education, Richmond	Private
Protestant Episcopal Theological Seminary, Alexandria	Private
St. Paul's College, Lawrenceville	Private
Shenandoah College, Winchester	Private
Shenandoah Conservatory of Music, Winchester	Private
Union Theological Seminary, Richmond	Private

DESEGREGATED IN POLICY

All White

Christopher Newport College (Jr.) of the College of William and Mary, Newport News	Public
Richard Bland College (Jr.) of the College of William and Mary, Petersburg	Public
Emory and Henry College, Emory	Private
Hollins College, Roanoke	Private
Marymount College (Jr.), Arlington	Private
Randolph-Macon Woman's College, Lynchburg	Private

SEGREGATED

All White

Longwood College, Farmville	Public

INSTITUTIONS	CONTROL
VIRGINIA—Continued	

SEGREGATED—Continued

All White—Continued

Madison College, Harrisonburg	Public
Mary Washington College of the University of Virginia, Fredericksburg	Public
Virginia Military Institute, Lexington	Public

SOURCE: U.S. Commission on Civil Rights, "Desegregated-Segregated Status of Institutions of Higher Education in the United States," Staff Paper, Washington, D.C., February 1964.

BIBLIOGRAPHY

ALLMAN, REVA W. "An Evaluation of the Goals of Higher Education by 294 College Seniors of Alabama." *The Journal of Negro Education*, 29 : 148–203, Spring 1960.

AMERICAN ASSOCIATION OF UNIVERSITY PROFESSORS. "The Economic Status of the Professions, 1962–1963." *AAUP Bulletin*, pp. 141–187, Summer 1963.

"THE AMERICAN NEGRO IN COLLEGE, 1962–63." *Crisis*, 70 : 418–430, August–September, 1963.

APTHEKER, HERBERT. *The Negro People in America*. New York: International Publishers, 1946. 80 pp.

ASCOLI, MAX. "This Negro Revolution." *The Reporter*, 29 : 22, October 10, 1963.

ASHMORE, HARRY S. *The Negro and the Schools*. Chapel Hill: The University of North Carolina Press, 1954. 239 pp.

ATWOOD, RUFUS B. "The Origin and Development of the Negro Public College, with Special Reference to the Land-Grant College." *The Journal of Negro Education*, 31 : 240–250, Summer 1962.

ATWOOD, RUFUS B., H. S. SMITH, and CATHERINE O. VAUGHAN. "Negro Teachers in Northern Colleges and Universities in the United States." *The Journal of Negro Education*, 18 : 561–567, Fall 1949.

BLAUSTEIN, ALBERT P., and CLARENCE FERGUSON, JR. *Desegregation and the Law: The Meaning and Effect of the School Segregation Cases*. New Brunswick, N. J.: Rutgers University Press, 1957. 333 pp.

BOKELMAN, W. ROBERT, and LOUIS A. D'AMICO. "Changes in Faculty Salaries and Basic Student Charges in Negro Colleges: 1960–61 and 1961–62." *The Journal of Negro Education*, 31 : 507–510, Fall 1962.

BOND, HORACE MANN. *The Education of the Negro in the American Social Order*. Englewood Cliffs, N.J.: Prentice Hall, Inc., 1934. 501 pp.

BOND, HORACE MANN. "The Origin and Development of the Negro Church-Related College." *The Journal of Negro Education*, 29 : 217–226, Summer 1960.

BONDS, A. B., JR. "The Role of Men in Church and Civic Affairs." June 1963. (Mimeographed, 7 pp.)

BOTTOMS, L. W. "The Policies and Rationale Underlying the Support of Negro Colleges and Schools Maintained by the Presbyterian Church in the United States." *The Journal of Negro Education*, 29 : 264–273, Summer 1960.

BOYKIN, L. L. "Trends in American Higher Education with Implications for the Higher Education of Negroes." *The Journal of Negro Education*, 26 : 193–199, Spring 1957.

BRADLEY, GLADYCE H. "Friendships Among Students in Desegregated Schools." *The Journal of Negro Education*, 33 : 90–92, Winter 1964.

BRAZZIEL, WILLIAM F. "Curriculum Choice in the Negro College." *The Journal of Negro Education*, 29 : 207–209, Spring 1960.

BRAZZIEL, WILLIAM F. "Some Influences of Value and Needs on Academic Achievement in a Low Socio-Economic College Sample." *Journal of Human Relations*, 11 : 639–649. Autumn 1963.

BRICE, EDWARD WARNER. "Enrollment in Institutions of Higher Learning Attended Predominantly by Negroes During the Past Decade." *Negro Educational Review*, 10 : 108–120, July 1959.

BROWN, AARON. "The Negro Graduate, 1950–1960." *Negro Educational Review*, 11 : 71–81, April 1960.

BROWN, INA CORINNE. "Anthropological and Sociological Factors in Race Relations" in *Negro Education in America*. New York: Harper & Row, Publishers, Incorporated, 1962. 315 pp.

BROWN, CHARLES I. "The Married Students at Bennett College." *The Journal of Negro Education*, 32 : 183–187, Spring 1963.

BROWNLEE, FREDERICK L. "The Negro Church-Related College: A Critical Summary." *The Journal of Negro Education*, 29 : 401–407, Summer 1960.

BRYANT, LAWRENCE C. "Graduate Degree Programs in Negro Colleges, 1927–1960." *Negro Educational Review*, 11 : 177–184, October 1960.

BRYANT, LAWRENCE C. "Graduate Training in Negro Colleges." Section B. *The Journal of Negro Education*, 30 : 69–71, Winter 1961.

BURGESS, ELAIN M. *Negro Leadership in a Southern Community*. Chapel Hill: North Carolina Press, 1960. 231 pp.

CAMPBELL, E. FAY. "The Policies and Rationale Governing Support of Negro Private Colleges Maintained by the United Presbyterian Church in the United States of America." *The Journal of Negro Education*, 29 : 260–263, Summer 1960.

CHAO, T. T., and MALVIN MOORE, JR. "A Correlation Study on Grades Between High Schools and Fayetteville State Teachers College." *Savannah State College Bulletin*, 17 : 42–49, December 1963.

CLARK, KENNETH BANCROFT. *The Negro Protest*. Boston: Beacon Press, 1963. 56 pp.

CLARK, KENNETH BANCROFT, and LAWRENCE PLOTKIN. *The Negro Student at Integrated Colleges.* New York: National Scholarship Service and Fund for Negro Students, 1963. 59 pp.

CLARK, THOMAS D. *The Emerging South.* New York: Oxford University Press, 1961, 317 pp.

CLIFT, VIRGIL A. "Appropriate Goals and Plans for the Future" and Preface to *Negro Education in America.* New York: Harper & Row, Publishers, Incorporated, 1962, pp. 287–308.

COLLINS, ERNEST M. "Integration in the State Supported Colleges and Universities of the South." *The Journal of Negro Education,* 32 : 239–246, May 1961.

D'AMICO, LOUIS A., and MAENYLIE M. REED. "A Comparison of Tuition and Fees Charged in Negro Institutions of the Southeast and of the Nation." *The Journal of Negro Education,* 33 : 186–190, Spring 1964.

DANIEL, ROBERT P. "The Relationship of the Negro Public College and the Negro Private and Church-Related College." *The Journal of Negro Education,* 29 : 388–393, Summer 1960.

DANIEL, WALTER G. "Editorial Comment: A Memorandum on the Education of Negroes." *The Journal of Negro Education,* 33 : 97–102, Spring 1964.

DANIEL, WALTER G. "Liberal Arts and Teacher Education in the Negro Public College." *The Journal of Negro Education,* 34 : 404–413, Summer 1962.

DANIEL, WALTER G. "Negroes as Teaching Assistants in Some Publicly Supported Universities." *The Journal of Negro Education,* 31 : 202–204, Spring 1962.

DANIEL, WALTER G. "The Relative Employment and Income of American Negroes." *The Journal of Negro Education,* 32 : 349–357, Fall 1963.

DAVIS, ALLISON. *Social Class Influence upon Learning.* Cambridge: Harvard University Press, 1948. 100 pp.

DAVIS, JOHN W. "The Future of the Negro Public College." *The Journal of Negro Education,* 31 : 421–428, Summer 1962.

DECKER, PAUL M. "A Study of Job Opportunities in the State of Florida for Negro College Graduates." *The Journal of Negro Education,* 29 : 93–99, Winter 1960.

DENNIS, LAWRENCE E., and THEODORE J. MARCHESE (eds.). *Expanding Opportunities: The Negro and Higher Education.* American Council of Education Committee on Equality of Educational Opportunity, Washington, D.C., Volume I, May 1964. 8 pp.

DERBIGNY, IRVING A. *General Education in the Negro College.* Stanford University, Calif. : The Stanford University Press, 1947. 249 pp.

"Desegregation and the Negro College." *The Journal of Negro Education.* Yearbook. Volume 27, Summer 1958.

Desegregation in Higher Education (revised). Atlanta: Southern Regional Council, 1963. 11 pp.

Doctorate Production in U.S. Universities 1936–56. Washington: National Academy of Sciences–National Research Council, Pub. 3,582, 1958, pp. 70–141.

DODDY, HURLEY H. "The Progress of the Negro in Higher Education." *The Journal of Negro Education,* 32 : 485–492, Fall 1963.

DODDY, HURLEY H. "The Status of the Negro Public College: A Statistical Summary." *The Journal of Negro Education,* 31 : 370–385, Summer 1962.

DODSON, DAN W. "Developments in Race Relations and Their Implications for the Education of Negroes in the United States, 1950–60." *Negro Educational Review,* 10 : 121–129, July 1959.

DRAKE, ST. CLAIR. *The American Dream and the Negro: 100 Years of Freedom.* Emancipation Proclamation Centennial Lectures, January–February 1963. 70 pp.

DUNBAR, LESLIE. *Some Thoughts on the Civil Rights Campaign.* 15 pp. (Unpublished.)

DUNNE, WILLIAM. "The Roman Catholic Church: The Rationale and Policies Underlying the Maintenance of Higher Institutions for Negroes." *The Journal of Negro Education,* 29 : 307–314, Summer 1960.

"Educational Desegregation, 1956." *The Journal of Negro Education.* Yearbook. Volume 25. Summer 1956.

EELLS, WALTER CROSBY. *Degrees in Higher Education.* Washington, D.C.: The Center for Applied Research in Education, Inc., 1963. 118 pp.

EPPS, EDGAR C. "Ethnic Differences in Occupational and Educational Aspirations." *Florida Agriculture and Mechanical College Bulletin,* pp. 28–35, Summer 1961.

FELLMAN, DAVID (ed.). *The Supreme Court and Education.* New York: Bureau of Publications, Teachers College, Columbia University. 1960. 120 pp.

FEN, SING-NAN. "Liberal Education for Negroes." *The Journal of Negro Education,* 30 : 17–24, Winter 1961.

FEN, SING-NAN. "The Learning of Social Relations in School." *The Journal of Negro Education,* 32 : 87–91, Winter 1963.

"Financing Higher Education." Southern Regional Education Board: Atlanta. Number 13. 1963.

FROE, OTIS D. "Some Research Concerned with Non-Intellective Factors in Student Achievement at Morgan State College." K. M. Wilson, ed. Atlanta: Southern Regional Education Board, 1962.

"Future of Private Negro Colleges." *Ebony.* 16 : 88–90, July 1961.

GALLAGHER, BUELL. *American Caste and the Negro College* (with a foreword by William H. Kilpatrick). New York: Columbia University Press, 1938. 461 pp.

GINZBERG, ELI. "The Future of Negro Land-Grant Colleges." Speech given March, 1962, United States Department of Agriculture, Washington, D.C.

GINZBERG, ELI. *The Negro Potential.* New York: Columbia University Press, 1956. 144 pp.

GIST, NOEL P., and WILLIAM S. BENNETT, JR. "Aspirations of Negro and White Students." *Social Forces*, 42 : 40–80, October 1963.

GOFF, REGINA M. "Culture and the Personality Development of Minority Peoples" in *Negro Education in America*. New York: Harper & Row, Publishers, Incorporated, 1962, pp. 124–150.

GOLDEN, HARRY. "The American Negro and Higher Education." *Crisis*, 70 : 405–409, August–September 1963.

GOODE, WILLIAM J. "Illegitimacy, Anomie, and Cultural Penetration." *American Sociological Review*, 26 : 910–925, December 1961.

GREGORY, FRANCIS A., CARL F. HANSEN, and IRENE C. HYPPS. "From Desegregation to Integration in Education." *Journal of Intergroup Relations*, 4 : 55–72, Winter 1962.

GROSSACK, MARTIN M., ed. *Segregation and Mental Health*. New York: Springer Publishing Co., Inc., 1963. 288 pp.

HARRINGTON, MICHAEL. "The New Lost Generation: Jobless Youth." *New York Times Magazine*, May 24, 1964, pp. 134+.

HARRINGTON, MICHAEL. *The Other America: Poverty in the United States*. New York: The Macmillan Company, 1963. 191 pp.

HARRIS, NELSON H. "Desegregation in Institutions of Higher Learning" in *Negro Education in America*. New York: Harper & Row, Publishers, Incorporated, 1962, pp. 235–269.

HARRISON, E. C. "Working at Improving the Motivational and Achievement Levels of the Deprived." *The Journal of Negro Education*, 32 : 301–307, Summer 1963.

HENDERSON, T. H. "The Future of the Non-Land Grant Negro Public College." *The Journal of Negro Education*, 27 : 397, Summer 1958.

HENDERSON, VIVIAN W. *The Economic Status of Negroes: In the Nation and In the South*. Atlanta: Southern Regional Council, 1963. 23 pp.

HINES, RALPH J. "Social Expectations and Cultural Deprivation." *The Journal of Negro Education*, 33 : 136–142, Spring 1964.

HOPE, JOHN, II. "The Negro College, Student Protest and the Future." *The Journal of Negro Education*, 30 : 368–376, Winter 1961.

HULLFISH, GORDON H. "Education and Social Relationships in a Democracy," and the Introduction to *Negro Education in America*. New York: Harper & Row, Publishers, Incorporated, 1962, pp. 153–170.

HYMAN, HERBERT H., and PAUL B. SHEATSLEY. "How Whites View Negroes, 1942–63." Reprint from *New York Herald Tribune*, November 10, 1963.

JONES, JESSE T. "Negro Education: A Study of the Private and Higher Schools for Colored People in the United States." Department of the Interior, Bureau of Education, *Bulletin*, 1916, Number 28. Washington, D.C., 1917.

JENKINS, MARTIN D. *A Program for the Improvement of Predominantly Negro Colleges*. Washington, D.C.: ACE Conference on Expanding Opportunities for Negroes in Higher Education, 1963. Manuscript. 10 pp.

JENKINS, MARTIN D. "Enrollment in Institutions of Higher Education of Negroes, 1941–42." *The Journal of Negro Education,* pp. 220–221, April 1942.

JENKINS, MARTIN D. "The Future of the Desegregated Negro College." *The Journal of Negro Education,* 28 : 419–429, Summer 1958.

JENKINS, MARTIN D. "The Negro College." *Howard University Magazine,* 6 : 13–16, January 1964.

JENNINGS, FRANK G. "For Such a Tide Is Moving." *Saturday Review,* pp. 74–87, May 16, 1964.

JOHNSON, CHARLES S. *The Negro College Graduate.* Chapel Hill: University of North Carolina Press, 1938. 329 pp.

JOHNSON, G. B. "Desegregation and the Future of the Negro College: A Critical Summary." *The Journal of Negro Education,* 27 : 430–435, Summer 1958.

JONES, LANCE G. E. *The Jeanes Teacher in the United States, 1908–1933: An Account of Twenty-five Years Experience in the Supervision of Negro Rural Schools.* Chapel Hill: University of North Carolina Press, 1937. 146 pp.

JONES, LEWIS E. *The Influence of Student Demonstrations on Southern Negro Colleges: Part II—Crises on the Campus.* A Report from the Department of Race Relations of Fisk University to the Field Foundation, Inc. 79 pp.

JOSEY, E. J. "Negro College Libraries and ACRL Standards." *Library Journal,* 88 : 2989–2996, September 1, 1963.

JOSEY, E. J. "Your College Library and Your College Education." *The Quarterly Review of Higher Education Among Negroes,* 31 : 9, January 1963.

KLEIN, ARTHUR JAY. "Survey of Negro Colleges and Universities." Prepared in the Division of Higher Education, U.S. Office of Education *Bulletin,* 1928, Number 7, Washington: U.S. Government Printing Office, 1929.

LEWIS, ALFRED B. "The Importance of Economics in the Civil Rights Struggle." *Crisis,* 70 : 534–536, 572, November 1963.

LOGAN, R. W. "The Evolution of Private Colleges for Negroes." *The Journal of Negro Education,* 27 : 213–220, Summer 1958.

LOMAX, LOUIS E. *The Negro Revolt.* New York: Harper & Row, Publishers, Incorporated, 1922. 271 pp.

LOMBARDI, DONALD N. "Factors Affecting Changes in Attitudes Toward Negroes Among High School Students." *The Journal of Negro Education,* 32 : 129–137, Spring 1963.

LOW, W. A. "The Education of Negroes Viewed Historically" in *Negro Education in America.* New York: Harper & Row, Publishers, Incorporated, 1962, pp. 27–60.

MARTIN, ROBERT E. "General Education: Its Problems and Promises in Education of Negroes" in *Negro Education in America.* New York: Harper & Row, Publishers, Incorporated, 1962, pp. 183–198.

MARTIN, WILLIAM H. "The Land-Grant Functions of the Negro Public College." *The Journal of Negro Education,* 31 : 396–403, Summer 1962.

MARTIN, WILLIAM H. "Unique Contributions of Negro Educators" in *Negro Education in America*. New York: Harper & Row, Publishers, Incorporated, 1962, pp. 60–93.

MATHEWS, MARCIA M. "The Difference Between Black and White." *Saturday Evening Post*, 232 : 13–15, January 16, 1960.

MAYS, BENJAMIN E. *What Is the Future of Negro Colleges?* Reprint from the *Southern School News*, April 1961. 12 pp.

MAYS, BENJAMIN E. "The Future of Negro Colleges." *Saturday Review*, pp. 53–54, November 18, 1961.

MC CONNELL, ROLAND C. "A Small College and the Archival Record." *The Journal of Negro Education*, 32 : 84–86, Winter 1963.

MC QUEEN, ROBERT, and BROWNING CHURN. "The Intelligence and Educational Achievement of a Matched Sample of White and Negro Students." *School and Society*, pp. 327–329, September 24, 1960.

MEISTER, MORRIS, ABRAHAM TAUBER, and SIDNEY SILVERMAN. "Operation Second Choice." *Junior College Journal*, Volume 33, Number 2, October 1962.

MILLARD, THOMAS L. "The Negro and Social Protest." *The Journal of Negro Education*, 32 : 92–98, Winter 1963.

MILLER, CARROLL L. "The Negro Publicly Supported Junior College." *The Journal of Negro Education*, 31 : 386–395, Summer 1962.

MILLS, JAMES ALEXANDER. "Changes in the Faculties of Negro Colleges, 1948–1958," *The Quarterly Review of Higher Education Among Negroes*, 30 : 153–157, July 1962.

MITCHELL, JAMES J. "Negro Higher Education: Years of Crises." *The Quarterly Review of Higher Education Among Negroes*, 30 : 18–21, January 1962.

MITCHELL, JAMES J. "What Can We Do to Encourage Young Negroes to Become Americans?" *The Quarterly Review of Higher Education Among Negroes*, 31 : 159–162, October 1963.

MORLAND, KENNETH J. *Token Desegregation and Beyond*. Atlanta: Southern Regional Council, 1963. 27 pp.

MUSE, BENJAMIN. *Virginia's Massive Resistance*. Bloomington: Indiana University Press, 1961. 184 pp.

MUSSEN, P. H. "Some Personality and Social Factors Related to Changes in Children's Attitudes Towards Negroes." *Journal of Abnormal Social Psychology*, 45 : 423–441, July 1950.

MYRDAL, GUNNAR. *An American Dilemma: The Negro Problem and Modern Democracy*. With the assistance of Richard Sterner and Arnold Rose. New York: Harper & Row, Publishers, Incorporated, 1944. 1,483 pp.

MYRDAL, GUNNAR. *Challenge to Affluence*. New York: Pantheon Books, 1963. 172 pp.

"Negro Education in the United States: A Special Issue." *Harvard Educational Review*, Summer 1960.

"Negro Higher and Professional Education in the United States." *The Journal of Negro Education*, Yearbook. Volume 17, Summer 1948.

"The Negro Private and Church Related College." *The Journal of Negro Education*, Yearbook, Volume 29, Summer 1960.

"Negroes in College: What the Figures Show." *U.S. News and World Report*, 55 : 81, November 25, 1963.

"The Negro Public College." *The Journal of Negro Education*, Yearbook. Volume 31, Summer 1961.

NELSON, HAROLD A. "Expressed and Unexpressed Prejudice Against Ethnic Groups in a College Community." *The Journal of Negro Education*, 31 : 125–131, Spring 1962.

NELSON, WILLIAM STUART. "Can Negro Colleges Meet the Challenge of the Modern World?" *Negro Digest*, 12 : 8, June 1963.

NELSON, WILLIAM STUART. "The Image of the College and World Affairs." *The Quarterly Review of Higher Education Among Negroes*, 31 : 79–104, July 1963.

NORMAN, ARTHUR. "A New Approach to Negro Education." *The Journal of Negro Education*, 30 : 35–40, Winter 1961.

O'DELL, J. H. "The Negro People in the Southern Economy." *Freedomways*, 3 : 526–548, Fall 1963.

OPPENHEIMER, MARTIN. "Institutions of Higher Learning and the 1960 Sit-Ins: Some Clues for Social Action." *The Journal of Negro Education*, 32 : 286–288, Summer 1963.

PARKER, F. "Negro Education in the U.S.A.: Doctoral Dissertations." *Negro History Bulletin*, 24 : 192, 25 : 24, May and October 1961.

PATTERSON, F. D. "Colleges for Negro Youth and the Future." *The Journal of Negro Education*, 27 : 110–111, Spring 1958.

PAYTON, C. R. *Negro College Students.* Unpublished doctoral research project, Teachers College, Columbia University, 1962.

PETTIGREW, THOMAS F. "Negro American Intelligence: A New Look at an Old Controversy." *The Journal of Negro Education*, 33 : 6–25, Winter 1964.

PHELPS-STOKES FUND. *Education for Human Development.* New York, 1962. 11 pp.

PHILLIPS, WALDO B. "Counseling Negro Pupils: An Educational Dilemma." *The Journal of Negro Education*, 29 : 504–507, Fall 1960.

PITTMAN, JOSEPH A. "A Study of the Academic Achievement of 415 College Students in Relation to Remedial Courses Taken." *The Journal of Negro Education*, 29 : 426–437, Fall 1960.

PRICE, J. ST. CLAIR. *Improving the Academic Performance of Negro Students.* Washington, D.C.: Research Committee, Association of Colleges and Secondary Schools, 1959. 66 pp.

PURYEAR, PAUL L. "Equity Power and the School Desegregation Cases." *Harvard Educational Review*, 33 : 421–438, Fall 1963.

"Racial Segregation in Education." *School and Society*, May 7 and May 21, 1960.

RAMAKER, ROBERT. "Negro Colleges Train Too Many Teachers, Too Few Technicians; Job Openings for Grads Go Begging." *Wall Street Journal*, 154 : 1, July 15, 1959.

"The Relationship of the Federal Government to Negro Education." *The Journal of Negro Education*, Yearbook. Volume 7, July 1939.

ROTH, ROBERT M. "A Self Selection Process by Northern Negroes Existing in a Southern Negro College." *The Journal of Negro Education*, 28 : 185–186, Spring 1959.

ROUNDTREE, J. G. "Education and the Negro." *Negro Historical Bulletin*, 27 : 106–108, February 1964.

ROUSSENE, RONALD J. "Teachers of Culturally Disadvantaged Youth." *The Journal of Negro Education*, 32 : 114–121, Spring 1963.

SAWYER, BROADUS. "The Baccalaureate Origins of the Faculties of Twenty-one Selected Colleges." *The Journal of Negro Education*, 31 : 83–87, Winter 1962.

SAWYER, BROADUS. "The Graduate Training of Twenty-one Selected College Faculties." *The Journal of Negro Education*, 32 : 193–197, Spring 1963.

SCALES, EDRIDGE. "A Study of College Student Retentions and Withdrawal." *The Journal of Negro Education*, 29 : 438–444, Fall 1960.

SEXTON, PATRICIA CAYO. *Education and Income: Inequalities of Opportunity in Our Public Schools.* Foreword by Kenneth B. Clark. New York: Viking Press, 1961. 298 pp.

SHOCKLEY, A. A. "Does the Negro College Library Need a Special Negro Collection?" *Library Journal*, 86 : 2048–2050, June 1, 1961.

SHOEMAKER, DON (ed.). *With All Deliberate Speed: Segregation-Desegregation in Southern Schools.* New York: Harper & Row, Publishers, Incorporated, 1957. 239 pp.

SHUEY, A. M. *Testing of Negro Intelligence.* Lynchburg, Virginia: J. P. Bell Company, 1958. 351 pp.

SILBERMAN, CHARLES. "The City and the Negro." *Fortune*, March 1962.

SINGH, HARBANS. "A Proposal for a College for Gifted Negro Students." *The Quarterly Review of Higher Education Among Negroes*, 30 : 158–159, July 1962.

SISK, GLENN. "The Negro Colleges in Atlanta." *The Journal of Negro Education*, 33 : 131–135, Spring 1964.

SMITH, PAUL M., JR. "The Realism of Counseling for Scholarship Aid with Freshmen in the Negro College." *The Journal of Negro Education*, 33 : 93–96, Winter 1964.

SOUTHERN ASSOCIATION OF COLLEGES AND SCHOOLS. *Suggested Recommendations for Improvement of Professional Preparation.* Atlanta, Georgia: The Association.

SOUTHERN REGIONAL COUNCIL. "Public Education in Mississippi." Atlanta, Georgia: The Council, August 19, 1963. 6 pp.

STALLINGS, FRANK H. *Racial Differences in Academic Achievement.* Atlanta, Georgia: Southern Regional Council, February 26, 1960. 5 pp.

A *Step Toward Enlarging the Pool of Qualified Negro Candidates for Higher Education.* A Cooperative School-College Program at Princeton University. November 15, 1963. 30 pp.

"Strengthening Negro Colleges." *School and Society*, 92 : 94, March 7, 1964.

TAEUBER, KARL E., and ALMA F. TAEUBER. "The Negro Population in the United States." New York: Phelps-Stokes Fund. (Unpublished.)

TAYLOR, DALMAS A. "The Relationship Between Authoritarianism and Ethnocentrism in Negro College Students." *The Journal of Negro Education*, 31 : 455–459, Fall 1962.

THIRTY-FIRST ANNUAL CONFERENCE ON EDUCATION. *Perceptions of the Cultural Problems of Negro Youth in the Public Schools of Texas.* Prairie View, Texas: The Research Committee of Prairie View Agricultural and Mechanical College of Texas. March 1961.

THIRTY-THIRD ANNUAL CONFERENCE ON EDUCATION. *The Changing World of Work: Implications for Education.* Prairie View, Texas: The Research Committee of Prairie View Agricultural and Mechanical College of Texas. March 1, 1963. 53 pp. and bibliography.

THIRTY-FOURTH ANNUAL CONFERENCE ON EDUCATION. *Testing in Relationship to the Educational and Social Adjustment of the Culturally Deprived.* Prairie View, Texas: The Research Committee of Prairie View Agricultural and Mechanical College of Texas. March 6, 1964. 52 pp. and bibliography.

THOMPSON, CHARLES H. "Problems in the Achievement of Adequate Educational Opportunity" in *Negro Education in America.* New York: Harper & Row, Publishers, Incorporated, 1962, pp. 171–182.

THOMPSON, CHARLES H. "The Present Status of the Negro Private and Church-Related College." *The Journal of Negro Education*, 29 : 227–244, Summer 1960.

THOMPSON, DANIEL C. "Problems of Faculty Morale." *The Journal of Negro Education*, 29 : 37–46, Winter 1961.

THOMPSON, DANIEL C. *Teachers in Negro Colleges.* Unpublished doctoral dissertation, Columbia University, 1955.

TRENT, WILLIAM J., JR. "Cooperative Fund Raising in Higher Education." *The Journal of Negro Education*, 24 : 6–15, Winter 1955.

TUMIN, MELVIN MARVIN (ed.). *Race and Intelligence.* New York: Anti-Defamation League of B'nai B'rith, 1963. 56 pp.

"The Underprivileged Reader, a Report on 'Access to Public Libraries' Survey," Presented at the American Library Association Conference, July 15, 1963. *Wilson Library Bulletin.*

UNITED STATES OFFICE OF EDUCATION. *National Survey of the Higher Education of Negroes.* Misc., No. 6, Vols. 1–4. Washington, D.C.: Government Printing Office, 1942–43.

Vol. 1. CORINNE BROWN. *Socio-economic Approach to Educational Problems.*

Vol. 2. *General Studies of Colleges for Negroes.*

Vol. 3. LLOYD BLAUCH and MARTIN D. JENKINS, *Intensive Study of Selected Colleges for Negroes.*

Vol. 4. AMBROSE CALIVER. *A Summary.*

VIORST, MILTON. "Howard University: Campus and Cause." *Harper's*, pp. 51–60, November 1961.

VONTRESS, CLEMMONT E. "The Negro Against Himself." *The Journal of Negro Education*, 32 : 237–242, Summer 1963.

WALKER, G. H. "Analysis of Negro Junior College Growth." *Junior College Journal*, 30 : 264–267, January 1960.

WALTER, PAUL A. *Race and Cultural Relations.* New York: McGraw-Hill Book Company, 1962.

WEAVER, GEORGE L. "The New Challenge to Negro Colleges." *Negro Digest*, 11 : 33–37, July 1962.

WELLS, GUY H. "The Supreme Court Decision and Its Aftermath" in *Negro Education in America.* New York: Harper & Row, Publishers, Incorporated, 1962, pp. 210–234.

WILSON, LOGAN. *Integration and Higher Education.* Speech delivered at the American Conference of Academic Deans, January 13, 1964. Manuscript, 11 pp.

WITTY, P. "New Evidence on the Learning Ability of the Negro." *The Journal of Abnormal and Social Psychology*, 40 : 401–404, October 1945.

WOLFE, D. P. "Education's Challenge to American Negro Youth." *Negro History Bulletin*, 26 : 115–118, December 1962.